RATIONAL INVESTING IN IRRATIONAL TIMES

Also by Larry E. Swedroe

What Wall Street Doesn't Want You to Know
The Only Guide to a Winning Investment Strategy You'll Ever Need

RATIONAL INVESTING IN IRRATIONAL TIMES

How to Avoid the Costly Mistakes
Even Smart People Make Today

◆

LARRY E. SWEDROE

◆

TRUMAN TALLEY BOOKS
ST. MARTIN'S PRESS
NEW YORK

www.stmartins.com

Library of Congress Cataloging-in-Publication Data

Swedroe, Larry E.
    Rational investing in irrational times : how to avoid the costly mistakes
    even smart people make today / Larry Swedroe.
       p. cm.
    ISBN 0-312-29130-2
  1. Portfolio management. 2. Investment analysis. I. Title.

HG4529.5 .S937 2002
332.6—dc21

2001050755

10 9 8 7 6 5 4

This book is dedicated to my mother,
also affectionately known as The Creator.
I would like to thank her for always believing in me,
for always supporting me,
and for being the best mother anyone could ask for.
I love you.

In this business there are fifty ways to screw up. If you're a genius, you can think of twenty-five of them, and you ain't no genius.

—*Body Heat* (the movie)

Only two things are infinite, the universe and human stupidity, and I'm not sure about the former.

—Albert Einstein

Contents

PART TWO:
Ignorance Is Bliss

PART THREE:
Mistakes Made When Planning an Investment Strategy

CONTENTS

PART FOUR:
Mistakes Made When Developing a Portfolio

CONTENTS

Conclusion

Introduction

The green—in our eyes and in other people's wallets—brings out the worst in us. I don't mean morally, I mean our worst instincts as investors. We think we make rational decisions. More often, we veer from hope to fear and back again, without putting our brains into gear at all.
—Jane Bryant Quinn, *The Washington Post*, August 1, 1999

If you want to see the greatest threat to your financial future, go home and take a look in the mirror.
—Jonathan Clements, *Wall Street Journal*, April 27, 1998

I joined Buckingham Asset Management, a financial advisory firm, in 1996, as both a principal of the firm and its director of research. I had spent my entire career either managing various types of financial risk, including interest rate, foreign exchange, and credit, or advising corporations on the same types of risk. I joined Buckingham (a registered investment advisor to investors) and its affiliated BAM Advisor Services (a provider of turnkey asset management services to approximately one hundred other advisory firms around the country) because the firm's investment philosophy is based on what I strongly believed to be the winning investment strategy. Also important to me is that Buckingham is a fee-only advisor, and therefore does not present the conflicts of interests with which commission-based advisors must deal.

My main role as director of research is to communicate to our clients (investors and other advisors) the principles of modern portfolio theory (MPT) and the efficient market theory (EMT) upon which our investment philosophy is based. It is also my role to keep our clients advised of the latest academic research. However, my most important role is to help investors understand how to apply the principles of MPT and the EMT to their own unique circumstances and personalities so that they have the greatest chance of reaching their financial and life objectives.

Upon joining Buckingham, one of my first tasks was to find a book that would explain the principles of MPT in a simple way so that investors could find answers to these important questions:

- How do investors generally believe markets work?
- How do markets really work?
- How can you apply the knowledge of how markets really work to develop a winning game plan tailored to your unique situation?

Despite a long search, I could not find a book that fully addressed those three important issues. Most investment books promise spectacular results with easy-to-follow formulas. Unfortunately, none of those types of books stands up to scrutiny. I was searching for a work that did not promise instant wealth, but did provide the road map to a long-term winning investment strategy.

Since my search proved unsuccessful, in mid-1996 I set out to write such a book, one that would appeal not only to sophisticated investors, but also to intelligent investors with little or no knowledge of financial markets. I believe that my first book, *The Only Guide to a Winning Investment Strategy You'll Ever Need*, meets all the criteria I identified. While explaining the principles of modern portfolio theory, it clearly lays out the case against active management and for passive management, and it explains why diversification is the winning strategy. The book also attempts to destroy many of the sacred cows of investing—the myths in which Wall Street and the media need you to believe in order for them to maximize their profit (at your expense). And, finally, it shows how you can use this information to help you construct a portfolio unique to your personal circumstances.

In May 1998, *The Only Guide to a Winning Investment Strategy You'll Ever Need* was published to very favorable reviews, including a strong endorsement from the *Wall Street Journal*, which named it among the three top investment books of 1998 that, uncharacteristically, were "worth the paper they are printed on, and then some."[1] I am most pleased that even several years later I still regularly receive e-mail, letters, and phone calls with appreciation from people not only in the United States but around the globe as well.

In January 2001 my second book, *What Wall Street Doesn't Want You To Know*, was published. It was highly praised by John Bogle, the founder and former Chairman of the Vanguard Group, and both *The New York Times* and the *Financial Times* of London. Like its predecessor, this book attempted to present the evidence on how markets have worked and the logic of why they should continue to operate in a similar manner in the future. It built on and extended the evidence in my first book, presenting the results of the latest academic research on financial markets as well as much of what I had learned since my first book was completed.

During my time as an investment advisor I have seen investors and advisors alike make a wide variety of mistakes in their investment decisions. I decided that I could help investors greatly improve the likelihood of achieving their financial objectives by writing a third book that would:

- Describe the many mistakes I have witnessed.
- Explain why they are mistakes.

- Explain why investors make them.

- Explain how to avoid them.

This book is divided into four parts: Understanding and Controlling Human Behavior Is an Important Determinant of Investment Performance; Ignorance Is Bliss; Mistakes Made When Planning an Investment Strategy; and Mistakes Made When Developing a Portfolio. It also contains a glossary of technical terms. Oscar Wilde said: "Experience is the name everyone gives to their mistakes." My hope is that you will benefit from my experiences. I hope that by providing you with the knowledge contained in this work you will avoid the most common mistakes investors make, learn the winning investment strategy, and reach your financial and life goals. The book is about making you an informed investor. Being aware of how vulnerable you are to your own psychology, and how behavioral mistakes cause you to stray from proven investment principles, should help you to improve your investment performance. Understanding just how powerful psychological forces can be may help you to control them. At the very least, being armed with as much information as possible should improve your odds of success. Forewarned is forearmed.

PART ONE

◆

Understanding and Controlling Human Behavior Is an Important Determinant of Investment Performance

We also know how cruel the truth often is, and we wonder whether delusion is more consoling. —Henri Poincaré

It ain't what a man don't know as makes him a fool, but what he does know as ain't so. —Josh Billings

If you can keep your head when all about you are losing theirs, maybe you haven't heard the news.
—Adam Smith, *The Money Game*

We have met the enemy and he is us. —Pogo

MISTAKE 1

◆

Are You Overconfident of Your Skills?

People exaggerate their own skills. They are optimistic about their prospects and overconfident about their guesses, including which managers to pick. —Richard Thaler

Jonathan Burton, in his book, *Investment Titans*, invited his readers to ask themselves the following questions:

- Am I better than average in getting along with people?
- Am I a better-than-average driver?

Burton noted that, if you are like the average person, you probably answered yes to both questions. In fact, studies typically find that about ninety percent of respondents answer positively to those types of questions. Obviously, ninety percent of the population cannot be better than average in getting along with others, and ninety percent of the population cannot be better-than-average drivers. As Burton observed, we do not live in Lake Wobegon where everyone is above average. While, by definition, only half the people can be better than average at getting along with people, and only half the people can be better-than-average drivers, most people believe they are above average. Overconfidence in our abilities may in some ways be a very healthy attribute. It makes us feel good about ourselves, creating a positive framework with which to get through life's experiences. Unfortunately, being overconfident of our investment skills can lead to investment mistakes.

Examples of the "Lake Wobegon effect" are the results of two surveys published in the September 14, 1998, edition of the *Wall Street Journal*. In its June 1998 survey, the *Journal* found that the average investor expected the market to return 13.4% for the next twelve months. Of course, on average, each investor expected to individually earn almost two percent more than the market. The survey was repeated in September with similar results. Investors on average expected the market to return 10.5% for the next twelve months, yet they expected their own portfolios to return almost 13%. Another great example is a February 1998 survey by Montgomery Asset Management. It found that seventy-four percent of investors interviewed expected their funds to consistently outperform the market.[1] It is simply impossible for the average investor to beat the market since investors collectively are the market. The logic is inescapable: The average investor must, by definition, earn market rates of return, less the expenses of his or her efforts.

Professor Richard Thaler of the University of Chicago and Robert J. Shiller, an economics professor at Yale, note that "individual investors and money managers persist in their belief that they are endowed with more and better information than others, and that they can profit by picking stocks. Ninety percent think they're above average."[2] This insight helps explain why individual investors believe they can pick stocks that will outperform the market; time the market so that they're in when it is rising and out of it when it is falling; and identify the few active managers who will beat their respective benchmarks.

Even when individuals think that it is hard to beat the market, they are confident that they themselves can be successful. Here is what the noted economist Peter Bernstein had to say: "Active management is extraordinarily difficult, because there are so many knowledgeable investors and information does move so fast. The market is hard to beat. There are a lot of smart people trying to do the same thing. Nobody's saying that it's easy. But possible? Yes."[3]

Remember that to profit from the market's mistakes you must either have information that the market doesn't have (and remember if it is inside information you cannot legally trade on it), or you must interpret the information better than the collective wisdom of the market. Obviously, not everyone can be above average in doing so. And to beat the market you must be well above average since you incur expenses in the effort.

Let's take a look at some further evidence on investor overconfidence. Brad Barber and Terrance Odean of the Graduate School of Management, University of California at Davis, have done a series of studies on investor behavior and performance. The following is a list of their main findings.

- Individual investors—individual investors underperform appropriate benchmarks.[4]

- Men versus women—though the stock selections of women do not outperform those of men, women produce higher net returns due to lower turnover (lower trading costs). Also, married men outperform single men.[5] The obvious explanation is that single men do not have the benefit of the spouse's sage counsel to temper their own overconfidence. It appears that a common characteristic of human behavior is that on average men have confidence in skills they don't have, while women simply know better.

- Frequent traders versus less active investors—individuals who traded the most (presumably due to misplaced confidence) produced the lowest net returns.[6]

- Individuals who switched from telephone trading with a discount broker to e-trading—presumably, these individuals switched to Internet trading because of their past success. Unfortunately, they performed worse after the switch. Their overconfidence led to increased trading and the greater costs associated with increased turnover led to lower returns.[7]

How expensive is overconfidence? DALBAR, an independent financial services research firm, found that for the fifteen-year period ending in 1998, where as the S&P 500 returned almost 18% per annum, the average individual investor buying and selling individual stocks and no-load mutual funds (average holding period for the funds was less than three years) earned an average return of just over 7%. The average individual investor in the study earned a cumulative return of 140%. Had he instead simply invested in the S&P 500, his cumulative return would have been 820%. Overconfidence can be very expensive.[8]

Overconfidence causes investors to see other people's decisions as the result of mood, feelings, intuition, and emotion. Of course, they see their own decisions resulting from objective and rational thought. Overconfidence also causes investors to seek only evidence confirming their own views, and ignore contradicting evidence. As veteran bond market reporter John Liscio put it, "Forecasters, by definition, are biased and untrustworthy recorders of current economic events. In other words, they tend to uncover evidence that supports their forecasts, and they ignore or analytically dismiss anything that challenges it. And, even if the headline data appear to contradict their disclosure of the universe, they will undoubtedly uncover some statistic or extenuating circumstance that dovetails neatly with their worldview."[9]

Examining the results of the Mensa investment club provides an amusing bit of evidence on overconfidence. Their results make the Beardstown Ladies look like Warren Buffett. The June 2001 issue of *Smart Money* reported that over the past fifteen years the Mensa investment club returned just 2.5%, underperforming the S&P 500 Index by almost 13% per annum. Warren Smith, an investor for thirty-five years, reported that his original investment of $5,300 had turned into $9,300. A similar investment in the S&P 500 Index would have produced almost $300,000. One investor described their strategy as buy low, sell lower. The Mensa members were overconfident that their superior intellectual skills could be translated into superior investment returns.

Wall Street Journal columnist Jonathan Clements made the following observation: "Beat the market? The idea is ludicrous. Very few investors manage to beat the market. But in an astonishing triumph of hope over experience, millions of investors keep trying."[10] Overconfidence helps explain this triumph of hope over experience. Investors may even recognize the difficulty of the task; yet they still believe that they can succeed with a high degree of probability. As author and personal finance journalist James Smalhout puts it, "Psychologists have long documented the tendency of *Homo sapiens* to overrate his own abilities and prospects for success. This is particularly true of the subspecies that invests in stocks and, accordingly, tends to overtrade."[11]

It appears that overconfidence is a common limitation of the human mind. It is not a trait limited to investors. Various studies have found that lawyers, psychologists, physicians, engineers, negotiators, and of course security analysts are all overconfident of their skills. Clinical psychologists, for example, believed that their diagnosis was correct ninety percent of the time, when it was correct in just fifty percent of cases. One study found that even when people describe themselves as being ninety-nine percent confident, they were correct just eighty percent of the time.[12]

Recognizing our limited ability to predict the future is an

important ingredient of the winning investment strategy. Being aware of the tendency toward overconfidence, you can avoid the mistake of trying to outperform the market. Meir Statman, a finance professor at the University of Santa Clara, California, provides the following advice on how to avoid the mistake of overconfidence: "Start keeping a diary. Write down every time you are convinced that the market is going to go up or down. After a few years, you will realize that your insights are worth nothing. Once you realize that, it becomes much easier to float on that ocean we call the market."[13]

MISTAKE 2

◆

Do You Project Recent Trends Indefinitely into the Future?

We've found people tend to buy what has done well recently. But, in fact, studies have shown that they cost themselves money with poorly timed purchases and sales.

—Scott Cooley, analyst at *Morningstar*,
St. Louis Post-Dispatch, February 11, 1999

The biggest investment mistake people make is focusing on last year's mutual fund performance and not on what really drives returns.

—Barbara Raasch, partner at Ernst and Young,
BusinessWeek, February 22, 1999

As we age, our long-term memory skills tend to remain strong, while our short-term memory skills erode. Unfortunately, individuals don't benefit from that tendency when it comes to investing. It seems to be a simple human failing to fall prey to "recency"—the tendency to give too much weight to recent experience, while ignoring the lessons of long-term historical evidence. This leads to overconfidence (a mistake we have already identified) and the treating of the unlikely as impossible (a mistake we will discuss later).

Investors subject to recency make the mistake of extrapolating the most recent past into the future, almost as if it is ordained that the recent trend will continue. The following are some examples of recency.

- For the period 1998 through 1999, growth stocks, especially technology-related stocks, dramatically outperformed value stocks. While the S&P 500 (a large growth index) returned almost 25% per annum, large value stocks returned 8.3% per annum and small value stocks returned just 4% per annum. How did investors react? According to a *Wall Street Journal* article, in the first three quarters of 2000 there were over $60 billion of redemptions from value funds. On the other hand, over $160 billion poured into growth funds and over $40 billion poured into tech funds.[1] The year 2000, however, witnessed an almost complete reversal. Large and small value stocks were each up in excess of ten percent, while the S&P 500 fell over nine percent and technology stocks experienced one of the worst bear markets ever, with the tech-heavy NASDAQ falling almost seventy percent from its March 2000 peak by April 2001. Investors chasing the recent events ignored the historical evidence that value stocks have provided greater returns over the long term. For example, for the seventy-year period 1928–97, small and large value stocks returned 14.5% and 12.7%, respectively, while the S&P returned 10.7%, and large growth stocks returned just 9.9%.

- In 1999, with the NASDAQ soaring to record heights, there were net redemptions of $8 billion of small bank certificates of deposits (CDs). Small CDs are those with a face value of less than $100,000. Investors were redeeming their safe CD investments, presumably to invest in NASDAQ and other growth stocks in order to benefit from the performance of the NASDAQ—which they were certain (to their later great regret) would continue.[2]

- From January through November 2000, with the market at much lower levels, there were net purchases of small CDs of $77 billion. The same was true for large CDs. In 1999 individuals purchased $32 billion of large CDs. Through November 2000, individuals had purchased $62 billion of these instruments.[3] Investors had become more conservative, extrapolating the recent bear market into the future.

- In March 2000, when the NASDAQ crossed 5,000, trading volumes at on-line brokerage firms were at very high levels as individuals poured money into the market. However, in November, when the NASDAQ had given up about one-half its value, trading volume was much lower, at least for individual investors. Again, individuals seem subject to recency and chasing the latest trend.[4]

Firm	Daily Number of Trades March	Daily Number of Trades December
Ameritrade	173,000	101,000
Datek	135,699	97,971
Schwab	415,000	230,000

Another example of recency is the prevalent belief among U.S. investors that the United States is the only safe place to invest. The argument goes something like: We have the best economy. Just look at returns over the past eleven years, from 1990 through

2000. While the S&P 500 returned 15.4% per annum, the EAFE (Europe, Australasia, and Far East) Index returned just 4.9%. Why would you invest internationally when you can invest all your money in the United States, the world's greatest economy? This is the same argument Japanese investors were making in 1989 about investing internationally. For the twenty-year period 1970–89, Japanese small-and large-cap stocks returned 29.5% and 22.2% per annum, while the S&P 500 returned 11.6% per annum. Japanese investors, influenced by recency and extrapolating the recent past into the future, then earned returns of −10% and −3.6% per annum for the next eleven years, while the S&P 500 returned 15.4% per annum.

Another good example of recency: For the thirty-one-year period 1969–99 the performance of the S&P 500 and the EAFE indices were virtually identical, with the S&P 500 outperforming by just 0.09% per annum (12.93% to 12.84%). However, for the eighteen years from 1971 to 1988, EAFE outperformed the S&P 500 by 6.2% per annum (17.2% to 11.0%). If you were subject to recency as we entered 1989, you would have been loading up on international stocks and selling the S&P 500.

Perhaps the best examples of the dangers of recency are provided by three studies. The first is a Morningstar study that tracked the performance of the least popular fund categories from 1987 through 2000. They defined popularity by the amount of cash flowing in or out (redemptions) of funds. The least popular funds are those that are either receiving the least amount of inflow or experiencing the most amount of outflow. As it turns out, the three least popular categories of funds have beaten the average fund seventy-five percent of the time, and more amazingly, they have beaten the most popular funds ninety percent of the time.[5]

A second Morningstar study, covering the period 1987–94,

compared returns each year with the returns for the next one, two, and three years. Morningstar found that funds from the three *least* popular equity categories (based on net cash inflows) outperformed funds from the three *most* popular categories twenty-two out of twenty-four times.[6] This is particularly interesting since the vast majority of fund flows go to the top past performers.

The third study, conducted by Financial Research Corporation, looked at fund flows following the best and the worst four quarters for each of Morningstar's forty-eight investment categories. What they found is that investors follow a consistent pattern of buying high and selling low—not exactly a prescription for investment success. In the quarters following high returns, an average of $91 billion in net new cash flowed into funds—investors bought high. On the other hand, after the worst performing quarters, cash inflows dropped to just $6.5 billion—investors missed out on the opportunity to buy when the stocks were on sale.[7]

The problem created by recency can be stated as causing individuals to adopt a buy high/sell low investment strategy, known as "convex investing." The problem is illustrated in the following diagram:

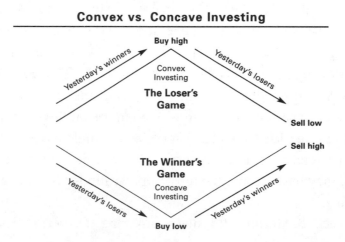

Convex vs. Concave Investing

12

If you are subject to recency, you are trying to buy yesterday's returns. You are like generals always fighting the last war. Unfortunately, you can only buy tomorrow's returns. This problem can be avoided by ignoring the media, the financial press, and "expert" advice from Wall Street urging investors to act on the mistaken assumption that somehow this time it's different, the trend will continue. Before jumping on any bandwagon, check the long-term historical evidence and the logic of the conclusions (and watch out for overconfidence). Those who do jump on the bandwagon are highly likely to be found abandoning it in the near future.

MISTAKE 3

◆

Do You Believe Events Are More Predictable After the Fact Than Before?

There is an old saying that on Monday morning we all make great quarterbacks. With the benefit of hindsight, the right play to call and the winning strategy are always obvious. Unfortunately, it seems to be a human failing that we are either unable or unwilling to recall what our beliefs were before the events actually occurred. We have a tendency to exaggerate our pre-event estimate of the probability of an event occurring. This "hindsight bias" may lead us to believe that even events that the "experts" failed to foresee were not only painfully obvious but also possibly even inevitable. Every day we hear after-the-fact analysis explaining market moves in a way that sounds as if an event were predictable. To demonstrate that this phenomenon is a result of hindsight bias, consider the following:

In the eleven years from 1990 through 2000, Japanese large-cap stocks produced annualized dollar returns of −3.6% per annum. While this was occurring, the S&P 500 returned 15.4% per annum. Although many investors may believe that it was easy to foresee the types of returns that occurred, let's see just how obvious it actually was without the benefit of hindsight. Taking Mr. Peabody's way-back machine (of Rocky and Bullwinkle fame), let's travel back in time to see what investors were actually thinking.

It's 1989, and Japan is the envy of the world. Asset prices are rising rapidly. The Nikkei is at 40,000, having risen almost 500% for the decade and no top is in sight (sound familiar?). Land values have risen so high that the land under the Imperial Palace is worth more than all the real estate in California. The Japanese "managed capitalism" model, with a few government officials deciding how capital will be allocated, is the envy of the world, a model other countries should adopt. Its system of interlocking directorates gives Japanese companies immense competitive advantages, with the result that Japan's technology and product quality is clearly viewed as superior to ours, dominating us in almost all industries. Japan is running huge budget and trade surpluses. On the other hand, the United States is running huge budget deficits, our economy is growing very slowly, the market is about to fall again in 1990, and Sony's co-founder Akio Morita states: "America no longer makes things, it only takes pleasure in making profits from moving money around. America is by no means lacking in technology. But it does lack the creativity to apply new technologies commercially. This, I believe, is America's biggest problem. On the other hand, it is Japan's strongest point. America assuredly faces gradual decline."[1] Tokyo was sure to become the financial center of the world. The Japanese even bought up such important U.S. symbols as Rockefeller Center and the Pebble Beach Golf Course. Financial publications were saying, "You ain't seen nothing yet." We were reading such scary books as *The Land of the Rising Sun*. The United States was surely headed the way of the Roman and British empires.

Of course, the world turned out to be quite a different place than most experts were predicting. This is just one example of how investors perceive events to have been more predictable after the fact than was the case before the fact. An eerily similar story could be told about the collapse of the NASDAQ in March

15

2000. Other than a few financial economists who were shouting that the market was irrationally exuberant, most investors were pouring money into technology stocks and funds right at the peak—and doing so at record rates. Only one percent of Wall Street analysts' recommendations were to sell.[2]

Here is a good summary of what most investors were hearing, reading, and believing at the time the NASDAQ was peaking:

It's a new world order. It's the new new thing. Investors should own great companies at any price. Never discard the right company just because the price is too high. It's different this time. The Internet is changing the world. It's a great revolution, supercharging the economy. The United States clearly is the leader in technology and productivity is growing at the fastest rate ever. We dominate the Internet and biotech and financial services sectors. That is where the future is. Besides, the U.S. free enterprise system has proven it's the best model. Others have to now catch up. Just look at returns over the last few years. The opportunity is enormous. You can't afford to miss out. The future for New Age companies like AOL, Amazon, Cisco, Priceline, and the like is so bright and obvious how can you possibly go wrong?

Needless to say, experts are now pointing out the inherent flaws in the "new economy" as if these should have been self-evident all along. Hindsight bias is very dangerous. It causes investors to recall their successes but not their failures. It also causes investors to believe that investment outcomes are far more predicable than they actually are. Meir Statman put it this way: "Hindsight bias makes it easy to believe not only that the future is preordained, but that anyone with half a brain could have seen it."[3]

Hindsight bias promotes both overconfidence and a perception that investing entails far less risk than it actually does. This mistake can be avoided by remembering that stock market returns are highly unpredictable. Since we live in an *ex ante facto* (before the fact) world, without the benefit of clear crystal balls, the best solution to the unpredictability of the market is to build a globally diversified portfolio (so you don't have too many eggs in one basket) of index/passive asset class funds (so you keep all costs and taxes as low as possible and earn market rates of return) that reflects your unique ability, willingness, and need to take risk. Another suggestion that might help you avoid hindsight bias is to keep a diary of your forecasts, as Meir Statman proposed. This will prevent you from remembering only your successes and will also likely make you a bit more humble about your forecasting abilities, thus avoiding the mistake of overconfidence. Finally, take the advice of columnist Jason Zweig: "Whenever some analyst seems to know what he's talking about, remember that pigs will fly before he'll ever release a full list of his past forecasts, including the bloopers."[4]

MISTAKE 4

◆

Do You Extrapolate from Small Samples and Trust Your Intuition?

People often draw faulty conclusions from information. One reason is that they mistakenly trust their intuition that processes and interprets the information. Another reason is that the information may be complicated. When information involves investment decisions, mistakes in judgment can be very costly. A Hebrew University psychologist, Amos Tversky, tried the following experiment in human behavior.[1]

Imagine that two bags are filled—out of sight—with the same number of poker chips. Bag A has two-thirds chips that are white and one third that are red. In bag B the proportions are reversed. Your task is to guess which is the bag with mostly red chips. From bag A you are allowed to withdraw only 5 chips, 4 of which turn out to be red. From bag B you are allowed to withdraw 30 chips, 20 of which turn out to be red. Which bag would you guess has the most red chips?

If you are like most people, you would probably guess bag A, since eighty percent of the chips you withdrew were red, versus just sixty-seven percent from bag B. However, statistics tell us that you are more likely to be right if you chose bag B. The reason is that because the sample size from bag B is much larger, you have more confidence in the result. Statistical theory tells us that the 20 out of 30 bag is much more likely to be the bag with more red chips than the 4 out of 5 bag.

What does this have to do with investing? Like those guessing bag A, investors often make decisions based on very small samples. For example, from 1996 through 1998, growth stocks outperformed value stocks and large-cap stocks outperformed small-cap stocks. The S&P 500 Index rose 28.3% per annum and outperformed the DFA 9–10 (microcap) fund, the DFA Small Value Fund, and the DFA Large Value Fund by 18.1%, 12.8%, and 8.5% per annum, respectively. The press and airwaves were filled with gurus stating that investors should avoid those "lousy" small-cap and value stocks, as they were obviously poor investments. Small-cap and value funds (and emerging market funds, and real estate funds, among others) experienced outflows of funds, and large-cap growth funds experienced inflows.

Think of the period from 1996 to 1998 as bag A, from which

you were only able to draw a small sample, one with few observations. Think of the seventy-three years of data for which information on equity markets is available as bag B. While large-cap and growth stocks have outperformed over the very recent past, over the longer term we know that small-cap stocks have outperformed large-cap stocks and value stocks have outperformed growth stocks. From 1927 to 1998 while the S&P 500 rose 11.2%, the asset classes of 9–10 (micro-cap, the smallest twenty percent of stocks as defined by CRSP, the Center for Research in Security Prices at the University of Chicago), small value, and large value rose 13.1%, 14.8%, and 13%, respectively.

Investors ignoring the much larger data set are making the same mistake as those who chose bag A on the basis of a very small sample: They are trusting their intuition that the small sample is representative of the entire data set. The only difference between the two is that choosing bag A didn't cause you to lose any money. Basing investment decisions on very small samples can lead to very costly outcomes, particularly if a small and probably recent data series causes you to abandon a well-thought-out investment strategy.

A powerful illustration of incorrectly basing investment decisions on small data sets is the following tale. Every investor knows that stocks provide higher returns than bank certificates of deposits. However, remember that for the twenty-five-year period 1966–90 riskless one-month bank CDs outperformed large-cap growth stocks. If after twenty-five long years you abandoned your strategy of investing in the higher expected returning asset class of equities and switched to bank CDs, you would have missed the greatest bull market in history. Despite that lesson, some investors are all too willing to abandon their investment strategies based on much shorter-term results—often on just a few months of data, let alone just a few years.

It appears that making irrational decisions based on short-term results is an all too human pattern of behavior that affects a large number of investors. You can avoid the mistake of relying on small samples of data by making sure your decisions are based on long-term historical evidence, not on short-term data that is probably a random outcome by its very nature.

MISTAKE 5

◆

Do You Let Your Ego Dominate the Decision-Making Process?

Behavioral finance is a new and fascinating field, taking what psychologists have learned about human behavior and applying it to investing. The insights provided by behavioralists help explain why investors act the way they do, sometimes in what appears to be irrational ways. As Jonathan Clements of the *Wall Street Journal* said: "When it comes to investing, we're a bunch of irrational, inconsistent, neurotic wimps."[1] One insight from the field of psychology is that individuals allow their egos to influence their investment decisions, leading to costly errors. Let's briefly explore some of the ways in which egos can get in the way of rational decision making.

1. There is a tremendous body of evidence that the vast majority of actively managed funds underperform their benchmarks, and that the longer the time frame the greater the likelihood of underperformance. While a few active funds do manage to beat their benchmarks, even an organization like Morningstar, with its extensive resources, has admitted

that its star ratings have no predictive value for future performance. (They are very good, of course, at "predicting" past performance.) Therefore, what logic is there for you to believe you can forecast which of the few actively managed funds that outperformed in the past will continue to do so? Consider that the only way you can be successful where Morningstar, and all other such rating services and newsletters, have failed is either to use a different system or to interpret the data differently and more correctly. If you are going to use past performance to predict the future winners, the evidence is strong that your approach is highly likely to fail. What other way is there to identify future winners? Faced with the facts, some individuals are even willing to admit that it is very hard to identify such future winners. Their egos, however, lead them to conclude that somehow they will succeed where others fail. They thus end up playing a loser's game, where the odds of winning are so low that they are better off not playing.

2. Listen to Edward C. Johnson III, chairman of Fidelity Advisors: "I can't believe that the great mass of investors are going to be satisfied with just receiving *average* returns. The name of the game is to be the best" (emphasis mine).[2] This is what a typical stockbroker's pitch might be when confronted with an investor who asks about investing in index funds as a good strategy: "If you index [passively invest] you will get average rates of return. You don't want to be average, do you? Don't you think you can do better than that?" Both stockbrokers and Edward Johnson are appealing to what seems to be the very human need to be "better than average." Listen carefully once again to Jonathan Clements: "It's the big lie that, repeated often

21

enough, is eventually accepted as truth. You can beat the market. Trounce the averages. Outpace the index. Beat the street. An entire industry strokes this fantasy."[3]

The mistake Wall Street wants you to make is to fail to understand that by simply earning market returns, you will earn greater after-tax returns than the average investor. The reason is that the average actively managed fund underperforms its benchmark by almost two percent per annum on a pretax basis, and by far more on an after-tax basis. In other words, by earning market returns you will outperform the average investor, and that includes professional investors. The only sure way to be above average is not to play Wall Street's game of active investing.

3. The need to protect their ego also helps explain why individuals choose to invest in actively managed funds instead of passive investment vehicles. If the active manager they chose beats the benchmark, the investor takes credit for being smart enough to have chosen the manager. If the manager underperforms, the manager gets the blame and is fired. From the ego's perspective it is an "I win/I don't lose" game. If investors choose a passively managed investment vehicle, they have no one to blame except themselves. This becomes an "I win/I lose" game. The ego prefers not to play a game it might lose.

4. The same I win/I don't lose game applies to stock picking. If the stocks that individuals choose outperform, they take the credit. If they underperform, they blame the broker, publication, or guru that recommended the stock. The ego is protected in either case.

You can avoid costly investment mistakes by not letting your ego enter into the investment decision-making process. As John

Bogle, the founder of Vanguard, put it: "The realistic epitome of investment success is to realize the highest possible portion of the market returns earned in the financial asset class in which you invest—the stock market, the bond market, or the money market—recognizing and accepting that that portion will be less than 100%."[4] The best way to accomplish that objective is to invest in passively managed and tax-managed funds. Bogle notes that they will be "a vast improvement over the 85% or so that the typical mutual fund has provided."[5]

MISTAKE 6

◆

Do You Allow Yourself to Be Influenced by a Herd Mentality?

Sober nations have all at once become desperate gamblers, and risked almost their existence upon the turn of a piece of paper. To trace the history of the most prominent of these delusions is the object of the present pages. Men, it has been well said, think in herds; it will be seen that they go mad in herds, while they only recover their senses slowly, and one by one.
    —Charles MacKay, *Extraordinary Popular Delusions and the Madness of Crowds*, 1841

By the mere fact that he forms part of an organised crowd, a man descends several rungs in the ladder of civilisation. Isolated, he may be a cultivated individual; in a crowd, he is a barbarian that is a creature acting by instinct. He possesses the spontaneity, the violence, the ferocity, and also the enthusiasm and heroism of primitive beings, whom he further tends to resemble by the facility with which he allows himself to be impressed by words and images—which would be entirely without action on each of the isolated individuals composing the crowd—and to be induced to commit acts contrary to his most obvious interests and his best-known habits. An individual in a crowd is a grain of sand, which the wind stirs up at will. —Gustave LeBon, *The Investor's Anthology*

We need to learn to set our course by the stars, not by the lights of every passing ship. —General Omar Nelson Bradley

Psychologists have long known that individuals allow themselves to be influenced by the herd mentality, or the "madness of crowds," as Charles MacKay described it back in the 1840s. The herd mentality may be defined as a desire to be like others, to be part of the "action" or "scene." This mentality manifests itself in the fashion world where, like the length of a skirt or the width of a tie, fashions seem to come in and go out of favor with no apparent reason. The English novelist and playwright Henry Fielding put it this way:

Fashion is the great governor of this world; it presides not only in matters of dress and amusement, but in law, physics, politics, religion, and all other things of the gravest kind; indeed, the wisest of men would be puzzled to give any better reason why particular forms in all these have been at certain times universally received, and at other times universally rejected, than that they were in or out of fashion.[1]

Unfortunately, when it comes to investing, perfectly rational people can be influenced by a herd mentality. The potential for large financial rewards plays on the human emotions of greed and envy. In investing, as in fashion, fluctuations in attitudes often spread widely without any apparent logic. But whereas changing the length of a skirt or width of a tie won't affect your net worth in any appreciable manner, allowing your investment decisions to be influenced by the madness of crowds can have a devastating impact on your financial statement.

Investing, especially in speculative assets, has become much more of a social activity over the past decade. The dramatic growth of investment clubs, like the Beardstown Ladies, and the proliferation of Web chat boards is supporting evidence. Today, investors often spend many of their non-working hours on-line, reading, discussing, or simply gossiping about their investments. Of course, they discuss their successes with far greater frequency than they do their losses—contrary to the cliché that misery loves company. How can investment "fashions," or the madness of crowds, be destructive to your financial health? Let's see.

Influenced by the herds, investors start betting huge sums on investments they know little or nothing about (perhaps can't even spell), or would not have even previously considered. If a particular madness lasts long enough, even very conservative investors may abandon long-held beliefs—feeling they have missed out on what the crowd deems "easy money" or a sure thing. They forget basic principles such as risk and reward and the value of diversification. This is the "Uncle Jim syndrome"—If Uncle Jim can make all that money owning Priceline, E-loan, and Amazon, why can't I? I'm at least as smart as he is.

While it doesn't happen often, perhaps once every generation or so (just long enough for people to forget the last bubble and for a new generation of "suckers" to become of investment age), bubbles do seem to appear with regularity. We are all familiar with the most recent technology (especially dot-com) debacle, but that bubble was not unique. In the 1960s, for example, we had a "tronics" bubble, when any stock with "-tronics" as a suffix soared to heights never even imagined. There have been enough manias that several wonderful books have been written on the subject. To avoid repeating mistakes of the past, you may consider reading Robert Shiller's *Irrational Exuberance*, Edward Chancellor's *Devil Take the Hindmost*, and Charles MacKay's *Extraordinary Pop-*

ular Delusions and the Madness of Crowds. MacKay's book is particularly noteworthy as it was written in 1841—proving that while fashions change, human behavior doesn't.

Since fashions affect social behavior, is it not logical to believe that they affect investment behavior as well? Shiller in his book makes the strong case that mass psychology may at times be the dominant cause of stock price movements. While the market is very rational over the long term, for short periods it can become quite irrational. The "madness of crowds" takes over and a new "conventional wisdom" is quickly formed. Charles MacKay put it this way: "Every age has its peculiar folly: some scheme, project, or fantasy into which it plunges, spurred on by the love of gain, the necessity of excitement, or the force of imitation." Sir Isaac Newton was reported to have said about the investment mania of his day, the South Seas Company: "I can calculate the motions of heavenly bodies, but not the madness of people."[2]

Shiller argues that: "Anyone taken as an individual is tolerably sensible and reasonable—as a member of a crowd, he at once becomes a blockhead."[3] In mass, blockheads can play a major role in the stock market. What are known as positive feedback loops lead to self-fulfilling prophecies—in the short term. Buying attracts more buying, and prices go up simply because they are going up. Buoyed by rising prices, investors become more confident, enticing more money into the market. Like a Ponzi scheme, the strategy works until it no longer works. Herding can create bubbles and, unfortunately, the devastating impact that results from the bursting of those bubbles. Let's see just how devastating the impact can be.

Going to our videotape (playback) machine, we can see that the twentieth century witnessed three periods when price-to-earnings (P/E) ratios reached historically lofty levels. The first occurred at the turn of the century. Prices had exploded as real earnings growth boomed. Corporate profits had doubled over the previous five years. The future was certainly optimistic, fueled by the dawning of a new era—a high-tech future. Sound familiar? The coincidence is almost eerie. What actually occurred? By June 1920, the stock market had lost sixty-seven percent of its real June 1901 value. The second occurrence of lofty valuations occurred in 1929, after a spectacular bull market had sent P/E ratios far above previous peaks. By June 1932, the market had fallen over eighty percent in real terms. The third instance occurred in 1966. P/E ratios soared to levels reached only in the two previous "bubbles." By December 1974, real stock prices fell fifty-six percent and would not return to their January 1966 level until May 1992.

The most recent bubble reached its peak in March 2000 when the NASDAQ crossed the 5,000 level. Caught up in the mania of a high-tech revolution, investors had driven price-to-earnings ratios to heights never seen before. By March 2001 the NASDAQ had fallen seventy percent, its greatest drop ever.

How do we explain what Federal Reserve chairman Alan Greenspan called the "irrational exuberance" of investors? Investors influenced by the herd can console themselves that if they are proved to be wrong, at least they are wrong along with everyone else. The consequences, both professionally and for one's own self-esteem, are far less than if you are wrong and alone in your choice of action. There is safety in numbers. This may help explain why even so-called professionals get caught in the herd. How many Wall Street analysts and strategists were advising investors to sell technology stocks in March 2000? As we saw, the number of analyst sell recommendations was about one percent.

In *Irrational Exuberance*, Robert Shiller provides a number of other behavioral and societal explanations for the most recent example of herding and the resulting bubble.

1. *The arrival of the Internet.* Its pervasiveness gives a much greater impression of the impact of technology than anything ever experienced before.

2. *The triumph of American capitalism and the decline of foreign rivals.* Merrill Lynch's motto, "We're Bullish on America," sums it up.

3. *Cultural changes favoring business success.* Increased materialism fueling demand for stocks.

4. *Change in political climate favoring business and investing*—A Republican Congress and capital gains tax cuts.

5. *The baby boom and its perceived effect on the market.* This is what I call the "Harry Dent syndrome."

6. *Dramatic expansion of media coverage on financial markets.* This creates portfolio envy for those "missing the boat."

7. *Overly optimistic analyst earnings forecasts.* In late 1999, seventy percent of stocks had buy recommendations, while only one percent had sell recommendations.

8. *Expansion of deferred compensation plans, providing many more equity opportunities than were previously available to the general public.* This created *interest value* or *curiosity value* not based on rational decision making.

9. *The growth of mutual funds.* This explosive growth was accompanied by a like growth in advertising to attract the herd.

10. *The decline of inflation and the effects of money illusion.* Stock indices are not inflation adjusted, giving the illusion of greater real returns.

11. *Explosion of day trading, discount brokers, and 24-hour trading.* All making trading more accessible.

12. *The rise in gambling opportunities*. This contributes to a speculative environment.[4]

Unfortunately, for rational investors who are able to resist the madness of crowds, there does not seem to be a way systematically to profit from manias. The reason is that there is no way to predict just how irrational prices might get. For example, hindsight reveals that Amazon may have looked irrationally priced at 50, tempting rational investors to short the stock. Unfortunately, it became even more "irrationally" priced, reaching over 100. A "rational" investor shorting the stock at 50 would have been proven correct in the long term, but he might also have been long dead, as margin calls might have forced him to cover his position well before the "inevitable" collapse occurred. As John Maynard Keynes said, "Markets can remain irrational longer than you can remain solvent." Burton Malkiel, professor of economics at Princeton University, put it this way: "We know in retrospect that stock prices tend to overreact and valuations revert to the mean. But it's never possible to know in advance when the reversion will occur. Even bubbles are only clear in retrospect."[5]

Understanding human behavior and having the discipline to avoid the temptation of following the crowd and the noise of the moment is a very important part of the winning investment strategy. Perhaps it is hard for human beings to stand still when all around us are taking action, even when we know it is in our best interests to do nothing. The keys to staying disciplined, and avoiding becoming "irrationally exuberant," are:

- Having a thorough understanding of how markets work. Bubbles inevitably burst, since valuations cannot be justified by any likely economic assumptions. Always remember that while stock valuation is not a science, stocks are nothing more than financial instruments whose values are based on future earnings. Knowledge is power.

- Having a well-thought-out road map to achieving your financial goals. The road map, in the form of an investment policy statement (IPS), including a rebalancing table, will help to keep you from taking "scenic tours" of interesting investments best avoided.

- Having an understanding of how human behavior can impact investment decisions. Remember Anatole France's warning: "If fifty million people say a foolish a thing, it is still a foolish thing." Forewarned is forearmed.

MISTAKE 7

◆

Do You Confuse Skill and Luck?

Investors attribute successes to their own brilliance, and they attribute failures to bad luck. If you keep doing that, at the end of the day you think you're a genius.
> —Nicholas Barberis, *Wall Street Journal*, February 4, 2001

Lucky fools do not bear the slightest suspicion that they may be lucky fools—by definition, they do not know that they belong to such a category. They will act as if they deserve the money. The lucky fool [is] defined as a person who benefited from a disproportionate share of luck but attributes his success to some other, generally very precise, reason. —Nassim Nicholas Taleb, *Fooled By Randomness*

People see skill in performance where there is no skill. The idea that any single individual without extra information or extra market power can beat the market is extraordinarily unlikely.

> —Daniel Kahneman, *Dow Jones Asset Management*,
> November/December 1998

Imagine the following scenario: 10,000 individuals are gathered together to participate in a contest. A coin will be tossed and they must guess whether it will come up heads or tails. Anyone who correctly guesses the outcome of ten consecutive tosses will be declared a winner and will receive the coveted title of "coin-tossing guru." According to statistics, we can expect after the first toss, 5,000 participants will have guessed right and 5,000 guessed wrong. After the second round, the remaining participants will be expected to be 2,500; and so on. After ten repetitions we would expect to have ten remaining participants who would have guessed correctly all ten times and earned their guru status. What probability would you attach to the likelihood that those ten gurus would win the next coin-toss competition? Would you bet on them winning? The answers are obvious. What does this have do with investing?

Today, there are more mutual funds than there are stocks. With so many active managers trying to win, statistics alone dictate that some will succeed. However, beating the market is a zero sum game—that is, since all stocks must be owned by someone, for every active manager who outperforms the market there must be one who underperforms. Therefore, the odds of any specific manager being successful are at best 50/50 (before considering the increased burden of higher expenses active managers must overcome in order to outperform a benchmark index fund or exchange traded fund). Using our coin-toss analogy, we would expect that randomly half the active managers would outperform in any one year, about one in four to outperform two years in a row, and one in eight to do so three years in a row. The reason for choosing the 10,000 number for the coin toss is that we are not far from having that number of actively managed funds. So that after ten years we would randomly expect that ten funds out of the 10,000 would outperform their benchmark. Admitting that there were far fewer funds in 1991, at the start of the period, the fact is that in the ten years ending in 2000, only one single manager succeeding in beating the index each year, Bill Miller of Legg Mason. The evidence, as you can see in the following chart, is that even fewer active managers outperform than would be randomly expected to do so.

Active vs. Passive Management

Security Selection: Do active managers perform better than a random flipping of coins?

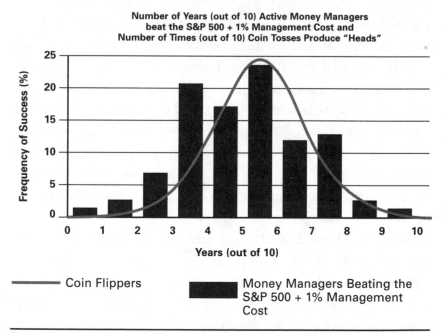

Number of Years (out of 10) Active Money Managers beat the S&P 500 + 1% Management Cost and Number of Times (out of 10) Coin Tosses Produce "Heads"

Coin Flippers

Money Managers Beating the S&P 500 + 1% Management Cost

Source: SEI Investments (1984–1993) Manager returns are calculated without subtracting fees.

While no one would use the results of our coin-tossing contest to predict the next winner, a manager who beats her index for even one year is instantly accorded guru status, complete with write-ups in financial publications and appearances on CNBC.

There is an old saying that even a blind squirrel will on occasion find a nut. Since there is no evidence of any persistence in fund performance, and there is no way to predict the future winners, investors appear to be interpreting the *accidental success* (picking a stock or mutual fund manager that outperforms) to be the result of skill. Investors make the similar mistake of interpreting *accidental failure* to be the result of bad luck.

The October 8, 2001, issue of *BusinessWeek* included a perfect example of the phenomenon of being fooled by randomness. The article, entitled "Chicks' Picks Come Home To Roost," was a mea culpa by reporter Toddi Gutner. A year earlier she had written a column about the Chicks Laying Nest Eggs—ten female friends and relatives using the Internet to run an investment club. Their portfolio had beaten the S&P 500 Index by thirty percent for the period October 1998 through September 2000. Instead of attributing this to randomness, the author gave them guru status—"have proved to be no financial birdbrains." The author never questioned that it might have been randomness. Instead, it had to be skill. The reason it had to be skill is that if it were a random event there would be no story.

The Chicks went on to publish a book imparting their wisdom, *Chicks Laying Nest Eggs: How 10 Skirts Beat the Pants Off Wall Street . . . And How You Can Too*. Giving Gutner credit, she admitted in her column that she is now thinking she is the birdbrain. She reported that the Chicks' portfolio has lost thirty-five percent from its inception nearly three years earlier through September 17, 2001. This compares to a loss of just sixteen percent for the S&P 500. The problem is that she goes on to look for reasons for their failure. Their failure was most likely the result of the same randomness as was their success. Not recognizing this will likely result in making the same mistake in the future—being fooled by randomness.

You can avoid this type of mistake by checking to see if an outcome is statistically significant, or if it is more likely to have been a random, and therefore unpredictable occurrence. In addition, you should make sure that there is logic supporting the conclusion. Sometimes even outcomes that are statistically significant are the result of random events. For example, in the vast majority of years that the team from the National Football Conference won the Super Bowl, the stock market rose. Although the correlation between stock prices and the NFC winning the Super Bowl might be high, no one would intelligently risk their capital on the continuation of such a correlation.

In conclusion, I would like to relate the following tale. It illustrates why investors make the mistake of interpreting accidental success (picking a stock or mutual fund manager that outperforms) to be the result of skill. While browsing the Internet one day, I came across the following posting on a Morningstar site called the "Rekenthaler Report." A poster was seeking the input of John Rekenthaler, Morningstar's director of research.

John: How do funds like Dodge & Cox Stock which hold 80+ securities get blindsided by negative info such as the recent Bausch & Lomb news when they have a relatively small portfolio and a stable of analysts who are supposed to be on top of the companies they own. Similarly, another fund I own, Sequoia, a focused fund with around a dozen holdings, was blindsided by adverse news from one of its big holdings—Progressive Corp—about casualty losses and other negative info. Do these people get complacent and fall asleep at the switch because they are value funds and have buy and hold investors and stop doing their homework? All we get at annual meetings are "mea culpas" and excuses. I'd like to hear your thoughts on this.[1]

Why is it that investors assume that analysts and fund managers get "blindsided" by *unexpected bad news*, yet they give the very same people credit for being *gurus* when they benefit from *unexpected good news*? "News" is exactly that—*new* information—that is randomly either better or worse than the market expected.

The dictionary defines surprise as causing an effect through being unexpected at a particular time or place. And if, as Joseph Mezrich, the Head of Quantitative Strategies Group at Morgan Stanley Dean Witter, concluded, *"Surprise is a persistently important factor in stock performance"*[2] then it would seem that efforts to outperform the market, by such actively managed funds as Dodge & Cox and Sequoia, are likely to prove futile. The logic is simple. First, if there are no surprises in terms of new information, then the market will have already incorporated the expected results into prices. On the other hand, if the new information is a surprise, then by definition the impact of the new information is not predictable (since, after all, it is a surprise). In other words, the effect of surprises on market prices may be explainable, but not exploitable.

To summarize, active managers attempt to identify stocks that will outperform the market. If a major determinant of investment returns is the unknowable, in the form of new and surprising information, just how likely is it that active management will be able to add value, or outperform, after expenses? Unless you believe that you can forecast the unforecastable (surprises), the logic is inescapable: active management is a loser's game. Wall Street, however, must keep alive the myth that active management works. If not, investors would stop playing the active management game—and while investors would achieve far greater returns, Wall Street's earnings would fall as its commission revenue would shrink, as would the revenue from expensive actively managed funds. This is why some refer to much of Wall Street's advice as "investment pornography"—information that is meant to tempt you into action, when inaction is the best course. Let's look at one such example.

Mezrich declares that surprises are a "persistently important determinant of returns," yet he goes on to state that "In a scenario of slowing growth, negative earnings surprise becomes an important risk factor in stock selection. The ability to anticipate where the risk of earnings surprise is greatest should help performance."[3] Let's carefully analyze his comments. First he states that in a scenario of slowing earnings growth, earnings surprises become important in stock selection. Is Mr. Mezrich the only one aware that the economy is slowing and therefore it is likely that corporate earnings are also going to slow and earnings forecasts will have to be adjusted downward? In fact, the Federal Reserve lowered interest rates just prior to his statement. The Fed explicitly stated its motivation was the apparent risk of an economic slowdown. Mezrich proceeds to state that the ability to identify the risks of negative earnings surprises is key to performance. Again, is he the only one who knows the economy is weakening and earnings in certain sectors will now likely be less than previously anticipated? Finally, he states that surprises, meaning non-forecastable events, determine returns. Well, which is it? Is news forecastable or isn't it? If it is forecastable, it is already factored in prices and expected returns. On the other hand, if it is not forecastable—surprises do determine returns—then you cannot predict them.

Should we be surprised by Mezrich's comments? Not really, because, after all, we know that there is no evidence or even logic that active management is likely to prove to be the winning investment strategy. The whole field is filled with smoke, mirrors, and black magic.

MISTAKE 8

◆

Do You Avoid Passive Investing Because You Sense a Loss of Control?

As they begin their investment journey investors using mutual funds can choose one of two paths. They can choose either actively managed funds or passively managed vehicles such as index funds and exchange traded funds (ETFs). The evidence is clear that the vast majority of individual investors would improve their outcomes if they adopted the passive strategy; yet most investors choose the active path. There are many possible explanations for this outcome. We have already explored some, including overconfidence.

An important factor in this choice is that investors feel that they are somehow in control of actively managed funds. Wall Street firms' understanding of this psychology is reflected in their advertisements for on-line trading espousing the "you're in control" theme. On the other hand, these same investors feel that passive investing involves a sense of loss of control over the risk and returns of their portfolios. A passive investor simply builds a diversified portfolio of passively managed/index funds or ETFs that reflects her unique ability, willingness, and need to take risk, and then rebalances when the market's moves have caused her portfolio to drift out of balance. The sense is that the market, not the investor, is "in control."

It's a very human trait to want to take control and do something. Although using actively managed funds and actively managing their portfolios gives investors a sense of control, the reality is completely different. You simply need the right pair of looking glasses to have the correct perspective.

Financial economists have found that almost all investment returns are determined by a portfolio's exposure to the three risk factors of equities; size (small versus large); and value (growth versus value). When fixed-income instruments are in the portfolio, then the determinants include the maturity (or more correctly the duration) and credit quality of the fixed-income assets. The problem is that when investors choose actively managed funds to build their portfolios they cede control over the determinants of return to fund managers. Active managers try to time the market and select which stocks will outperform. If an active manager believes that a bear market will arrive the fund will sell stocks and buy treasury bills, or possibly even sell stocks short. A small-cap fund might decide to buy large-cap stocks, a value fund might decide to buy growth stocks, and a domestic fund might decide to buy international stocks. These types of changes are called "style drift," and it is style drift that causes investors to lose control over their asset allocation, and thus the risk and reward of their portfolio. Let's use our videotape to see the implications of style drift.

It was 1995 and you decided to invest the equity portion of your portfolio in the world's largest mutual fund, Fidelity Magellan. By February 1996 Magellan's allocation to equities had fallen to just seventy percent, twenty percent was in bonds, and ten percent was in short-term marketable securities. Magellan's manager was making a big bet (with your assets) that long-term bonds and short-term marketable securities would outperform the equity markets. How did his bet affect your asset allocations? Assume that you had $100,000 to invest and desired an 80% equity/20% fixed-income allocation, and you invested your $80,000 equity allocation in Fidelity Magellan.

However you actually only had $56,000 ($80,000 × 70%) invested in equities.

	Desired Allocation	Actual Allocation
Equity Allocation	80% $80,000	56% $56,000
Fixed Income Allocation	20% $20,000	44% $44,000
Total Portfolio	100% $100,000	100% $100,000

Your asset allocation was subjected to style drift. By placing funds with an active manager you ceded control, allowing someone else to modify your strategy. The key issue is not the outcome of Magellan's decision, but is instead your loss of control over your portfolio's asset allocation. However, it is worth noting that the market subsequently soared to new highs, bonds fell in value, and the fund's manager, the highly regard Jeff Vinik, moved on "to pursue other career alternatives." Notably, for the period February 1985 to June 1995, the composition of Fidelity Magellan's fund "varied over time to such a degree that it would have been virtually impossible for investors to determine the asset classes in which they were investing, or the risks to which they were being exposed."[1]

Because investors in passively managed funds never have to worry about style drift, they retain complete control over the risks and rewards of their portfolio. Yet investors often make the mistake of equating the use of passive investment vehicles with losing such control. By understanding that the efforts of active managers to select stocks and time the market have little impact on a portfolio's returns, you can avoid the mistake of using actively managed funds to provide yourself with a false sense of control.

We need to cover one other "take control" strategy: the purchase by investors of individual stocks instead of actively managed funds. This strategy would seem to be the ultimate in controlling your own portfolio. However, in pursuing this course, you create two problems. First, you cannot achieve the extensive diversification that the use of mutual funds accomplishes. Second, the evidence tells us that investors who select their own stocks underperform appropriate benchmarks by significant margins.

Terrance Odean, of the University of California at Davis, studied the performance of individual investors by examining over 100,000 trades covering the period 1987–93. He found that stocks individual investors buy trail the overall market and stocks they sell beat the market after the sale. The study further showed that this underperformance increased as the time frame increased. Investors shot themselves in the foot with their trades even before taking into account the transaction fees and taxes, which would further depress trading performance. The author's conclusion: Individuals shouldn't try to pick stocks.[2]

Odean and Brad Barber also studied the performance of those investors who "take control" through do-it-yourself on-line trading. They investigated the performance of individual investors who were clients of a discount brokerage firm that used the telephone to implement their own stock picks and then switched to e-trading. They studied over 3,000 accounts, half of which switched to e-trading. The assumption is that those that switched were motivated by their excellent investment results, and that trading more would only improve their results. Unfortunately, it appears that these investors confused luck and skill. Those who switched to e-trading did substantially increase their trading activity—annualized turnover leaped about seventy percent within the first month and two years later was still eighty percent greater than the turnover of investors who continued to use the telephone. The result of all that trading activity: after all expenses except taxes, e-traders trailed the market by 3.5% per annum.[3]

Thus the evidence is clear that if you are considering taking control by buying individual stocks you would do yourself a great service if you first considered whether your objective is to take control or to earn the greatest possible return for the risks you are willing to accept.

MISTAKE 9

◆

Do You Avoid Admitting Your Investment Mistakes?

Behavioral finance studies have found that the average individual is very risk-averse. For example, studies have found that to entice the average person to accept an even money bet, like a coin toss, you must offer him at least two to one odds. Similarly, behavioral finance has found that the pain of a loss is at least twice as great as the joy we feel from an equivalent size gain. These behavioral traits lead to an investment mistake called "regret avoidance."

Individuals are very reluctant to admit their investment mistakes. This causes them to hold on to securities that have losses, because as long as they continue to hold the losers they can maintain the illusion that a loss is only a theoretical loss until it is realized. The act of selling, on the other hand, would be viewed as an admission that they had made an error. This perception, plus the amount of mental pain involved when losses are realized, causes investors to be reluctant to sell, and thereby avoid the regret of the loss. Like a gambler at the craps tables in Las Vegas, they will try to play until they get even. How many times have you said to yourself, or heard others say, "I will sell it when it gets back to what I paid for it"?

Avoiding the facts, however, doesn't change them. Regret avoidance leads to two investment mistakes. The first mistake is that an asset should be held only if it makes sense to do so in the overall context of the portfolio's asset allocation. What you paid for the security should have no bearing (except for the tax consideration) on whether you should continue to hold it. The right question to ask is: If I did not own any amount of a particular stock, would I buy any at the current price to fit into my portfolio plan? If the answer is no, then you should sell it, because every day you continue to own the security at current prices you are effectively making a decision to buy it.

There is a second mistake that regret avoidance causes. Whenever you have an asset in a taxable account with a significant unrealized loss, you should sell the asset to realize the loss for tax purposes. It is even more important to do so if the loss is short term, as the tax deduction obtained with the loss will be at the higher ordinary income tax rate, rather than the lower long-term capital gains rate. By "harvesting" the loss you will be able to use the loss to offset other gains in the portfolio, thereby reducing your tax bill.

If the asset with an unrealized loss still fits within the overall strategic asset allocation of the portfolio, one of two options should be considered when selling the stock or mutual fund. The first option is to simply sell and repurchase the same security after thirty days. This allows you to avoid the "wash sale" rule, which states that repurchasing the same or a substantially similar security within thirty days causes the two trades to be considered a wash, rendering the loss non-deductible. This strategy does run the risk that the stock/fund might rise substantially during the thirty-day waiting period. On the other hand, the stock/fund might fall substantially. The other strategy is to swap the asset for a similar, but not substantially identical, security. For example, if you own an S&P 500 Index fund with a loss, you might sell it and simultaneously buy a Russell 1000 fund. The two funds should perform very similarly. Another example might be that if you owned Merck, you might sell it and buy another pharmaceutical company such as Pfizer. After another thirty-one days have passed, if you desire, you can reverse the swap and once again hold your original asset.

You can prevent the paralysis induced by regret avoidance by remembering that tax-managing a portfolio is a very important part of the investment process. While we all would like to only have winners in our portfolio, realizing losses to obtain the tax benefit is part of the winning strategy. Once the loss is realized, you are less likely to make the mistake of buying the same security again if it no longer fits into your overall portfolio plan. If the losing asset is not in a taxable account, then the sell decision should be made as part of a regular portfolio review. Remember to ask yourself whether or not the asset still fits within the overall plan and if you would buy it today if you didn't currently own it.

There is one other mistake that is related to regret avoidance, one that relates to load mutual funds. First, there is no reason to purchase mutual funds that carry loads when there are perfectly good low-cost, no-load alternatives. There is no evidence that load funds outperform no-load funds. The load itself is just another hurdle the fund has to overcome in order to outperform its benchmark. Investors who already own load funds are reluctant to sell them because selling the fund would force them to admit that they made a mistake in paying the load in the first place. They *feel* that the load fee would be wasted if they sold the fund. Unfortunately, the load has already been paid; it is what economists call a sunk cost—it is gone whether you hold the fund or sell it. Once again, if you own a load fund, you should ask yourself: If I didn't already own it, and the fund were to waive the load, would I buy it? If the answer is no, sell it.

MISTAKE 10

◆

Do You Let the Price Paid Affect Your Decision to Continue to Hold an Asset?

Put yourself in the following situation: You are a wine connoisseur. You decide to purchase a few cases of a new release at $10 per bottle, and you store the wine in your cellar to age. Ten years later the dealer from whom you purchased the wine informs you that the wine is now selling for $200 per bottle. You have a decision to make. Do you buy more, sell your stock, or drink it?

Faced with this type of decision, very few people would sell the wine—but very few would buy more. Given the appreciation in the wine's value, many might choose to save it to drink on special occasions. But the decision not to sell, while not buying more, is not completely rational. The wine owner is being influenced by what is known as the "endowment effect." The fact that the wine is something you already own (an endowment) should not have any impact on your decision. If you would not buy more at a given price, you should be willing to sell at that price. Since you wouldn't buy any of the wine if you didn't already own any, the wine represents a poor value to you and thus should be sold.

The endowment effect causes individuals to make poor investment decisions. It causes investors to hold on to assets that they would not purchase if they didn't already own any, either because they don't fit into the asset allocation plan, or they are viewed as so highly priced that they are poor investments from a risk/ reward perspective. The most common example of the endowment effect is that people are very reluctant to sell stocks or mutual funds that were inherited, or were purchased by a deceased spouse. I have heard people say, "I can't sell that stock, it was my grandfather's favorite and he'd owned it since 1952." Or, "That stock has been in my family for generations." Or, "My husband worked for that company for forty years, I couldn't possibly sell it." Another example of an investor subject to the endowment effect is stock that has been accumulated through stock options or some type of profit-sharing/retirement plan.

Financial assets are like the bottles of wine. If you wouldn't buy them at the market price, you should sell them. Stocks and mutual funds are not people—they have no memory, they don't know who bought them, and they won't hate you if you sell them. An investment should be owned only if it fits into your current overall asset allocation plan. Its ownership should be viewed in that context.

You can avoid the endowment effect by asking this question: If I didn't already own the asset, how much would I buy today as part of my overall investment plan? If the answer is, "I wouldn't buy any," or, "I would buy less than I currently hold," then you should develop a disposition plan. There is one further consideration to be given to disposing of an "endowment asset": There may be substantial capital gains taxes involved. If this is so, you might consider donating the stock to your favorite charity. By donating the financial asset in place of cash you would have donated anyway, you can avoid paying the capital gains tax.

MISTAKE 11

◆

Are You Subject to the Fallacy of the "Hot Streak"?

In investment performance, the past is not prologue.
—Charles Ellis, *Winning the Loser's Game*

There is an amusing and insightful story from the world of statistics that has relevance to the field of investing. Each year a statistics professor begins her class by asking each student to write down the sequential outcome of a series of one hundred imaginary coin tosses. One student, however, is chosen to flip a *real* coin and chart the outcome. The professor then leaves the room and returns in fifteen minutes with the outcomes waiting for her on her desk. She tells the class that she will identify the one real coin toss out of the thirty submitted with just one guess. With great persistency she amazes the class by getting it correct. How does she perform this seemingly magical act? She knows that the report with the longest consecutive streak of *H* (heads) or *T* (tails) is highly likely to be the result of the real flip. The reason is that, when presented with a question like which of the following sequences is more likely to occur, *HHHHHTTTTT* or *HTHTHTHTHT*, despite the fact that statistics show that both sequences are equally likely to occur, the majority of people select the latter "more random" outcome. They thus tend to write imaginary sequences that look much more like *HHTTHTHTTT* than *HHHTTTHHHH*.

Streaks randomly occur with much greater frequency then people believe. For example, the odds of flipping a coin twenty times and getting either four heads or four tails in a row are fifty percent. Because people underestimate the frequency of streaks,

46

they tend to assign far too much meaning to events that are highly likely to be random occurrences. One study even demonstrated that a "hot hand" in basketball was likely to be nothing more than a random event.[1] A statistician following a basketball team around for an entire season found that the odds of a career fifty percent shooter hitting the next shot were fifty percent, even if this player had just hit five shots in a row. The hot hand, at least for basketball, is a myth.

Erroneously overreacting to what are random events can lead to not only poor coaching decisions but poor investment decisions as well. Consider the following. In the 1990s the Janus funds achieved legendary status for their performance. Their flagship fund, the Janus Fund, returned 20.5% per annum, beating the S&P 500 by 2.3% per annum. The "Get Rich Quick Fund," however, did far better, returning 24.3% per annum. What was its strategy? Get Rich Quick bought all stocks that began with the letter M.[2] While no one would conclude that Get Rich Quick had found the Holy Grail of investment strategies, investors are all too quick to conclude that Janus's results were due to skill and not a random outcome—given how many players compete, a few are bound to outperform the benchmark.

A common investment error is to jump on the bandwagon of an actively managed fund that has been successful in beating its benchmark a few years in a row. Investors perceive that there is a causal relationship (the fund manager is an investment guru) when the performance is far more likely to be the result of a random event. If the odds of beating the benchmark in one year are fifty percent then beating a benchmark three years in a row is just as likely as tossing three heads in a row. It is expected to occur twelve and one half percent of the time. With thousands of managers trying, it is likely that many will succeed. Unfortunately, if success is a random event, it has no predictive value.

In his book *A Random Walk Down Wall Street*, Burton Malkiel reported that he did extensive testing on whether an investor, by choosing the "hot" funds, could outperform the market. The results showed the ineffectiveness of a strategy that chose the top ten, twenty, thirty, or more funds, based on the performance of the previous twelve months, and then one year later switched to the new top performers. This strategy produced results that were below both those of the S&P 500 Index and the average mutual fund. Similar results were found when Malkiel tried ranking funds by their past two-, five-, and ten-year track records. And I think most investors would be surprised at the results of another study of the performance of mutual funds all the way back to 1962. Its author, Mark Carhart, came to the amazing conclusion that the top ten percent performers in any one year are more likely to fall to the bottom ten percent than repeat in the top ten percent.[3]

The best example of the failure of the "hot hand" strategy is the 44 Wall Street Fund. Thanks to manager David Baker, in the 1970s it generated even greater returns than Peter Lynch's Magellan Fund and ranked as the top performing diversified U.S. stock fund of the decade. Unfortunately for investors believing they had found what we would now call the next Peter Lynch or the next Warren Buffett, in the 1980s, 44 Wall Street ranked as the single worst performing fund, losing 73%.[4] During the same period, the S&P 500 grew at 17.5% per annum. The fund did so poorly that in April of 1993 it was merged into the Cumberland Growth Fund, which was then merged into the Matterhorn Growth Fund in April of 1996. Belief in the hot hand, even with ten years of evidence, can be quite expensive. Each dollar invested in Baker's fund fell in value to just 27 cents. On the other hand, each dollar invested in the S&P 500 Index would have grown to just over $5. Even if you believe that past performance is a guide to future performance, at best it is a very difficult guide to read.

You can avoid the mistake of overreacting to events and following the "hot hand" by carefully considering whether the outcome might have been simply random. As investment manager Marty Whitman points out: "The gutters of Wall Street are strewn with the bodies of people who looked good for five years."[5] Examining long-term data can help reduce the risk of making this type of mistake. Using the coin-toss analogy, while three coin tosses that come up all heads would be considered random, if one hundred coin tosses resulted in ninety-five percent heads, we would be wise to consider that we are not dealing with a fair coin.

MISTAKE 12

◆

Do You Confuse the Familiar with the Safe?

People overconfidently confuse familiarity with knowledge. For every example of a person who made money on an investment because she used a company's product or understood its strategy, we can give you five instances where such knowledge was insufficient to justify the investment.
—Gary Belsky and Thomas Gilovich,
Why Smart People Make Big Money Mistakes

When AT&T was broken up, shareholders were given shares in each of what were called the Baby Bells. A study done a short while later found, however, that the residents of each region held a disproportionate number of shares of their local regional Bell. Each group of regional investors was confident that their regional Baby Bell would outperform the others. How else can you explain each investor having most of their eggs in one baby basket? This is not Lake Wobegon where all Baby Bells can outperform the average of the group. Other examples of familiarity breeding investment are that Georgia residents own sixteen percent of all Coca-Cola stock, and people in Rochester tend to own stock in Kodak and Xerox.[1] This story is a good analogy for the way domestic investors view non-domestic assets.

It seems to be a global phenomenon that most investors hold the vast majority of their wealth in the form of domestic assets. Although the following data is a bit dated, not that much has changed. In 1990, the domestic ownership shares of the world's five leading stock markets were United States ninety-two percent, Japan ninety-six percent, United Kingdom ninety-two percent, Germany seventy-nine percent, and France eighty-nine percent.[2] With the relative freedom of capital to travel around the world, the lack of global diversification cannot be explained by capital constraints. The only explanation is that investors in each country believe that their domestic market provides the best/safest investment opportunities. Investors in all five countries were taking the unnecessary risk of having almost all their eggs in their domestic basket, without any rational reason for doing so. It is simply a behavioral issue.

A 1991 study found that the expected real return to U.S. equities was 5.5% in the eyes of U.S. investors, but only 3.1% and 4.4% in the eyes of Japanese and British investors, respectively. Similarly, the expected return on Japanese equities was 6.6% in the eyes of Japanese investors, but only 3.2% and 3.8% in the eyes of U.S. and British investors, respectively.[3] Familiarity breeds overconfidence, or an illusion of safety, and lack of familiarity breeds a perception of high risk.

Many investors avoid adding international investments to their portfolios because they believe international investing is too risky. Is this perception accurate? A 1996 study found that portfolio allocations by U.S. investors to foreign and domestic securities are consistent with the belief by investors that the standard deviations of foreign securities are higher by a factor of 1.5 to 3.5 than their historical value.[4] Behavioral finance explains this phenomenon in the following way: "The distinction between foreign stocks and domestic ones is an illustration of the distinction between risk, where probabilities are known, and uncertainty, where probabilities are not known. Familiarity with a security brings the situation closer to risk than to uncertainty. Uncertainty averse investors prefer familiar gambles over unfamiliar ones, even when the gambles have identical risk."[5] For example, a study found that people who identify themselves as being familiar with sports, but not politics, prefer to bet on sports events rather than on political events. This preference exists even when subjects judge the odds in sport bets as identical to the odds in political bets.[6]

Academics recommend that investors add international assets to their portfolios because they actually *reduce* risk. International equities do not move in perfect tandem with domestic equities. Therefore, the addition of international stocks to a portfolio should reduce the volatility (risk) of the *overall* portfolio. A study published in the Fall 1998 issue of the *Journal of Investing* sought to determine whether international equity diversification actually provided that theoretical risk reduction benefit.

The study covered the period 1970–96. David Laster, of the Federal Reserve Bank of New York, examined the performance of portfolios with varying allocations to the S&P 500 Index and the EAFE Index. The study looked at portfolios with allocations of 10% S&P 500, and 90% EAFE; 20% S&P 500 and 80% EAFE; and so on. At the end of each year each portfolio was rebalanced, correcting for market movements, to its original allocations. Using a statistical method called "bootstrapping" (creating a series of monthly returns using randomly selected subperiods from the entire period), the study was able to effectively examine far more five-year holding periods than its twenty-seven-year period contained. Before reviewing the results of the study, it is important to note that during this period the S&P 500 Index outperformed the EAFE Index by 12.29% to 12.03% per annum. In addition, the correlation of returns between the two indices was 0.48, a fairly low figure. The study concluded that:

- Any combination of the S&P 500 Index and the EAFE Index outperformed either index individually—a result of the low correlation.

- Increasing the international allocation to as much as forty percent *increased* returns and *reduced* risk as measured by standard deviation (volatility).

- An allocation of forty percent international produced the highest Sharpe ratio—a measure of the amount of excess return (above the rate on riskless short-term U.S. treasury bills) for a given level of risk (with risk being defined as the standard deviation of returns).

- Increasing the international allocation from zero to just twenty percent reduced the likelihood of negative returns by one third.

- Investors with a ten percent international allocation could be ninety-eight percent confident that they would reduce risk by raising the international allocation.

- Investors with an allocation as high as twenty-two percent could be ninety percent confident that they would reduce risk by raising their international allocation.[7]

What is likely to surprise most investors is that adding international assets to a portfolio during a period when they underperformed actually resulted in higher returns and lower risk.

David Blitzer, Standard & Poor's chief investment strategist, provided further evidence on the wisdom of international diversification. Blitzer constructed a portfolio that was 60% U.S./40% international.[8] The international portion consisted of an equal eight percent weighting of five major countries, France, Germany, Japan, Switzerland, and the United Kingdom. He used the Morgan Stanley Capital International (MSCI) country indices for his data, and rebalanced the portfolios annually. The result of his study, which covered the period January 1970 through February 2000, was that no single country produced a higher return than did the overall portfolio, and the standard deviation (measure of volatility) of the portfolio was below that of any single country. Thus, by diversifying, investors earned higher returns while experiencing lower volatility than they could have done by investing either in the United States alone, or in any other country alone. Of course, to obtain that benefit an investor would have had to have the discipline to regularly rebalance, selling some of the recent winners and buying more of the recent losers.

	Annualized Return (%)	Standard Deviation (%)
Portfolio	14.2	14.0
United States	13.1	15.3
France	13.8	23.0
Germany	13.4	20.5
Japan	14.2	22.9
United Kingdom	13.4	24.0
Switzerland	13.5	19.1

One of the most common arguments against international investing is that the regulatory environment created by the SEC makes the United States a safer place to invest. Even if you fully agree, before believing that you can benefit from this information you must ask yourself if you are the only one that knows it. Obviously, the market is aware of this information, and security prices around the world surely reflect it. Here is something else to think about. Perhaps one of the contributing factors to the strong returns U.S. stocks have provided over the last fifty years is the improvement that the SEC has made in its oversight of the U.S. capital markets. It seems logical to conclude that this improvement has contributed to the lowering of the perception investors have of the risks of equity investing in the United States. The result was a lowering of the risk premium investors demand. That resulted in a *onetime* capital gain, and lower future expected returns (reflecting the now lower perceived risk). Now, applying that to foreign stocks, you might draw the following conclusions. The market knows that foreign stocks are riskier because of the more lax regulatory environment. The market therefore prices for that risk and you get higher expected returns as compensation. Let's now speculate on the following possible, if not likely, scenario.

The world has learned much about economic growth over the past fifty years as capitalism has triumphed. Countries need access to capital in order to grow their economies. If a country does not have adequate disclosure laws, investors won't provide capital. Therefore, is it not logical to conclude that the rest of the world will be moving to replicate U.S. regulatory standards? In fact, many foreign companies are already adopting U.S. accounting standards, as they want access to the U.S. capital markets. As more international companies and foreign markets adopt U.S. regulatory standards, the risk premiums demanded for international stocks might fall as investors recognize the change and lower their required risk premium. Investors in international stocks would then realize a capital gain from the fall in the risk premium.

Let's assume that you believe that the United States is safer because the economic and/or political prospects are better (keeping in mind that investors in other countries also appear to believe that their domestic market is safer). You should then conclude that the United States has lower expected returns. Although this would not mean that the United States was a poor place to invest, it is illogical to believe that the United States is a safer place to invest while also believing that the United States will provide higher returns. Risk and expected reward should be related.

There are other arguments for including international asset classes in a portfolio. U.S. investors have all of their intellectual capital in the domestic market. Their ability to generate income from employment is tied to U.S. economic conditions. They also might own a home, which may constitute a large percentage of their assets. If the dollar falls in value on the currency markets, not only will the cost of imports rise, but the competitive pressures from cheap imports will decrease, allowing domestic manufacturers to raise prices. This combination of events will lower living standards. Owning foreign assets acts as a hedge against such risk.

Allocating a significant portion of your portfolio to international asset classes will provide an insurance policy against potential problems in the United States. Since we don't have a clear crystal ball, diversification of risk is an important element of the winning strategy. If you need any more evidence of this, just refer back to the example of Japanese investors in 1989, as described in Mistake 3, "Do You Believe Events Are More Predictable After the Fact Than Before?" Those who do not learn from history are doomed to repeat the same mistakes.

In evaluating the risks of international investing it is worth considering these additional points. First, it is useful to remember that the United States was once an "emerging market." Many

European investors lost fortunes in perfectly legitimate enter-prises such as canals, railways, toll roads, and so on. There were also many incidents of fraud and defaults on debt obligations. Is it not logical to assume that many European investors swore off investing in a nation populated by such swindlers? Of course, fortunes were also made by those who did continue to invest in the United States. Second, many investors point out the political risks of investing overseas, including the risk of confiscation of property. While neither dismissing nor denying those risks, restricting investments to the United States does not eliminate that risk. How do you think investors in such companies as Philip Morris or Johns Manville felt about having their wealth effectively transferred by the U.S. court system to well-compensated attorneys and their plaintiffs? Is that not simply another form of expropriation?

Before concluding this chapter, let's discuss the potential inclusion of emerging market equities in a portfolio. Many investors shy away from investing in emerging markets because of the perception of high risk. It is true that investing in emerging markets is risky when viewed in isolation; but considering adding them to a portfolio is worthwhile for two reasons. First, since markets are efficient at pricing for risk, the greater risk of invest-ing in emerging markets should be offset by higher expected returns. Second, emerging markets are excellent diversifiers. For the five-year period ending 1999, the correlation between the IFC (International Finance Corporation) Emerging Markets Index and the S&P 500 was just 0.43. In the previous five years it was just 0.23. Equally important is the fact that emerging markets also have low correlation with EAFE (international large-cap stocks). For the same two five-year periods, the correlation between the IFC Emerging Markets Index and EAFE were 0.512 and 0.18. Given the low correlations with both U.S. markets and other international markets, the asset class of emerging markets makes an excellent diversifier for portfolios. The following example will illustrate the point.

To see the impact of adding emerging markets to a portfolio, I assumed a ten percent emerging market allocation being added to an S&P 500 fund to create a 90% S&P 500/10% emerging markets portfolio that would be rebalanced annually.

Annual Returns and Standard Deviation 1988–2000	
Emerging Markets*	18.5%/48%
S&P 500	16.7%/15%
10% Emerging Markets/ 90% S&P 500 portfolio	17.4% /16%

*Emerging Markets returns represent the live DFA Emerging Markets Fund and simulated returns prior to its going live in April 1994.

Note the very similar standard deviation of the portfolio as compared to the S&P 500, despite the very high standard deviation of the emerging markets asset class. Also note that with a 90/10 allocation, the weighted average return of the asset classes (without rebalancing) was 16.9%. Despite emerging markets making up just ten percent of the portfolio, rebalancing added 0.5% per annum to returns. This is due to the low correlation of returns between the two asset classes and the high volatility of returns of emerging markets.

Investing in international equities surely involves risk, but so does investing in domestic equities. And the evidence suggests that including international equities within a portfolio reduces the overall risks of the entire portfolio. Think about it this way: Diversification is a form of insurance. And we only insure against bad things not good things. International diversification provides us with insurance in case the U.S. capital markets and the dollar perform poorly.

MISTAKE 13

◆

Do You Believe You Are Playing with the House's Money?

In their wonderful book *Why Smart People Make Big Money Mistakes*, Gary Belsky, a writer at *Money* magazine from 1991 to 1998, and Thomas Gilovich, a psychology professor at Cornell University, relate the following legendary tale. By the third day of their honeymoon in Las Vegas, the newlyweds had lost their $1,000 gambling allowance. That night in bed, the groom noticed a glowing object on the dresser. He realized it was a five-dollar chip he had saved as a souvenir. The number seventeen was on the chip's face. Taking this as an omen, he donned his green bathrobe, rushed down to the roulette tables, and placed the five-dollar chip on the square marked seventeen. Sure enough, the ball hit seventeen. The thirty-five to one bet paid $175. He let his winnings ride, and once again the little ball landed on seventeen, paying $6,125. And so it went, until the lucky groom was about to wager $7.5 million. Unfortunately, the floor manager intervened, claiming that the casino didn't have the money to pay should seventeen hit again. Still clad in his bathrobe, the young man taxied to a better-financed casino. Once again he bet it all on seventeen, only to lose it all when the ball fell on eighteen. Broke and dejected, the groom walked back to his hotel room. "Where were you?" asked his bride. "Playing roulette." "How did you do?" "Not bad. I lost five dollars."[1]

The "Legend of the Man in the Green Bathrobe" illustrates what behavioral finance people call "mental accounting," the tendency to value some dollars less than others, and thus to waste them. In the case of the man in the green bathrobe, mental accounting allowed him to think of the $7.5 million he lost as the "house's money," not his. Investors make this same mistake. Let me explain.

A good friend had been either lucky or smart enough to buy Cisco at 5. The stock represented a relatively small portion of his net worth. When the stock reached 80, this was no longer the case. The sharp rise in the price of the stock had caused his position in Cisco to become a substantial portion of his portfolio. When I asked if he would buy any at the current price, he said, no. I then stated that if he wouldn't buy any, he must believe that it was either too highly valued or he was currently holding too much of the stock and it was too risky to have that many of his eggs in one basket. Despite the logic of my argument, he steadfastly refused to sell some shares for the following reason: His cost was only five, and the stock would have to drop about ninety-five percent before he would have a loss. I then asked him if he owned a green bathrobe.

A few months later Cisco had hit thirteen and he was still holding it. Now this man is one of the smartest people I know. He also had studied and was a big fan of the work of Amos Tversky and Daniel Kahneman, among the founding fathers of the field of behavioral finance. Yet mental accounting had caused him to make the same mistake as the man in the green bathrobe. He had considered his unrealized gain as the "house's money," instead of his own. Just as the man in the green bathrobe could have taken his chips and cashed them in, my friend could have sold the stock at 80 and converted his unrealized gain into nice green cash.

Making the mental accounting mistake of believing you are playing with the house's money can be avoided by developing and having the discipline to adhere to an IPS and a rebalancing table. This will force you to get up and walk away with the house's money if a position in a single stock, or asset class, grows beyond the maximum tolerance range established by your plan.

PART TWO

Ignorance Is Bliss

MISTAKE 14

◆

Do You Confuse Information with Knowledge?

Prominent media journalism is a thoughtless process of providing the noise that can capture people's attention.
—Nassim Nicholas Taleb, *Fooled by Randomness*

Something that everyone knows isn't worth knowing.
—Bernard Baruch

In the world of investing there is a major difference between information and knowledge. Information is a fact, data, or an opinion held by someone. Knowledge, on the other hand, is information that is of value. Confusing the two is a major mistake. Let's take a look at what I call the "information paradox."

At the core of the efficient market theory (EMT) is that *new* information is disseminated to the public so rapidly and completely that prices instantly adjust to new data. A good analogy is that financial markets operate much like our body's central nervous system in that they receive and relay information in an extremely rapid fashion. If this is the case, an investor can consistently beat the market only with either the best of luck or with inside information (on which it is illegal to trade). The logical conclusion seems *illogical* to most investors: if information is valuable, it has no value. Thus we have the information paradox.

There is a very simple and logical explanation of the paradox: The reason that valuable information has no value is that unless you are the only one to know it, the market has already incorporated it into prices. The only other way you can exploit information is to interpret that information differently from the way in

63

which the market collectively interprets it. The example below should illustrate the logic of the information paradox. Any investor who has ever purchased a stock based on a recommendation from a broker (or from a financial publication, a CNBC guest, and so on) will be able to relate to this situation.

The following dialogue is a hypothetical phone conversation between a broker and an investor. The conversation is hypothetical, but it will probably sound familiar (though perhaps exaggerated) to those who have dealt with brokers.

Broker: We just have to buy IBM.

Investor: Why should I buy IBM?

Broker: Our analyst that covers IBM is a genius. She graduated first in her MBA class at Harvard. She then graduated first in her class at MIT, receiving a Ph.D. in electrical engineering. She worked for ten years at IBM in product development and ten more in marketing and sales. She then joined our firm and has been our technology analyst. She has personally visited all IBM plants and research facilities; she has also visited with all competitors. She even visited with all of IBM's major customers to check on how they perceive IBM products and service and on the status of new orders. And she met with IBM's suppliers to check on the quality of their work. The stock is currently selling at 100. Given the great new pipeline of one hundred great new products and the growth in sales that will result, the stock is worth 200 if it's worth a penny.

Investor: That sounds great. Let's buy 1,000 shares.

Let's assume everything the broker said was absolutely true. There is a very logical reason for you to ignore all such prognostications—there is something very wrong with the picture. An alternative version of our hypothetical phone call will illustrate why. This version, however, is one that will not only be totally unfamiliar to all investors but is also one they will never hear. The reason is that while the broker will be no less truthful than in the previous example, here it is not in the broker's interest to disclose the truth.

Broker: Though we do have a very smart analyst covering IBM, there are sixty-five other very smart analysts covering IBM. They all have MBAs from top schools and lots of experience. They are all highly paid and motivated. They all work diligently to gather the facts. They all have the same information our analyst does. If the other analysts thought IBM was worth 200, obviously the stock would already be trading there. Do you think all those smart people would let a stock that is obviously worth 200 sit there at 100 without rushing to buy it at this obviously undervalued level? The reason IBM is trading at 100 is that the market as a whole thinks that it is only worth 100, not 200. However, our analyst thinks the rest of the world has got it wrong. Our analyst is *right* and the rest of the world is wrong. Only our analyst really knows this stuff, and the rest of the smart analysts are simply misinterpreting the information. We really need to buy IBM.
Investor: Dial tone . . .

I think it is safe to say that if you had heard the second conversation instead of the first, instead of buying IBM you would have laughed at the broker's "ill logic" and simply hung up. You will note, however, that although the second conversation is far more likely to reflect the truth about the analyst, this conversation never occurs. Why? It is not in the broker's interest for you to know the truth. He wouldn't make any money.

There is an alternative way to regard the advice of a stockbroker. Let's assume the broker actually has the investor's interest at heart and truly believes that his firm's analyst is a great analyst, can ferret out information others cannot, and can do a better job of interpreting the information. Though it is possible that all brokers may have their clients' interests at heart and also believe their firm's analyst is the best, all the analysts cannot be above average, let alone the best. Is it logical to believe that the analyst at Merrill Lynch is superior and knows more than the analyst at Goldman Sachs or Janus? Actually, it doesn't even matter. What really matters is that the evidence is clear that it is highly unlikely that any one individual over time will be able to identify securities the rest of the market has somehow mispriced.

There is another problem with following the broker's advice. Suppose that you do buy IBM and it proceeds to rise in value. Now what? Since IBM had about a 50/50 chance of outperforming the market, how do you know that the analyst's correct prediction was based on skill and not a matter of luck? Many analysts become famous on just a single recommendation. There are numerous examples, but perhaps the most famous and compelling is that of Elaine Garzarelli. While working at Shearson Lehman, Ms. Garzarelli correctly forecast the 1987 crash. Shearson Lehman began to widely tout her ability to call market moves and rewarded her for her successful prognostications with a mutual fund of her own to manage. Let's look at her record.

By June 30, 1994, the fund she was managing, the Smith Barney/Shearson Sector Analysis Fund, had risen in value by just 38% over the five years she was in charge, underperforming the Dow Jones Industrial Average by about 50%. In May 1996, with the Dow surpassing 5,700, this well-known market guru, who had left Shearson Lehman to form her own firm, advised her clients to invest aggressively. Almost immediately, the market underwent a sharp correction, falling over 400 points. She then reversed direction, advising her clients to sell. Once again the market reversed course. By November, the DJIA had crossed 6,500. In January 1997, with the market approaching 7,000, Ms. Garzarelli reversed position once again and advised her clients to buy. By April, the market had dropped to under 6,400.

The next time you watch CNBC and listen to an analyst or fund manager tout even a hundred good reasons why to buy a specific stock or equities in general, keep the information paradox in mind. Even though you are likely to be impressed with the intellectual capacity of the person and the information presented, as well as the logic of the recommendation, keep three points in mind before you leap into action:

1. Capturing *incremental* insight is very difficult, if not impossible, to achieve. The reason is that security analysts are competing with so many other smart and highly motivated people researching the same stocks. It is this tough competition that makes it so difficult to gain a competitive advantage. Imagine an art auction where you are the only expert among a group of amateurs. In that circumstance, it might be possible to find a bargain. On the other hand, if you are one of a group of mostly experts, it is far less likely that you will find bargain prices. The same is true of stocks. Competition among all the professional active managers ensures that the market price is highly likely to be the correct price.

2. Think about where you just heard the new insightful information—*on national television*. In the unlikely scenario this information was a secret, it no longer is. The same analogy could be made for recommendations from any of the high-profile publications such as *Barron's, BusinessWeek, Fortune, Forbes, Money,* or *Smart Money*.

3. As Rex Sinquefield, the co-chairman of Dimensional Fund Advisors, points out: "Just because there are some investors

smarter than others, that advantage will not show up. The market is too vast and too informationally efficient."[1]

The information paradox also applies to the recommendations of such gurus as Harry Dent. If you read his books, you would say Mr. Dent makes sense. However, before they leap to invest in individual stocks or mutual funds based on Harry Dent's (or any guru's) insightful analysis investors need to consider: Is Harry Dent the only person who knows that the demand for health care will rise as the population ages? Aren't all investors aware of this? Don't the big institutional investors and mutual funds that manage the vast majority of financial assets know all the things Dent predicts are likely to occur? Doesn't the market already incorporate this knowledge into current prices? The alternative is to believe the market is simply asleep—a highly unlikely scenario. If the market is aware of this information, it has already been incorporated into prices. Therefore, the knowledge cannot be exploited.

How can you avoid the mistake of confusing information with knowledge? Simply remember the following: Every time you hear or read a recommendation on a stock or asset class (technology stocks, small caps, emerging markets, etc.), ask yourself, Am I the only one who knows this information? If the answer is no (and of course it is, unless it is inside information on which it is illegal to trade), then the market has already incorporated that information into prices—and the information cannot be exploited. Possession of an insight is not sufficient. You can only benefit if other traders do not have the insight yet. Unfortunately, valuable information about a company, asset class, or market has no value since it cannot be exploited.

MISTAKE 15

◆

Do You Believe Your Fortune Is in the Stars?

The brand that has emerged as dominant in the 1990s is not Fidelity, Putnam, or even Merrill Lynch—but instead is Morningstar. —R. Pozen, *The Mutual Fund Business*, 1998, p. 75.

I own last year's top performing funds. Unfortunately, I bought them this year. —Anonymous

Perhaps the most popular approach to selecting mutual funds is to rely on the very popular rating service provided by Morningstar that rates funds using a star system similar to the one used by film critics. Ads touting four- and five-star ratings are found everywhere. Investors must believe the stars have predictive value. One study covering the period January through August 1995 found that an amazing ninety-seven percent of fund inflows went into four- and five-star funds, while three-star funds experienced outflows.[1]

Diane Del Guerico and Paula A. Tkac of the Federal Reserve Bank of Atlanta investigated how changes in Morningstar's ratings influence mutual fund cash flows. The study, "Star Power: The Effect of Morningstar Ratings on Mutual Fund Flows," covered almost 3,400 domestic equity mutual funds for the period November 1996 to October 1999, and identified over 12,000 ratings changes.[2] The following is a summary of the key findings.

- The initiation of a five-star rating results in average inflow over the next six months that is fifty-three percent greater than normal.

- An upgrade from four- to five-stars increases the rate of inflows over the next six months by thirty-five percent.

- Even upgrades from two- to three-stars, and from three- to four-stars, generates positive abnormal inflows.

- A downgrade from five- to four-stars has a negative impact, though to a much lesser degree. Fund inflows fell from their norm by eight percent. One reason for the smaller impact of a downgrade is that existing investors might be reluctant to sell as capital gains taxes are likely to be incurred as a result of a sale. Another reason is that a five-star fund that is on a recommended list might not be removed from that list unless the fund continues to lag in performance.

- Downgrades from three- to two-stars and four- to three-stars also generates abnormal negative flow.

- The influence of ratings changes is observable virtually instantaneously—demonstrating that investors are paying close attention to the ratings, and placing a high value on their predictive ability.

The authors also note that funds are "more likely to advertise if they have a five-star rating to tout," and advertising impacts fund flows. The paper cited a study that found that funds that advertise in popular magazines such as *Barron's* or *Money* receive significantly greater inflows than a control sample of funds with similar performance.[3] Funds, of course, are only likely to advertise four- or five-star ratings.

For investors the essential question is whether or not chasing ratings is the winning strategy. Let's examine the evidence.

Morningstar gives the coveted five-star rating to the funds it believes are among the top ten percent of all funds, and a one-star rating to the bottom ten percent. Mark Hulbert's *The Hulbert Financial Digest* tracked the performance of the five-star funds for the period 1993–2000. For that eight-year period the total return (pretax) on Morningstar's top-rated U.S. funds averaged +106%. This compared to a total return of +222% for the total stock market, as measured by the Wilshire 5000 Equity Index. Hulbert also found that the top-rated funds, while achieving less than fifty percent of the market's return, carried a relative risk (measured by standard deviation) that was twenty-six percent greater than that of the market. If the performance had been measured on an after-tax basis, the tax inefficiency of actively managed funds relative to a passive index fund would have made the comparison significantly worse.[4]

A Financial Research Corp. study covering the period January 1, 1995–September 30, 1998 revealed that two- and three-star funds outperformed their four- and five-star counterparts for the entire period. The study's conclusion: "the linkage between past performance and future realizations is tenuous if not nonexistent."[5]

A similar study, by Christopher R. Blake, associate professor of finance at Fordham University's Graduate School of Business, and Matthew Morey, assistant professor of finance at Fordham, found that for the five-year period ending December 31, 1997, the average five-star fund underperformed the market by almost four percent per annum. The study also found that the differences between the performances of the three-, four-, and five-star funds were so small as to have very little statistical significance.[6] Blake and Morey concluded that while a low star rating was actually a good predictor of relatively poor future performance, high star ratings were not good predictors of future top performance. The top-rated funds did not outperform the next highest or even median-ranked funds.[7] Morningstar has even stated that there is no connection between past and future performance and stars, historic star ratings, or any raw data, and that the stars should not be used to predict short-term returns or to time fund purchases.[8]

Despite this strong admission, it is obvious from the heavy expenditures of advertising dollars by mutual funds that they believe investors perceive the star ratings as having predictive value.

Morningstar's ratings are so popular that there have been many studies on their ratings of funds and future performance. One of these, *The Persistence of Morningstar Ratings*, sought to determine if there was any useful information contained in the star ratings.[9] If there is persistence in fund ratings it would be valuable information. Unfortunately, the authors concluded, after studying variable annuities, equity funds, and bond funds, that there is little evidence of persistence of performance. The study found:

- For four- and five-star equity funds, year-to-year persistence is the equivalent of a coin flip. Less than half of all mutual funds rated four- or five-star at year-end 1997 still held that high rating at year-end 1998. Basically, there is a reversion to a three-star mean.

- Persistence for variable annuities is worse than a flip of the coin. Year-to-year persistence is only about forty percent.

- Persistence is the worst for taxable bond funds at just over twenty percent.

- For equity funds with just three-year ratings the year-to-year persistence of ratings was less than twenty-five percent. Keep this in mind when you think you have discovered a new guru.

You can avoid the mistake of relying on either Morningstar's rating system or the past performance of actively managed funds in general when choosing building blocks for your portfolio by remembering the evidence presented here and by listening carefully to the following comments from Morningstar's director of research, John Rekenthaler, a man for whom I have the highest regard, especially for his integrity in an industry not especially known for it.

1. *There's actually not much difference between mid-ranked funds and top-rated ones. Three-star, four-star and five-star funds have been found to perform pretty much alike.*[10] (In the interests of full disclosure, Rekenthaler did go on to point out that mid-rank and high-rank funds do better on average than the lower-rank funds. This is a similar finding to the results found by Blake and Morey. However, the persistency of poor performance of low rank funds is most likely a function of their high expenses, and not poor stock selection skills.)

2. *We should have more answers. There is surprisingly little that we can say for sure about how to find top-notch stock funds.*[11]

3. And, commenting on whether investors should pay attention to mutual fund advertisements: *to be fair, I don't think that you'd want to pay much attention to Morningstar's star ratings either.*[12]

Finally, listen to the words of Amy Arnott, the editor of Morningstar's publication. "Over the years, Morningstar's star system has been frequently—and sometimes willfully—misunderstood. Many commentators insist on treating the star rating as a predictive measure or a short-term trading signal. The rating, which is clearly labeled as a historical profile, does neither."[13]

MISTAKE 16

◆

Do You Rely on Misleading Information?

"Warning: Returns shown contain biases we are not required to report." The SEC should require this disclosure for the advertisements of many mutual funds, because without this type of disclaimer the vast majority of investors are unaware they are making investment decisions based on reported returns that are either outright misrepresentations of the returns earned by investors or at the very least misleading representations. The reported returns of many funds are distorted because of biases in the data. Let's look at the two biases for which mandatory disclosures should be required.

The first disclosure relates to what is known as "survivorship bias." Funds that have poor performance are made to disappear, most often by the fund sponsor merging a poorly performing fund into a better performing one. Unfortunately, only the performance reporting disappears; not the poor returns.

In the most comprehensive study ever done on mutual funds, covering the period 1962–93, Mark Carhart found that by 1993, fully one third of all funds in his sample had disappeared.[1] In 1996, 242 (5%) of the 4,555 stock funds tracked by Lipper Analytical Services were merged or liquidated. Let's see why survivorship bias is so important. In 1986 the then-existing 568 stock funds returned 13.4%. By 1996, the 1986 performance had magically improved to 14.7%. The 1.3% improvement was a result of the disappearance of twenty-four percent of the original funds, and the fact that only the 1986 performance of the funds still in existence ten years later was used in the new computation.[2] As another example, for the ten-year period ending in 1992, capital appreciation funds reported an average appreciation of 18.08% versus a return of only 17.52% for the S&P 500 Index. Once the survivorship bias is eliminated, and the returns of vanishing funds are considered, the returns of all capital appreciation funds that existed during the same ten-year period drops to 16.32%. Actual returns to investors were not only almost two percent per annum worse then they initially appeared to be; they were also about one percent below the return available to investors in S&P 500 Index funds.[3]

Two other studies provide confirming evidence. Lipper Analytical Services found that the return of all general equity funds for the ten-year period they studied was 15.7%. This was 1.5% below that of the funds that existed at the end of the period (the survivors) and almost two percent below the return of the S&P 500 Index.[4] The second study found that over the fifteen-year period ending December 1992, the annual return of all equity mutual funds was 15.6% per annum. When the study included all the funds that failed to survive the entire period, the annual return dropped to 14.8%. The cumulative difference in returns was 781% versus 689%.[5]

The survivorship bias problem has increased in recent years as mutual fund families try even harder to bury poor performance. In 1998 alone, 387 stock and bond funds were merged out of existence, an increase of forty-three percent over the previous year. An additional 250 funds were liquidated due to investor redemptions. In the first quarter of 1999, the number of vanishing stock funds jumped seventy-four percent.[6] The trend continued into 2000 as a record 735 mutual funds were liquidated or merged. And in the first quarter of 2001, the number of disappearing funds rose thirty-seven percent compared to the year-ago period.[7]

The story of Liberty Financial Companies is a good illustration of the potential impact on reported returns when funds are merged out of existence. Liberty had been experiencing a serious drain on its assets under management. In 1999, net outflows were over $600 million, and increased to over $850 million in the first three quarters of 2000. In an effort to stem investor defections from its funds, on October 5, 2000, Liberty announced that it was planning to merge out of existence seventeen of its ninety-five stock and bond funds. The seventeen funds represented $1.7 billion of investor assets. The assets of those seventeen funds were to be merged into ten existing funds in the Liberty family.[8] It is probably safe to assume that the funds that were merged out of existence were the ones with the poorest track records. By merging the funds out of existence Liberty magically made the performance statistics of those funds disappear. The reported returns of the now-merged funds will only contain the live returns of the surviving fund. Of course, the poor returns investors received from the defunct funds did not disappear, it is just that their performance is no longer reported by either the rating services or the funds into which they were merged. (No respect for the dead.) Clearly, future investors are not getting the whole story on the returns earned by investors in the Liberty family of funds.

The second bias in data comes from the use of what are known as "incubator funds." Incubator funds are newly created funds, seeded by mutual fund families with their own capital. The funds are not available to the public. Here is one way the game may be played. A fund family creates several small-cap funds, possibly even under the same manager. Each fund might own a different group of small-cap stocks. The fund family incubates the funds, safe from public scrutiny. After a few years they bring public only the fund with the best performance. Magically, the performance of the other funds disappears. Unfortunately, a recent SEC ruling allows fund families to report the pre-public performance of incubator funds. Thus we have the potential for huge distortion of reality.

In October 2000, MFS Investment Management of Boston had nineteen funds in incubation, almost all of them less than three years old. If MFS's prior experience is a good predictor of the future, only one half of these funds will become available to the public; the other half of the currently incubating funds will die a quiet death by liquidation.[9] Which funds do you think will be liquidated? You can readily see how the real performance of MFS's funds can be distorted without full disclosure.

To make matters worse, a large fund family might provide a tiny incubator fund with a relatively large allocation of a hot IPO (initial public offering). Given the small amount of assets in an incubator fund, the fund's returns could be supercharged, clearly a distortion of what might be expected once a fund went public. Fortunately, the SEC has recognized the potential for distortion and has finally begun to take some action. In 1999 it fined the Van Kampen Growth Fund, a unit of Morgan Stanley Dean Witter, $125,000 for not adequately disclosing the role IPOs had in the strong first-year gain of the fund. The fund was started as an incubator fund in 1996 and rose 62% that year. Another example of the abuse of the system came in May 2000, when Dreyfus agreed to pay nearly $3 million to resolve charges from both the New York state attorney general and the SEC that the firm had made inadequate or false disclosures about the role of IPOs in returns.[10] It would seem that the logical solution to this distorted reporting is to prohibit the advertising of returns before a fund is made available to the public.

You should keep in mind that the "IPO game" is also often

played by large fund families. To illustrate the point, let's look at hypothetical Fund Family XYZ, a very large mutual fund complex. They have many funds with hundreds of billions of assets under management. When an IPO is announced, they, like dozens of other fund families, receive their allocation. If they were to divide up the allocation among their many funds, the impact of any potential first-day rise in the IPO's price would be minimal on each fund. However, if they give the entire allocation to the smallest fund in the family, the impact might be dramatic. Guess which option they choose? Not surprisingly, the fund may turn in a great year, fueled by its IPO allocations. The fund then receives a coveted five-star rating. Believing that past performance is a predictor of future performance, and that star ratings have predictive value, the public rushes to buy the fund. Assets under management grow dramatically. That game is over, though a new one might begin. And, there is even another game played by fund families to juice the returns of both their new and smaller funds. The game is called "front-running." Here is how it works. A large fund family starts a new small-cap fund. The fund buys shares of stocks with a low market cap and limited liquidity. The other funds in the same family then pile in, buying more shares. The limited supply of stock allows the large fund family to drive up prices with relatively small purchases by each fund. The returns of the new fund look great, with limited impact on the larger funds in the family.

As you can see, even with fund families playing within current SEC rules, there exists the possibility for a significant distortion of both the actual returns received by investors and the potential for repeat performances. Fuller disclosure might help, but since many investors don't read the fine print, the public would be better served if the practices were simply prohibited. At least being aware of the potential for bias in the data might help prevent a poor investment decision.

There is another similar kind of bias in the mutual fund business: selection bias. Fund families only advertise their funds with good track records and high star ratings. For example, you probably are familiar with Fidelity's ad campaign in which Peter Lynch suggests that index funds are good investments, but if you want to try to beat the market Fidelity has a long list of four- and five-star funds from which to choose. Of course, not all Fidelity funds are four or five stars. Why wasn't the performance of their other funds presented? Have you ever seen an ad for a mutual fund that advertises its poor track record? Of course not. Why do funds advertise their winning records? The presumption is that investors will extrapolate the past successes into the future—despite the warning/disclaimer required by the SEC stating that "Past performance is not an indicator of future performance." With this in mind, a very interesting study was published in the April 2000 edition of the *Journal of Finance*.

Prem C. Jain of Tulane University and Joanna Shuang Wu of the University of Rochester examined the performance of 294 U.S. equity mutual funds that advertised in *Barron's* or *Money* magazine. They measured the performance of the mutual funds one year prior to the first advertisement date, and one year after. The authors looked at fund objectives when considering returns. They placed funds into the categories of aggressive growth; growth; growth and income; small; and other. Given the bias that funds would not advertise poor performance, not unexpectedly the advertised funds performed well above average prior to the advertisement date. The average one-year pre-advertised return of the 294 funds was almost six percent higher than the average return of comparable funds during the period of July 18, 1994–June 30, 1996. The returns of the advertised funds were also 1.8% above the return of the S&P 500. To ensure an apples-to-apples comparison, the study also compared the returns of the advertised funds to the returns predicted by Mark Carhart's four-factor (equities, size, value, and momentum) model. They found the funds provided a positive alpha (value added) of 1.43%. In all cases the t-stats were high. A high t-stat is evidence of high statistical significance. In other words, the results were highly unlikely to be of a random nature.

In the post-advertisement period, however, the same funds returned 0.8% below the return of all comparable funds. The funds also underperformed the S&P 500 by almost 8% per annum, and the Carhart four-factor model by almost 3.5% per annum. Not surprisingly, the study also found that advertised funds attracted significantly greater investments than other similar funds in the post-advertisement period. Investors were chasing yesterday's returns.

The study considered the possibility that the poor post-advertising performance might have been caused by manager turnover. However, during the study period, 246 of the 294 funds had no turnover in managers. The study also found that there was no difference in performance between the funds that experienced turnover and the funds that did not.

Whenever you hear a claim about the performance of a mutual fund or a group of funds make sure that the data presented contains none of the biases discussed above. In addition, you should take very seriously the SEC's warning on using past performance as a predictor. As we have seen, this warning is required for a good reason—past performance has little to no predictive power.

One last point before moving on: A lingering bit of conventional wisdom about investing that Wall Street needs and wants you to believe is that while the market for large-cap stocks may be highly efficient (thus making active management a loser's game), the market for small-cap stocks is not efficient. They claim that the inefficiency of this asset class allows active managers to exploit market mispricings. That bit of conventional wisdom is as correct as once was the belief that the Earth was the center of the universe. Morningstar studied the performance of the top quartile small-cap growth funds for the five-year period ending May 1996 to see how they performed in the succeeding five-year period.[11] Not a single one remained in the top quartile, and only one fund even managed to outperform the average for all funds in that asset class. Eight of the top ten performers changed managers. Morningstar's suggestion was that investors should be quick to fire a small-cap growth manager who isn't performing. The more prudent advice would be to not make the mistake of hiring one in the first place. Consider the following: During the ten-year period covered by the study (ending May 2001), even with survivorship and other biases in the data, the only passively managed small-cap fund of which I am aware that existed during the entire decade returned 16.1% per annum, finishing in the top twenty percent (DFA Micro Cap Fund). Passive investing is the winner's game regardless of the asset class.

MISTAKE 17

◆

Do You Only Consider the Operating Expense Ratio When Selecting a Mutual Fund?

Fees paid for active management are not a good deal for investors, and they're beginning to realize it.
—Michael Kostoff, executive director of the Advisory
Board Co., a Washington-based market research firm, in
InvestmentNews, February 8, 1999

Mutual fund fees are unconscionably high. They get higher every year, while funds get bigger every year—and that should make the fees smaller—by virtue of the economies of scale.
—Patrick Regnier, associate editor, *Morningstar Investor,*
St. Louis Post-Dispatch, July 6, 1997

We all know that active management fees are high. Poor performance does not come cheap. You have to pay dearly for it.
—Rex Sinquefield, Dimensional Fund Advisors

The shortest route to top quartile performance is to be in the bottom quartile of expenses.   —John Bogle

Many investors know that when it comes to investing, costs matter. To outperform their benchmarks, active managers must not only be able to select the right stocks and/or time the market successfully; they must do so while more than recovering the costs of their efforts.

When deciding on their choice of mutual funds, many investors consider only the operating expense ratio. The main reason for this error is probably the fact that the operating expense ratio is the only expense that is currently published. Unfortunately, not only is the operating expense ratio but one of many costs, in many cases it is the least of the costs involved, especially for taxable accounts. It is just that the cost of the other expenses, trading costs, taxes, and the cost of cash, goes unreported. These costs are nonetheless real, and are manifested in lower returns.

Let's examine the other expenses that mutual fund investors incur and their impact on returns.

The Cost of Cash

The least understood hidden cost is the "cost of cash." The cost of cash occurs when a mutual fund holds a cash position instead of being fully invested in the market. A study by Russ Wermers found that non-equity holdings reduced returns for the average actively managed equity fund by 0.7% per annum.[1] The greater the cash position held, the greater the impact. Unfortunately, the past average cash holding of an actively managed fund may not be a good predictor of the future. Therefore, you might use Wermers's estimate when considering an active fund. With index funds or other passive investment vehicles being virtually fully invested, the cost of cash will be negligible.

Trading Expenses

The average actively managed fund now has turnover of about ninety percent, and the cost of trading—commissions and bid-offer spreads—averages approximately one percent to buy and one percent to sell. For very large-cap stocks the bid-offer spreads are somewhat lower, at around 0.7%. For very small-cap stocks the spreads are much wider. For example, for the smallest twenty percent of stocks as ranked by the Center for Research in Security Prices at the University of Chicago (CRSP), with market caps below about $200 million, the bid-offer spread exceeds two percent. For the smallest ten percent, with market caps below $100 million, the spread exceeds four percent. You can estimate the costs of trading by multiplying the turnover by the bid-offer spread, and then multiplying that by 2. For the average fund, you will get an estimate of 1.8% ($90\% \times 2 \times 1\%$). Despite its unreliability as a predictor, the best you can do is to look at a fund's historical turnover as your best estimate of its future turnover. With index funds, however, past turnover is likely to be a better predictor of future turnover. Depending on the index it is attempting to replicate, the typical passively managed fund will have turnover of between three percent and twenty-five percent (lower for passive large-cap funds and greater for passive small-cap funds). If we assume an average turnover of about fifteen percent, then we can estimate the cost of trading at 0.3% ($1\% \times 2 \times 0.15$).

Our estimate of the negative impact of the trading (turnover) of active managers is supported by the results of a Morningstar study. Morningstar divided mutual funds into two categories: those with an average holding period greater than five years (less than twenty percent turnover) and those with an average holding period of less than one year (turnover greater than one hundred percent). Over a ten-year period Morningstar found that low turnover funds rose an average of 12.87% per annum, while high turnover funds gained only 11.29% per annum on average. Trading costs and the impact on prices of trading activity reduced returns of the high turnover funds by 1.58% per annum.[2]

Trading costs are generally much higher for funds that invest internationally. Not only do they incur bid-offer spreads that are generally higher than they are in the United States, and commissions that are greater, but some countries also impose what is called a stamp duty. In addition, custodial fees can be very high. For example, in the United Kingdom commissions average thirty-five basis points, the stamp duty is fifty basis points, and custodial fees are six basis points, for a total of ninety-one basis points, even before considering the cost of the bid-offer spread.[3]

Market Impact Costs

Active managers incur "market impact" costs. Market impact is what occurs when a mutual fund wants to buy or sell a large block of stock. The fund's purchases or sales will cause the stock to move beyond its current bid (lower) or offer (higher) price, increasing the cost of trading. Barra, a research organization, recently completed a study on market impact costs. The cost of market impact will vary, depending on many factors (fund size, asset class, turnover, etc.), but it can be quite substantial. Barra noted that a fairly typical case of a small- or mid-cap stock fund with $500 million in assets and an annual turnover rate of between eighty and one hundred percent could lose three to five percent per annum to market impact costs—far more than the annual expenses of most funds. In another example, over a specified period, the PBHG Emerging Growth Fund had the highest estimated market impact cost among small- or mid-cap funds at 5.73% per annum. Even large-cap funds can have large market impact costs, as illustrated by the 8.13% figure estimated for the Phoenix Engemann Aggressive Growth Fund.[4]

Without access to the specific data it is very hard to estimate a fund's market impact costs. However, you can at least consider high turnover as an indicator of the size of the impact; the smaller the market capitalization of the stocks the fund owns, the greater the impact.

Taxes

Unfortunately, we have not come to the end of the road of fund expenses. In fact, for taxable accounts we have not yet covered what is often the greatest expense, the burden of taxes on IRS form 1099 fund distributions. Take one example. For the fifteen-year period ending June 30, 1998, the Vanguard S&P 500 Index Fund provided pretax returns of 16.9% per annum. The fund lost 1.9% per annum to taxes. Its after-tax return of 15% meant that the fund's tax efficiency was 89%. The average actively managed fund provided pretax returns of 13.6% and after-tax returns of just 10.8%. Losing 2.8% per annum to taxes resulted in a tax efficiency of just 79%.[5] Fortunately, after-tax returns data is now available from services such as Morningstar; recently, they have become an SEC reporting requirement.

It may be said that the long-term goal of investing is to multiply the eggs in our baskets. Yet too many investors focus on producing more eggs (getting high returns) while paying little attention to the fox (costs) that perpetually robs the henhouse. If you ignore the fox, soon there will be nothing left to produce more eggs.[5] You can avoid this mistake by analyzing a fund's turnover and tax efficiency, then using information in this chapter to estimate the total costs of investing in a fund.

MISTAKE 18

◆

Do You Fail to Consider the Costs of an Investment Strategy?

Most investors, both institutional and individual, will find that the best way to own common stocks is through an index fund that charges minimal fees. Those following this path are sure to beat the net results (after fees and expenses) delivered by the great majority of investment professionals. Seriously, costs matter. —Warren Buffett, quoted in John Bogle, *Bogle on Investing*

Investment strategies that produce market-beating results are obviously attractive to investors. Attributing great skill to the creators of the strategy, investors frequently adopt that strategy— all too often with disappointing results. One reason, as we have already seen, is that the past is not a good predictor of future performance. Also, investors are prone to attribute to skill what might be a function of luck since many strategies rely on patterns that might be the result of random events. There is another reason: although strategies do not entail costs, implementing them does. Let's look at four examples which demonstrate that it is a long way from a market-beating strategy to market-beating results. The first involves *BusinessWeek*.

One of *BusinessWeek's* regular columns is called "Inside Wall Street," the stock selections of columnist Gene Marcial. The July 24, 2000, issue contained an analysis of his 1999 stock picks. The article concluded that Marcial's stock-picking results were "sensational." They came to this conclusion by showing that Marcial's picks trounced both the DJIA and the S&P 500 indices, while they only slightly trailed the NASDAQ.

BusinessWeek measured the price performance of each stock recommended in Marcial's column during 1999 and compared their price performance against the S&P 500, DJIA, Russell 2000, and NASDAQ benchmarks. Price performance was measured against these indexes one day after the column was printed as well as one month, three months and six months after publication of the stock tips.

It is worth noting that Marcial's picks were up an average 8.8% the day after they appeared in print, compared to an average daily increase of 0.5% in the S&P 500 Index. However, investors couldn't buy at the previous day's close. Also, studies have shown that when new information becomes known, virtually the entire price move occurs in the very first trade. Thus investors likely paid about nine percent more for Marcial's picks than the previous close, clearly reducing the value of his picks for those investors who attempted to capitalize on Marcial's skills.

Larry Putnam, a contributing writer for the Web site index-funds.com, took a closer look at *BusinessWeek's* claim that stock-picker Marcial "trounced" most indexes and slightly trailed the NASDAQ Index in 1999.[1] When analyzing mutual funds or stock picks it is important to make sure you are making apples-to-apples comparisons, something *BusinessWeek* failed to do and thus provided misleading information. Putnam compared the price performance of Marcial's 155 stock picks to their appropriate benchmarks. Here is a summary of what he found:

- 85 (or 55%) of Marcial's 155 picks traded on the NASDAQ and AMEX. These are typically smaller-cap and technology -related stocks.

- 70 picks (45%) traded on the NYSE. These are more typically large-cap growth stocks.

- When you compare Marcial's picks with a portfolio that is weighted 55% NASDAQ Index and 45% S&P 500 Index, his 155 picks should have increased in price an average of 25.5% for the six-month period.

Marcial's picks were up 26%. Compared to the predicted 25.5% increase, the 26% reported increase for Marcial's stock selections no longer look "sensational." In addition, Marcial's returns do not take into consideration the fact that investors were highly unlikely to have been able to take advantage of the nine percent first day price rise. They also ignore trading costs (bid-offer spreads) and commissions. This is particularly important when you consider that nearly half of Marcial's picks were priced under 15, and about one third were priced below 10. Stocks with such low prices are typically very small-cap stocks that carry much greater trading costs than do large-caps. For example, the bid-offer spread (an estimate of trading costs) for the largest ten percent of stocks is just 0.65%. However, for the smallest ten percent of stocks it is almost seven times as great at 4.3%. Then consider you have to add in commissions (buy and sell) as well.

Once you subtract all estimated trading costs, Marcial's supposedly impressive returns no longer look so hot. In fact, using any reasonable estimate of the costs of implementing a "Marcial" strategy would have produced returns that were substantially below an appropriate benchmark. Another consideration is that this analysis ignored the potentially large tax implications of such an active stock-picking strategy. Putnam's work points out how easily investors can be misled by ambiguous information.

One last point on the "Marcial strategy." While the strategy is too costly to implement, the fact that his picks went up by nine percent on average the day after the picks were made is still impressive. Remember, however, that a stock being picked by Marcial in his *BusinessWeek* column is in itself "news," capable of influencing the price—it was a positive surprise. It certainly seems plausible that were the same picks made by an anonymous, amateur stock-picker rather than being published in *Business-Week*, nothing so spectacular would have occurred.

Our second example involves the Value Line Investment Survey and what is known as the "Value Line Enigma." Value Line touts its market-beating track record in advertisements hawking its services. Even Fischer Black, one of the fathers of the EMT, once stated that Value Line's results were a big exception to that theory. Black concluded: "investment firms would improve performance if they fired all but one of their security analysts and then provided the remaining analyst with the Value Line service."[2] Mark Hulbert, publisher of the *Hulbert Financial Digest*, found that the Value Line Survey has been one of the very few that has beaten the market since he began monitoring the performance of investment letters in the mid-1980.[3]

The results are truly incredible—at least on the surface. Investing $1,000 in a broad-based index fund for the period 1965–96 would have produced an ending value of $27,246. That same $1,000 invested in Value Line's rank one picks (top-rated) would have reached $580,115. Pursuing a rank five strategy would have resulted in an ending value of just $4,912.[4]

One would think that if anyone could beat the market using Value Line's advice and strategy it would be Value Line itself. To test this hypothesis, an investor could compare the performance of Value Line's funds with the performance of a comparable benchmark in the form of Vanguard's S&P 500 fund. Value Line runs three large-cap growth funds. Using the Morningstar database, I examined their performance, both on a pre- and after-tax basis, for the fifteen-year period ending September 2000. The Value Line Fund returned 16.81% pretax and 13.7% after tax. The Value Line Leveraged Growth Fund returned 18.25% per annum pretax and 15.52% after tax. The Value Line Special Situations Fund returned 15.79% pretax and 13.31% after tax. The three funds together provided a pretax return of 16.95% and an after-tax return of 14.18%. These returns compare to a pretax return of 16.76% and an after-tax return of 16.11% for Vanguard's S&P 500 Index fund. Thus, despite the huge apparent success of Value Line's stock-picking skills, they were able to translate that success after implementation expenses into a pretax outperformance of just 0.19% and an after-tax underperformance of 1.93%. The greater turnover of Value Line's actively managed funds resulted in greater capital gains being realized and greater taxes having to be paid. This impacted the after-tax performance dramatically—and negatively.

One study reported in the *Journal of Financial and Quantitative Analysis* took a closer look at the costs and implications of implementing the Value Line strategy. Its results shed considerable light on the apparent contradiction between the advertised returns and the implementable results. James Choi studied the Value Line recommendations from 1965 to 1996.[5] Although he did find that Value Line's outperformance before expenses was huge, he found no abnormal returns after accounting for expenses. Choi pursued a rank one strategy. Since Value Line delivers its recommendations to investors on Fridays, the totals were based on the assumption that securities were bought and sold at Friday's close. It was also assumed that stocks were held equally weighted, and rebalanced monthly. Choi found that pre-expense outperformance was an amazing 0.45% per month. He also found that most of the outperformance was concentrated in small- and mid-cap stocks (where transaction costs are greatest). Note also that the smallest stocks, in which there is limited liquidity, are where a Value Line recommendation can have the greatest price impact. In other words, it might be a self-fulfilling prophecy. To estimate the cost of turnover Choi used the estimates of institutional trading costs provided by Donald Keim and Ananth Madhavan in their 1998 study "The Cost of Institutional Equity Trades."[6] The table below lists the one-way estimated trading costs. Note that the cost of trading in the smallest-cap stocks is from about six to eighteen times as great as it is for the largest-cap stocks.

Market Cap Quintile	NYSE/AMEX Buy	NYSE/AMEX Sell	NASDAQ Buy	NASDAQ Sell
1 (largest)	0.31	0.26	0.24	0.16
2	0.43	0.63	0.51	0.85
3	0.64	1.02	0.92	1.18
4	1.00	1.33	1.52	1.73
5	1.78	2.03	2.85	2.91

Once Choi accounted for the huge turnover (as high as twenty-six percent per month), the abnormally high positive returns turned negative. He also found that if you rebalanced as infrequently as once per year, while costs fell, so did returns. Choi's results fully explain the difference between the results of the

Value Line *strategy* and the underperformance of the Value Line funds.

Choi's findings are very similar to the results of another study, reported in the *Journal of Finance*, on the stock-picking skills of security analysts.[7] The authors used the Zacks database for the period 1985–96 and covered over 360,000 recommendations from 269 brokerage houses and 4,340 analysts. To form portfolios, the study used the consensus analyst recommendations. Each time an analyst changed a rating or initiated coverage the consensus recommendation was recalculated and the portfolio rebalanced. The authors found that analysts did have stock selection skills. Buying the stocks with the most favorable consensus recommendation earned an annualized return of 18.8% per annum. This compared to a return of 14.5% for the market and just 5.8% for a portfolio of the least favorable consensus stocks. After controlling for market risk, size, book-to-market, and momentum factors, a portfolio of the most highly recommended stocks provided abnormal (above-market) gross returns of just over four percent per annum, and the least favorably recommended stocks provided abnormal gross returns of almost negative five percent per annum. It is important to note that the results were most pronounced for the smallest stocks. In contrast, among the very largest companies the study found no reliable differences between the returns of the most highly rated stocks and those with the least favorable recommendations. So the news is mixed on the ability of security analysts to identify future under- and outperformers. It appears that they are successful with very small stocks, but not successful at all with very large stocks. Unfortunately, the evidence shows that investors cannot exploit the stock selection skills that appear to be evident in the small-cap stocks. Let's examine why this is so.

As noted above, the abnormal returns were gross returns, before deducting all expenses. However, investors attempting to exploit the analysts' recommendations earn net, not gross returns. We must account for trading costs such as bid-offer spreads and commissions (mutual fund or other institutional investors would also incur market impact costs). The strategy of daily rebalancing based on changes of recommendations required turnover in excess of four hundred percent per annum. To estimate the cost of turnover the study used the estimates of institutional trading costs provided by Keim and Madhavan in their study, "The Cost of Institutional Equity Trades."[8] The estimated trading costs for a round-trip trade for large (seventy percent of total market cap for all stocks), medium (the next twenty percent of the total market cap), and small-cap stocks (the last ten percent of stocks by market cap) are 0.727%, 1.94%, and 4.12%, respectively. The weighted average estimated trading cost for the portfolio for a round-trip trade was 1.31%. Given a 458% annual turnover rate, the abnormal return for the most highly recommended stock portfolio not only disappears, it turns negative. Even with the small-cap stocks, which produced the greatest abnormal return of almost seven percent per annum, the trading costs resulted in negative net returns. With turnover of 265%, and estimated round-trip expenses in excess of four percent, turnover costs reduce returns by almost eleven percent per annum, leading to net returns of about negative four percent per annum. The study also examined strategies of reducing turnover; for example, reducing rebalancing to monthly reduced turnover to below three hundred percent, but also reducing the abnormal gross returns. The result was still negative net returns. The authors investigated a large number of trading strategies but they did not find any that produced positive net returns.

The bottom line is that a strategy of exploiting the stock selection skills of professional analysts required high turnover rates. The costs of that high turnover are great enough to suggest that while market inefficiencies may exist, they are not easily exploitable by investors.

There is another possible explanation: there is no such thing as stock selection skill; there just seems to be. Remember, the stocks that had the highest recommendations were the ones the analysts told their brokers to buy for their clients. That in itself moved the prices of small-cap stocks—just as in the case of the stock picks of Gene Marcial of *BusinessWeek*. For the large-cap stocks, the broker recommendations could not have such an impact.

The third example is the previously mentioned study by Russ Wermers, whose results confirmed the findings of other studies on the stock-picking skills of security analysts. His study, covering the twenty-year period 1975–94, included a universe of 241 funds at the start of the period and 1,279 by the end.[9] In order not to inject survivorship bias into the data, Wermers' total database included 1,788 funds that existed at any time during the period. Here is a summary of his findings:

- The stocks active managers selected outperformed by 0.7% per annum. In thirteen of the twenty years encompassed by the study, active managers outperformed the S&P 500 Index. Outperforming the market is a zero sum game—if there are winners, there must be losers. Wermers's findings are consistent with the findings of Brad Barber and Terrance Odean. Their studies on the behavior and performance of individual investors found that the stocks individuals buy underperform the ones they sell. It seems that professional active managers are exploiting the mistakes of individual investors. You might keep that in mind next time you decide to buy a stock.

- The 0.7% advantage provided by stock selection skills (exploiting the mistakes of individual investors) was more than offset by expenses incurred in the effort.

Wermers's study found that the returns of active managers were reduced by approximately:

- 0.7% per annum due to holding non-equity assets. Active managers generally hold some amount of cash (or cash equivalents) in attempts to time the market, while waiting to find what they perceive to be an undervalued security, or as reserves to meet shareholder redemptions. Some managers even hold longer-term fixed-income investments in an attempt to outperform equities.
- 0.8% due to fund operating expenses.
- 0.8% due to transaction costs (bid-offer spreads, commissions, and market impact).

The total negative impact of expenses was 2.3% per annum. Unfortunately, there is further bad news, as the study did not include the impact of taxes, which would have had an additional negative impact on returns.

Another point is worth noting. On average, the active fund managers held riskier-than-average stocks. During the period in question, fund managers held on average a larger-than-market exposure to small-cap stocks. This boosted returns 0.6% per annum. However, once the style adjustment was made, the "excess" returns of the stock picks virtually disappeared. On a risk-adjusted after-expense basis, the underperformance increased to 2.2% (1.6% plus 0.6%) per annum. If taxes were then taken into account, the underperformance would exceed three percent per annum. It is important to note that Wermers also found that active managers showed no ability to time movements between asset classes.

The fourth and most amusing example of "it's a long way from strategy to outcome" is a story about Wade Cook Financial's Internet site. In May 2001, this site, which solicits investors to pay up to $7,995 for two-day stock-trading seminars, began disclosing that it lost eighty-nine percent trading its own money last year. The company's advertising claims that some of its students obtain investment returns of fifteen percent a month. Its 10-K report filed with the Securities and Exchange Commission disclosed that Wade Cook Financial lost $2 million in the market in 2000. "Either Wade is unable to follow his own system, which he claims is simple to follow, or the system doesn't work," said Deb Bortner, director of the Washington State Securities Division and president of the North American Securities Administrators Association.[10]

As John Bogle of Vanguard stresses, costs matter. The bottom line is this: It is often a long way from the theoretical results of a strategy to the actual results that can be obtained. Keep this in mind the next time you read about a market-beating strategy.

MISTAKE 19

◆

Do You Confuse Great Companies with Great (High-Return) Investments?

One of the most persistent, and incorrect, beliefs among investors is that "growth" stocks have provided, and are expected to provide, higher returns than "value" stocks. Growth stocks are stocks of the glamorous high price-to-earnings (P/E) or low book-to-market (BtM) companies, while value stocks are the stocks of distressed companies, trading at low P/E ratios and high BtMs. The problem arises from the confusion between *earnings* generated by growth companies and *returns* earned by their shareholders. Let me explain. It is true that growth companies *outearn* value companies. For example, for the thirty six-year period ending in 1999, the return on assets (ROA) for growth stocks was almost ten percent per year. This was almost twice as high as the ROA for value stocks. During the same period, however, the annualized compound return to investors in value stocks was over sixteen percent per annum—almost forty percent higher than the less than twelve percent return to growth stock investors.

The simple explanation for this seeming anomaly is that investors discount the future expected earnings of value stocks at a much higher rate than they discount the future earnings of growth stocks. This more than offsets the faster earnings growth rates of growth companies. The high discount rate results in low current valuations for value stocks and higher expected future returns relative to growth stocks. Why do investors use a higher discount rate for value stocks when calculating the current value? The following example should provide a clear answer.

Let's consider the case of two similar companies, Wal-Mart and JCPenney. Most investors would say that Wal-Mart is a far better run company and a safer investment. If an investor could buy either company at the same market capitalization, say $20 billion, the obvious choice would be Wal-Mart. It not only has far higher current earnings but also is expected to produce much faster growth of future earnings. Investors recognizing this opportunity would buy shares of Wal-Mart, driving its price up, and sell shares of JCPenney, driving its price down. Now let us say that Wal-Mart's price rises relative to JCPenney until the two have the same *expected* (not guaranteed) future rate of return— say $40 billion for Wal-Mart and $10 billion for JCPenney. Given that Wal-Mart is perceived to be the better company, and therefore a less risky investment, investors would still choose Wal-Mart. The reason is that although we now have equal expected returns, there is less perceived risk in owning Wal-Mart. So our process of investors buying Wal-Mart and selling

JCPenney continues. It does so until the expected return of owning JCPenney is sufficiently greater than the expected return of owning Wal-Mart to entice investors to accept the risk of owning JCPenney instead of owning Wal-Mart—say $200 billion for Wal-Mart and $5 billion for JCPenney. The size of the price differential (and thus the difference in future expected returns) is directly related to the difference in perceived risk. Given that Wal-Mart is perceived to be a much safer investment than JCPenney, the price differential may have to be very large to entice investors to accept the risk of owning JCPenney.

Would these price changes make Wal-Mart "overvalued" or "highly valued" relative to JCPenney? The answer is "highly valued." If investors thought Wal-Mart was overvalued relative to JCPenney, they would sell Wal-Mart and buy JCPenney until equilibrium was reached. Instead, the high relative valuation of Wal-Mart reflects low perceived risk. Wal-Mart's future earnings are being discounted at a very low rate, reflecting the low perceived risk. This low discount rate translates into low future expected returns. Risk and reward are inversely related, at least in terms of expected future returns—"expected" since we cannot know the future with certainty. JCPenney's future earnings are discounted at a very high rate. It therefore has a relatively low valuation, reflecting the greater perceived risk. However, it also has high expected future returns.

Value stocks are the stocks of distressed companies. There are three very common characteristics of value stocks that all have simple intuitive risk interpretations (are associated with firms in distress). These three characteristics are: high volatility of dividends; high ratio of debt to equity; and high volatility of earnings. This high perceived risk translates into high-risk premiums demanded by investors, and thus low current prices and high future expected returns.

Hopefully, you now understand why growth stocks have provided, and are likely to continue to provide, lower returns than value stocks, despite having much higher growth rates of earnings. It is a simple risk story.

There is a related problem that investors have regarding growth stocks. They wonder: How can growth stocks, with their very high prices, be considered safe investments? For example, as we entered the new millennium, the P/E ratio of the large-cap growth dominated S&P 500 was approximately 30, and the P/E of the even more growth-oriented NASDAQ 100 was almost 150. Value stocks, on the other hand, had a P/E ratio of only about 12. Investors who wonder how stocks that have such a high valuation can be considered safe are confusing *business* (operating) risk with *price* risk. JCPenney has more *business* risk than Wal-Mart. Therefore, the price of JCPenney's stock falls until investors are compensated for the *business* risk. The distinction is in the risk of the *companies*, not the risk of their *stock prices*.

On the other hand, *stock* risk, or *price* risk, increases with increases in price. This concept can be clarified by an analogy related to the fixed-income markets. Long-term bonds have greater price risk than short-term bonds—the longer the maturity, the greater the risk. For example, if interest rates rise one percent, a one-year note will fall in value by one percent, a ten-year note by about seven percent, and a 30-year bond by about thirteen percent. Here is the analogy to growth and value stocks. Growth stocks are like long-term fixed-income instruments. Because of their high P/E and low BtM ratios, much of their value is derived from expected earnings far into the future. For value stocks, on the other hand, because of their low P/E and high BtM ratios, most of their current value is derived from liquidation value and expected earnings in the near future. As we saw, when interest rates go up, long-term (long duration) fixed-income assets fall in value more than short-term fixed-income assets. The same is true of equities. Growth stocks are longer duration assets than value stocks. Thus, when the rate at which you discount future earnings rises (because either the risk-free rate or the risk premium rose), the longer duration growth stocks will fall in price more than the shorter duration value stocks. So, growth stocks have more price risk than value stocks in the same manner that long-term treasury bonds have more price risk than short-term Treasury notes.

There is another reason that growth stocks might be considered to have more price risk. The less the perceived likelihood of a company failing to reach its projected earnings, the lower will be the risk premium, and the higher the stock price. Taken to an extreme, a stock with very little perceived risk might be said to be "priced for perfection." Simply put, there is little room for any upside surprise. If everything goes as expected, you get low returns (because of the low-risk premium). On the other hand, if almost anything goes wrong, the risk premium might rise sharply, and because of the long duration the stock could fall dramatically. This is the type of price risk that existed in the NAS-DAQ 100 stocks that were trading at astronomical P/E ratios prior to our entering the new millennium. Conversely, with value stocks being so distressed, there is far less likelihood of disappointment (when the risk premium would rise further) and lots of opportunity for upside surprise (the risk premium would fall and the price would rise dramatically).

In addition, if all the risk already perceived occurs, investors in value stocks will still earn high returns as that risk was already reflected in the price when the stock was purchased. Some value stocks are so distressed, due to such high perception of risk, that almost nothing else can go wrong that has not been already anticipated. Thus the stock might have a high upside potential should the risk premium fall. This was exactly what happened to emerging market stocks during the so-called Asian Contagion. Emerging market stocks were priced almost as if they were more likely to submerge rather than emerge. The DFA Emerging Markets Fund fell almost twenty percent in 1997 and another ten percent in 1998. Eventually the perception of risk was lowered as investors recognized that the emerging markets were not going to submerge. With the fall in the risk premium, the DFA Emerging Markets Fund rebounded over seventy percent in 1999.

Let's look at another example of why growth stocks with their high P/E ratios have a high degree of *price* risk. Keep in mind that a high P/E ratio reflects both the market's expectation for rapid growth in earnings and investor perception of low *business* risk. Anyone that follows the market closely has observed that frequently when a growth stock misses its forecasted earnings by even just a few cents, its stock falls dramatically—seemingly far out of proportion to the small shortfall in earnings. The explanation is simple. Let's assume we have a high-flying technology stock with projected earnings of $1 per share and selling at 100. Let's also assume that earnings come in at only ninety cents. The shortfall in earnings might cause the price to drop to 90, given the 100 P/E ratio. However, the shortfall in earnings will also likely affect the risk premium, causing it to rise. Let's assume that the rise in the perception of *business* risk causes the risk premium to rise so that the P/E ratio now falls to a still sky-high 80. Instead of falling just twenty percent as the P/E ratio fell, the price falls further due to the combination of the fall in the P/E ratio and the shortfall in earnings. The stock will actually fall to 72, or a drop of twenty-eight percent. It is the rise in the risk premium (perception of business risk) that causes the sharp fall, not the ten percent shortfall in earnings.

Hopefully we have resolved the seeming conundrum of the risk-iness of value and growth stocks, as well as their expected returns. To summarize, it is the perception of a high degree of *business* risk, and thus a high-risk premium applied to valuations, that causes the price of value companies to be distressed. The same high-risk premium creates high expected future returns. It is the perception of low *business* risk, and thus a low-risk premium applied to valuations, that causes the price of growth stocks to be elevated. It is high prices that create much higher *price* risk in the longer duration growth stocks than the shorter duration value stocks.

There is a simple principle to remember that can help you avoid making poor investment decisions. Risk and expected return should be related. If prices are high they reflect low perceived risk, and thus you should expect low future returns; and vice versa. This does not make a highly priced stock a poor investment. It simply makes it a stock that is perceived to have low risk and thus low future returns. Thinking otherwise would be like assuming government bonds are poor investments when the alternative is junk bonds.

MISTAKE 20

◆

Do You Understand How the Price Paid Affects Returns?

Probably the question heard most frequently is: "How high can stocks go?" To the unsophisticated observer there appears to be no maximum price. —New York Times, August 21, 1929

Investors must keep in mind that there's a difference between a good company and a good stock. After all, you can buy a good car but pay too much for it.
—Loren Fox, *Upside*, July 6, 1999

When forecasting investment returns, many individuals make the mistake of simply extrapolating recent returns into the future. Bull markets lead investors to expect higher future returns and bear markets lead them to expected lower future returns. However, you need to understand that the price you pay for an asset has a great impact on future returns. This bit of wisdom seemed to have eluded Henry Blodgett, Merrill Lynch's Internet analyst, when he made the following statement in a report on Internet Capital Group: "Valuation is often not a helpful tool in determining when to sell hypergrowth stocks."[1] He made this statement on January 10, 2000, shortly before the Internet bubble collapsed.

A two-step process determines equity prices. First, future earnings are forecast. Then the present value of those earnings is calculated by discounting them at the *risk-free rate* (the rate on riskless short-term instruments such as a one-month Treasury bill) plus a *risk premium* (the size of which is commensurate with the amount of perceived risk). The lower the riskless rate or the risk premium, the higher the present value, and vice versa. Let's explore how this works.

If the risk premium of an asset class falls (as investors perceive less risk), two things occur. First, investors in that asset class benefit from a onetime increase in the price of the asset as future earnings are now discounted at a lower rate. This is similar to the impact of falling interest rates on bond prices. The second impact is on future expected returns. Since risk premiums are a reflection of future expected returns, the falling risk premium reflects lower future returns. Of course, the reverse would be true if the risk premium of an asset class rose as investors perceive greater risk. The first impact would be a drop in equity prices as future expected earnings are now discounted at a higher rate, reflecting the now higher risk premium. The second impact would be that investors would now receive greater expected future returns, reflecting the greater risk premium. This process is exactly the opposite of what investors perceive when they extrapolate the recent outperformance of an asset class into the future.

Let's examine some of the historical data to see if we can make any useful observations about the size of risk premiums and future expected returns, or at least the changes in them. We will examine the valuation characteristics of P/E ratios and book-to-market (BtM) values.

The average historical P/E ratio for the market has been around fifteen. For the period 1926 through the second quarter of 1999 an investor buying stocks when the market traded at P/E ratios of between fourteen and sixteen earned a median return of 11.8% over the next ten years.[2] This is remarkably close to the long-term return of the market. The S&P 500 returned 11.0% per annum for the seventy-four-year period 1926–2000.

Let's now look at the returns investors received when they bought stocks when the perception of risk was low, for instance, during good economic times and a bull market; and when the perception of risk was high, during a recession or financial crisis and a bear market. Investors purchasing stocks when the P/E ratio was greater than twenty-two (when investors are highly optimistic and there is great enthusiasm for buying stocks) earned a median return of just five percent per annum over the next ten years.[3] High P/E ratios generally reflect a strong economy and a bull market. During such times investors perceive relatively low levels of risk, which translates into high prices and low-risk premiums. Those low-risk premiums, however, also translate into low future expected returns—exactly the opposite of what most investors expect.

Let's now look at the returns investors received when they purchased stock when the perception of risk was high. Investors who purchased stocks when P/E ratios were below ten earned a median return of 16.9% per annum over the next ten years.[4] Low P/E ratios generally reflect a weak economy and a bear market. During such times investors perceive relatively high levels of risk, which translates into low prices and high-risk premiums. Those high-risk premiums, however, also translate into high future expected returns. Investors buying stocks when the P/E ratios were below ten (when perceived risk was high, and seemingly no one wanted to own stocks) outperformed investors who bought stocks when P/E ratios were above twenty-two (when perceived risk was low, and seemingly everyone was jumping on the equity bandwagon) by almost twelve percent per annum.

In that light it is worth noting that from 1995 to 1999 we experienced a collapse in the risk premium for the large-cap stocks that dominate the S&P 500 and NASDAQ 100 indices. At year-end 1994, the P/E ratio for the S&P 500 was just under sixteen, not much higher than its historical average. However, by the end of the first quarter of 2000, it had risen to just under thirty, well above the twenty-two P/E ratio that historically has produced five percent returns over the succeeding ten years. The NASDAQ was trading at a P/E ratio of well over one hundred. Also worth noting is that the P/E ratios for the other asset classes had remained virtually unchanged. For large value stocks (as represented by the Dimensional Fund Advisors U.S. Large-cap Value Fund) the P/E ratio rose from 10.3 to just 11.3. For small-cap stocks (as represented by the DFA Micro Cap Fund) the P/E ratio actually fell from 14.1 to 13.7. And, for small-cap value stocks (as represented by the DFA 6–10 Value Fund) the P/E remained virtually unchanged, falling from 11.7 to 11.6.

The decreased perception of risk for large-cap growth stocks can also be seen by examining BtM values. For the S&P 500, the BtM fell by almost fifty percent, from 0.4 to 0.21. However, using the same DFA funds as benchmarks, for the asset classes other than large-cap growth we see a similar tale to what we found by looking at P/E ratios. The BtM of large-cap value stocks actually rose from 0.85 to 1.02, the BtM of small caps remained unchanged at 0.61, and the BtM of small-cap value stocks rose from 0.93 to 0.98. Low BtMs reflect low perception of risk (and low-risk premiums), and vice versa.

What conclusions, if any, should you draw from the above information? First, investors in 2000 who chased yesterday's returns by buying the then currently popular large-cap growth stocks were *highly likely* to be disappointed since those high prices reflected low perceptions of risk and thus low future *expected* returns. Second, while the prices of the large-cap growth stocks had risen to levels that have historically resulted in low future returns, the prices of other asset classes had not changed in relative valuation since 1994, and were basically trading at around historically average levels. Thus, between 1995 and 1999, the valuation of large-cap growth stocks relative to the valuations of other asset classes increased significantly. This lowered the future expected return of large-cap growth stocks relative to other asset classes. Of course, in the short term, anything could have happened. For example, the already low-risk premiums for large-cap growth and technology stocks could have fallen even further. This is how bubbles occur. Remember that although the market is very rational in the long term, it can be quite irrational in the short term.

You can avoid the mistake of simply extrapolating recent returns into the future by understanding and remembering how market prices are determined and how risk premiums impact future returns. It also helps to avoid the extremes in overconfidence and despair that bull and bear markets bring. And finally, it helps to remember the old cliché to buy low and sell high. Buying in bear markets is how you buy low. The simplest way to implement the buy low/sell high strategy is to build a portfolio that is highly diversified by asset class, and then regularly rebalance it. Through the process of periodically rebalancing your portfolio, you will automatically be selling the asset classes whose risk premiums have fallen and prices have thus risen (on a relative basis), and buying those whose risk premiums have risen and prices have thus fallen (on a relative basis).

MISTAKE 21

◆

Do You Believe More Heads Are Better Than One?

The bull market of the 1990s, the dramatic growth of the number of individual investors participating in the market through 401(k) and other retirement plans, and the explosion of media coverage have combined to fuel the interest in investing. Along with the "success" (at least until an accounting mistake was found) of the Beardstown Ladies, these factors have also probably fueled the interest in investment clubs. The question is: Are more heads better than one when it comes to investing? Terrance Odean and Brad Barber sought the answer to that question in their study, "Too Many Cooks Spoil the Profit: The Performance of Investment Clubs." The study covered 166 investment clubs, using data from a large brokerage house, from February 1991 to January 1997.[1] Here is a summary of their findings, which include all trading costs:

- The average club tended to buy high beta (highly volatile) small-cap growth stocks.
- The average club had annual turnover of sixty-five percent.

- The average club lagged a broad market index by 3.8% per annum, returning 14.1% versus 17.9%.

- Sixty percent of the clubs underperformed the market.

- When performance was adjusted for exposure to the risk factors of size and value, alphas (performance above or below benchmark) were negative even before transactions costs. After trading costs the alphas were on average −4.4% per annum.

Though these findings are not surprising given all the evidence on the failure of active managers to beat their benchmarks, they do conflict with data from the 35,000 member National Association of Investment Clubs (NAIC). The study noted that several articles in the *Wall Street Journal* and *New York Times* claimed that NAIC surveys show that instead of sixty percent of the clubs underperforming, sixty percent outperform. There are three good possible explanations. First, as with actively managed funds, there is likely to be survivorship bias in the data—clubs that perform poorly might break up. Second, there is likely to be reporting bias in the data—clubs that perform poorly are less likely to report results than clubs that do well. In fact, only about five to ten percent of all investment clubs return the NAIC's survey.[2] Third, there may be more Beardstown Ladies out there—clubs that simply miscalculate returns.

There were some other interesting findings:

- Despite trading less than individuals (sixty-five percent annual turnover as compared to seventy-five percent for individual investors), and therefore incurring lower trading expenses, clubs produced lower returns than individual investors—proving that at least when it comes to investing, fewer heads may be better.

- The clubs would have been far better off if they never had traded during the year—beginning-of-the-year portfolios outperformed their actual holdings by 3.5% per annum. The reason was that the stocks they sold outperformed the stocks they bought by over four percent per annum. The conclusion is that investment clubs have something in common with individual investors—trading is hazardous to their financial health.

Barber and Odean concluded: "Investment clubs serve many useful functions. They encourage savings. They educate their members about financial markets. They foster friendships and social ties. They entertain. Unfortunately, their investments do not beat the market." Of course, every investment club probably believes it will be one of the minority that manages to outperform.

MISTAKE 22

◆

Do You Believe Active Managers Will Protect You from Bear Markets?

I am the first to admit that during bear markets not only do actively managed funds begin with an advantage over passively managed ones, but that the value of index funds will go down during bear markets. The advantages that active managers have in bear markets are a result of their maintaining reserves both to meet redemption requests and to hold investment funds available as they seek the next great stock to buy. This cash reserve, because cash is a poorly performing asset class in bull markets, is one of the reasons active managers underperform in bull markets. In bear markets, however, cash becomes king. Theoretically anticipating bear markets, active managers can reduce their exposure to equities and protect their investors from the type of losses that index funds experience (since index funds are always virtually one hundred percent invested). Unfortunately, for active managers anyway, the videotape reveals that active managers offer no such protection. Let's look at some of the evidence.

Just prior to the worst bear market in the postwar era (1973–1974), mutual fund cash reserves stood at only four percent. They reached about twelve percent at the ensuing low. In mid-1998, when the Asian Contagion bear market arrived, cash reserves were just five percent. Compare this to the thirteen percent level reached at the market low in 1990, just prior to beginning the longest bull market in history.[1] It seems fund managers are very good at executing a buy high and sell low strategy.

A Lipper Analytical Services study provided further evidence on the failure of active managers to outperform in bear markets, despite their advantages. Lipper studied the six market corrections (defined as a drop of at least ten percent) from August 31, 1978, to October 11, 1990, and found that while the average loss for the S&P was 15.12%, the average loss for large-cap growth funds was 17.04%.[2]

Fund managers fared no better in the bear market of July–August 1998. The average equity fund lost 19.7%. This compares to losses of just 17.4% and 15.4% for a Wilshire 5000 Index fund and an S&P 500 Index fund, respectively.[3] As they said in the old Wendy's commercial, "Where's the beef?" Susan Dziubinski, editor of Morningstar's *FundInvestor* newsletter, put it this way: "The average fund can't keep up with its index when it's sunny or rainy."[4]

And, finally, consider this evidence. Goldman Sachs studied mutual fund cash holdings from 1970 to 1989. The study found that mutual fund managers miscalled *all* nine major turning points.[5]

In the face of all of so much evidence, only people who are unwilling to give up on long-held opinions will continue to believe that active managers can protect investors from bear markets.

MISTAKE 23

◆

Do You Fail to Compare Your Funds to Proper Benchmarks?

After just one third of actively managed mutual funds outperformed the S&P 500 Index in 1999, seventy-two percent did so in 2000. Active managers and their faithful immediately declared that it was once again a stock-pickers market, and that active management would prove to be the winning strategy. Unfortunately, this is an old canard that is trotted out every so often in an attempt to keep both alive the myth that active management is the winning strategy and to keep investors paying high fees for poor, inconsistent, and tax-inefficient performance. However, when proper light is shed on the subject, the canard is exposed as having no basis in fact.

Active managers point to their successes in periods like 1977–79, when eighty-five percent, sixty-nine percent, and eighty percent, respectively, of the actively managed funds outperformed the S&P 500, and 1991–1993 when fifty-five percent, fifty-four percent, and sixty percent, respectively, did so, as "proof" of their ability to outperform the market. The claim is that those were stock-pickers kind of years—as opposed to the years 1994–98 when no more than twenty-two percent of the active funds accomplished that feat. The problem with the claim of being a stock-picker's market is that it doesn't hold up to scrutiny. The reason is that the claimants are using an apples-to-orange comparison to make their case. The conclusions are drawn because of confusing indexing with the exclusive use of the S&P 500.

Going to the videotape we find that for the thirty-six-year period 1963–98 there were just fourteen years (thirty-nine percent) when more than fifty percent of active managers beat the S&P 500 Index.[1] Of those fourteen years, thirteen were years when small caps (as represented by the CRSP 6–10 index through May of 1986, and the DFA 6–10 Fund thereafter) beat large caps. The one exception was 1974, when fifty-three percent of active managers beat the S&P 500 Index and small caps underperformed that index by about two percent.

The explanation for the seeming outperformance of active managers in those fourteen years is that the average actively managed fund holds stocks with a smaller average market cap than the weighted market cap of the S&P 500 Index. And it is asset allocation, not stock selection or market timing, that determines almost all returns. This can be seen when we compare the performance of actively managed funds to the performance of a small-cap benchmark in the fourteen years when more than fifty percent of the actively managed funds outperformed the S&P 500 Index. Here is what we find:

- A small-cap index (or fund) outperformed the average actively managed fund in twelve of the fourteen years.

- The only two years when the average actively managed fund beat both the S&P 500 and a small-cap benchmark were 1966 and 1974—both years of bear markets in both small- and large-cap stocks.

- There were seven other years when small-cap stocks out-performed large-cap stocks. In not a single one of those periods did more than fifty percent of active managers beat the S&P 500 index.[2]

The data should come as no surprise. When small-cap stocks outperform large-cap stocks, managers holding stocks with an average market cap less than that of the S&P 500 should (and do) perform relatively better. Unfortunately, the S&P 500 Index is the wrong benchmark. Actively managed funds should always be benchmarked in a way that ensures an apples-to-apples comparison. Small-cap funds should be compared to a small-cap index and large-cap funds should be compared to a large-cap index.

Another explanation for the "outperformance" of active managers in 2000 is that value funds outperformed growth funds (like the S&P 500). Thus, any actively managed value fund, or even an actively managed growth fund that had more exposure to the value asset class than does the S&P 500 Index, was highly likely to outperform that particular benchmark. For example, while the S&P 500 fell just over nine percent, the DFA Large Value and Small Value funds rose ten percent and nine percent, respectively. Those funds would be the proper benchmarks for value-oriented funds, not the S&P 500 Index.

Mark Carhart's classic study of the mutual fund industry determined that once you accounted for style factors (small cap versus large cap and value versus growth), the average actively managed fund underperformed its benchmark on a pretax basis by 1.8% per annum.[3] Another exhaustive study by Russ Wermers, published in the August 2000 issue of the *Journal of Finance*, came to a virtually identical conclusion.

To gain further perspective on active management, let's take a longer-term look at the performance against two benchmarks, the

Wilshire 5000 and the Russell 3000, that are broader indices than the S&P 500 Index. For the five-, ten-, and fifteen-year periods ending in 2000 only sixteen percent, sixteen percent, and seventeen percent of actively managed funds outperformed the Wilshire 5000, and only fourteen percent, fourteen percent, and fifteen percent of actively managed funds outperformed the Russell 3000.[4] This data should be enough to convince almost anyone that active management is a loser's game. It's not that you can't win; it's just that the odds of doing so are so low that it doesn't pay to play. But for those who need further evidence, this data does not even contain all the bad news. First, the evidence is based on pretax returns. Since actively managed funds are inherently more tax inefficient than index funds, it is a virtual certainty that on an after-tax basis the percentage of outperformers would have been much lower. Second, the data contains survivorship bias, which negatively impacts returns further as was previously explained.

To avoid making this type of mistake, make sure that you compare the performance of an actively managed fund against its appropriate passive benchmark. If it is a small-cap fund, make sure you compare it to a small-cap index such as the Russell 2000 or the S&P 600. If it is a small-cap value fund, it should be compared to a benchmark like the S&P 600/Barra Value Index, and so on. It is worth noting that behavioral finance people have found that investors often avoid making this comparison because of the "rising sea raises all boats" phenomenon. In other words, if the asset class in which your fund invests does well, it is highly likely that your fund has also done well. You of course feel good. However, the evidence suggests that despite doing well on an absolute basis, the likelihood is that the fund has underperformed its passive benchmark, especially on an after-tax basis. And the longer the time frame, the more likely it is that this will be true. By avoiding the comparison you are able to continue the illusion of outperformance.

MISTAKE 24

◆

Do You Focus on Pretax Returns?

If index funds look great before taxes, their performance is almost unbeatable after taxes, thanks to their low turnover and thus slow realization of capital gains.
— Jonathan Clements, *Wall Street Journal*, December 22, 1998

For all long-term investors, there is only one objective—maximum total real return after taxes. — John Templeton

While I was at Morgan Stanley Dean Witter I never once came across a broker talking to a client about the problems turnover creates with mutual fund investing. Nor capital gains tax. Nor the effect the tax has on lowering the investor's true rate of return. Simply put, the idea or notion of after-tax returns was shoved aside and under the rug.
— Ted Lux, ex-stockbroker, *Exposing the Wheel Spin on Wall Street*

My experience is that most investors focus on the pretax returns of their investments, despite the fact that investors in taxable accounts don't get to spend pretax returns, only after-tax returns. Most investors are simply not aware of just how devastating an impact taxes can have on returns. One reason that investors don't focus on taxes is that they are subject to what is called mental accounting: the returns earned go into one pocket, but come April fifteenth, when their accountant hands them their tax bill based on IRS form 1099 distributions, they pay the bill from a different pocket, never tying the two together. Let's see just how large a role taxes play in determining after-tax returns.

Although the effect of paying taxes may be minimal in any one year, it becomes substantial over protracted periods. A study commissioned by Charles Schwab demonstrated how great an impact this stealth attack has on returns. Schwab measured the performance of sixty-two equity funds for the period 1963–92. It found that while each dollar invested would have grown to $21.89 in a tax-deferred account, a taxable account would have produced only $9.87 for a high-bracket investor. Taxes cut returns by 57.5%.[1] For high-tax-bracket investors, the study also found that for the ten-year period ending December 1992, Vanguard's S&P 500 Index fund would have outperformed ninety-two percent of actively managed funds after taxes.[2]

A simulated study covering the twenty-five-year period ending in 1995 examined the effects of expenses and taxes on returns. This study assumed that a hypothetical fund (1) matched the performance of the S&P 500 Index (the average actively managed fund underperforms by almost two percent per annum); (2) had turnover of eighty percent; (3) and incurred expenses of one percent (the average fund has expenses of about 1.5%). The study found that the typical investor received only forty-one percent of the pre-expense, pretax returns of the Index. The government took forty-seven percent of the returns, even without considering state and local taxes, or if the investor were subject to the highest tax brackets. The fund sponsor received twelve percent of the returns. This study also found that reducing expenses to just thirty basis points would have raised the investor's share of returns from forty-one to forty-five percent. The study also examined the effect of reducing the turnover rate to the same turnover as the S&P 500 Index. By reducing turnover to three percent, the share of returns realized would have increased to sixty-four percent, increasing investor returns by fifty-six percent.[3]

Let's look at several studies that cover shorter investment horizons. Robert Jeffrey and Robert Arnott demonstrated the impact of taxes on returns in their study of seventy-one actively managed funds for the ten-year period 1982–91. They found that while fifteen of the seventy-one funds beat a passively managed fund on a pretax basis, only five did so on an after-tax basis.[4]

Morningstar studied the five-year period 1992–96 and found that diversified U.S. stock funds gained an average of 91.9%. Morningstar then assumed that income and short-term gains were taxed at 39.6% and long-term capital gains at 28%—after-tax returns dwindled to 71.5%, a loss of twenty-two percent of the returns.[5] As you can see, even over short investment horizons, taxes can destroy returns.

A study by the Schwab Center for Investment Research examined the historical tax efficiency of five hundred seventy-six large-cap actively managed funds and forty-four large-cap index funds for the three-year period ending December 1997.[6] The study calculated the tax efficiency of each fund by dividing its pretax return by its after-tax return. The study assumed a $10,000 investment and that the cash to pay the taxes was generated by selling shares. Tax rates of 39.6% for short-term gains and ordinary income and 28% for long-term gains were assumed. The Center concluded:

- The average large-cap fund was approximately eighty-six percent tax efficient, losing fourteen percent of its returns to taxes.
- The average large-cap index fund was approximately ninety-four percent tax efficient, losing only six percent of its returns to taxes.

It is important to note, especially for investors residing in high-tax areas, that state and local taxes were not considered.

The study also examined the amount of dollars that would have been lost to taxes over five-, ten- and fifteen-year holding periods. The results are shown in the following table.

Dollars Lost to Taxes, Assuming a $10,000 Initial Investment and a 10% Pretax Return		
Holding Period	Actively Managed Funds	Index Funds
5 years	$999	$434
10 years	$3,118	$1,381
15 years	$7,302	$3,290

Another important study investigated the likelihood of actively managed funds outperforming passively managed ones.[7] This study, entitled "How Well Have Taxable Investors Been Served in the 1980s and 1990s?", investigated:

- The pre- and after-tax efficiency of actively managed funds.
- The likelihood of pre- and after-tax outperformance.
- The relative size of outperformance versus the relative size of underperformance.

The study included all funds with over $100 million in assets. Here is a summary of its findings:

- For the ten-year period 1982–91, on a pretax basis, twenty-one percent of the funds outperformed their benchmark, Vanguard's S&P 500 Index Fund. The average outperformance was 1.8% per annum. The average underperformance was a similar 1.9%. On an after-tax basis, however, only about eight percent of the funds managed to beat their benchmark. The average outperformance was now just 0.9%, while the average underperformance increased to 3.1%. Keep this in mind: the ratio of about 3.5:1 (the 3.1% underperformance divided by the 0.9% outperformance) in favor of the underachievers is made all the more significant because there were about eleven times as many losers as winners. Thus, we find that not only are there far more losers than winners but also the average size of the underperformance is far greater than the size of the outperformance. Therefore, we need to look at the risk-adjusted odds of outperformance. We can calculate that by multiplying the odds of outperformance by the ratio of underperformance to outperformance. Doing so gives us risk-adjusted odds against outperformance of about thirty-eight to one.

- For the ten-year period 1989–98, on a pretax basis, just fourteen percent of the funds outperformed, with the average outperformance being 1.9%. The average underperformance was 3.9%. On an after-tax basis, only nine percent of the funds outperformed. The average outperformance was 1.8%. The average underperformance was 4.8%. The risk-adjusted odds against after-tax outperformance are about twenty-eight to one.

- For the full twenty-year period, twenty-two percent of the funds beat their benchmark on a pretax basis. The average outperformance was 1.4%, with the average underperformance being 2.6%. On an after-tax basis, just fourteen percent of the funds outperformed. The average after-tax outperformance was 1.3%, while the average after-tax underperformance was 3.2%. The risk-adjusted odds against outperformance are about seventeen to one.

- For the full twenty-year period the average fund underperformed its benchmark by 1.75% per annum before taxes and by 2.58% on an after-tax basis.

- For the entire time frame, only about three percent of active funds paid less capital gains taxes than did their benchmark. Only about ten percent of funds paid lower total taxes.

The story is actually worse than it appears, because the above data contains survivorship bias. For example, for the full twenty-year period the average fund underperformed its benchmark by about 1.75% per annum on a pretax basis and by 2.58% on an after-tax basis. However, thirty-three funds disappeared during the time frame covered by the study. When we adjust for survivorship bias, the underperformance increases to 2.12% and 2.82%, respectively. Thus, the risk-adjusted odds of outperformance are even lower than the dismal figures previously presented. One more point on survivorship bias: Since the study only covered funds with more than $100 million in assets, it is likely that the survivorship bias is understated. Funds that have successful track records tend to attract assets. Funds with poor records tend to lose assets or are "put to death," never reaching the $100 million threshold of the study. So, it seems logical to conclude that if the study covered all funds, instead of just those with assets over $100 million, the survivorship bias would have been even greater. We do know that far more than thirty-three funds disappeared during the period covered.

Individual investors are beginning to awaken to the important role that fund distributions play in after-tax performance. This has been one of the driving forces behind the rapid growth of index and other passively managed funds. Recently, many fund families, including Dimensional Fund Advisors, Charles Schwab & Co., and the Vanguard Group, have taken this issue to the next level by creating passively managed funds that are also tax-managed. These tax-managed funds strive both to minimize fund distributions and to maximize the percentage of distributions that will be in the form of long-term capital gains. They accomplish this by implementing the following strategies:

- Maintaining low turnover.
- Attempting to avoid realization of short-term gains.

- Harvesting losses by selling stocks that are below cost, in order to offset gains in other securities.

- Selling the appreciated shares with the highest cost basis.

- Trading around dividend dates.

KPMG Peat Marwick studied the benefit that such a tax-managed fund might provide.[8] To understand the impact of taxes on returns, the firm examined the hypothetical performance of $10,000 invested in two funds, one a tax-managed fund and the other an actively managed fund, both having pretax returns of ten percent. The example assumed that short-term gains and ordinary income would be taxed at 39.6% and long-terms gains at 20%, and the funds would be liquidated after twenty years. The following table lists the study's other assumptions.

	Tax-Managed Fund (%)	Actively Managed Fund (%)
Income and short-term distributions	0.0	3.0
Long-term distributions	1.0	4.0
Price appreciation (unrealized gains)	9.0	3.0
Total annual returns	10.0	10.0

After twenty years, the tax-managed fund would grow to $54,792, or twenty-five percent greater than the $43,941 produced by the actively managed fund. The difference in after-tax returns was 8.9% versus 7.7%. Taxes cost the tax-managed fund eleven percent of its pretax returns, as compared to twenty-three percent for the actively managed fund. Another way to look at it is that the pretax return of the actively managed fund would have had to be 11.6% (or sixteen percent greater) just to match the after-tax return of the tax-managed fund. Given that the average actively managed fund has underperformed its benchmark on a *pretax* basis by almost two percent per annum, the extra burden of taxes would seem to create an almost insurmountable hurdle.

KPMG took their study one step further. They considered what would happen if instead of liquidating the funds after twenty years, the investor either transfers them to his or her estate at death, or gifts them to a charitable institution. In either case, the capital gains taxes that were otherwise due on sale could now be avoided. In this case, the $10,000 would have grown to $64,870 in the tax-managed fund, thirty-nine percent greater than the $46,690 produced by the actively managed fund. The after-tax returns were 9.8% and 8.0%, respectively. The actively managed fund would have had to generate almost twenty-three percent per annum better pretax returns in order to match the after-tax returns of the tax-managed fund.

Using data from Morningstar, KPMG found that over a ten-year period the median actively managed fund lost sixteen per-cent of its pretax returns to taxes on an annual basis, with some funds losing as much as forty percent of their pretax returns to taxes. This result was not all that different from the hypothetical example they created.

Taxes are probably the largest expense investors incur, even greater than management fees or commissions. Therefore, ignor-ing the impact of taxes on the returns of taxable accounts is one of the biggest mistakes you can make. You can avoid this mis-take if you keep the following points in mind. The burden of taxes provides an almost insurmountable hurdle for active man-agers to overcome. Because of the important impact of taxes on returns, passively managed funds that are also tax-managed should be the investment vehicles of choice for taxable accounts. By choosing passively and tax-managed funds, you won't have to worry about the impact of taxes on your returns. If you do choose to use actively managed funds, they are best held in a tax-deferred account, where the high turnover won't impact after-tax returns.

MISTAKE 25

◆

Do You Rely on a Fund's Descriptive Name When Making Purchase Decisions?

How many legs would a sheep have if you called its tail a leg?
Four. Because calling its tail a leg doesn't make it one.
—Abraham Lincoln

Several academic studies have come to the conclusion that asset allocation—how investments are allocated among various asset classes in a portfolio—determines the vast majority of not only the returns but also the risks of a portfolio. A study by Gary P. Brinson, L. Randolph Hood and Gilbert L. Beebower, "Determinants of Portfolio Returns," demonstrated that ninety-four percent of returns result not from market timing or stock selection, but from "asset allocation" decisions.[1] In another study of thirty-one pension plans, representing $70 billion of total assets under management, Eugene Fama Jr. found that asset allocation determined over ninety-seven percent of returns.[2] And finally, a study by Roger G. Ibbotson and Paul D. Kaplan, analyzing the ten-year performance of ninety-four balanced mutual funds and the five-year performance of fifty-eight pension plans, concluded that approximately one hundred percent of a portfolio's absolute return is explained by asset allocation.[3] Whether the number is ninety-four or one hundred percent doesn't really matter. The evidence is very clear that asset allocation determines the vast majority of the risk and reward of a portfolio.

Given that conclusion, the most important decision that investors can make, the one that will determine the long-term performance of the portfolio, is the asset allocation decision. Once investors decide on their investment policy (asset allocation), they must choose which funds to use as the building blocks of their portfolio. One choice involves the decision of implementing the strategy with active or passive managers. If investors choose passive managers, they can be sure the specific investment style will be adhered to, as the fund will simply be replicating the asset class or index it represents. There is no such assurance with active managers. With active managers you cannot even rely on the fund's name when making a choice. Let's look at two examples.

Assume that an investor would like exposure to the asset class of U.S. large-cap value stocks. Believing that the fund's name describes its investment style, the investor chooses the PBHG Large-cap Value Fund. As of March 31, 2001, the fund's weighted average book-to-market value was 0.14. The ten percent of stocks that are the most "growthy" have a BtM of 0.14 or lower. This is certainly not a value-oriented fund. Using the academic definition of value, the top three deciles as ranked by BtM by CRSP, a fund would have to have a weighted average BtM of 0.92 or higher to be considered a value fund. Even using a more liberal definition of value as the top fifty percent of stocks as ranked by BtM, value would be defined as stocks with a BtM of about 0.6 or greater. By contrast, the DFA Large-cap Value Fund, a passive asset class fund, had a BtM of well over one. As another example, investors seeking exposure to the asset class of U.S. small-cap stocks might choose the Aquinas Small-Cap Fund, which in March 2001 had a median market cap of almost

$2.4 billion. I don't know of any definition of small-cap that would include a fund that had over fifty percent of the stocks in the fund having a market capitalization that large. In fact, that level would place their median market capitalization in the top thirty percent of all stocks as ranked by CRSP. In contrast, the passively managed DFA Small Cap Fund had a median market cap of less than $100 million, and their passively managed Micro Cap Fund had a median market cap of about $50 million.

To the surprise of most investors, even index funds can have somewhat misleading names. The best example is an index fund based on the S&P 500/Barra Value Index. The problem arises because of the choice of index. Let me explain. Barra ranks the 500 stocks in the S&P 500 Index by BtM. When they get halfway down the list by market capitalization, they call the stocks with the lowest BtM growth, and the remainder are called "value." The problem is that almost all the stocks in the index are growth stocks. The result is you have the S&P 500/Barra Growth Index being very "growthy" and the S&P/Barra Value Index being less "growthy." It certainly isn't value-oriented. The weighted average BtM of the S&P 500/Barra Value Index at year-end 2000 was 0.42. This placed it in the top thirty percent of all stocks as ranked by BtM. In contrast, the passively managed DFA Large Value Fund had a BtM of 1.06, placing it within the bottom thirty percent of all stocks as ranked by BtM. Investors seeking exposure to the asset class of U.S. large value stocks won't find it by buying an S&P 500/Barra Value Index fund.

My experience is that many people have trouble with this example. Perhaps the following will help. Suppose Barra decided to split the S&P 500 not into value and growth, but instead into small and large. It would then rank the 500 stocks by market cap and call the top half the S&P 500/Barra Large Index and the bottom half the S&P 500/Barra Small Index. Since all the stocks in the S&P 500 Index are large caps, the result would be that you would have one very large index and another less large index. A fitting analogy would be to take a black horse, paint it with white stripes, and call it a zebra. Of course, no matter what the color, the horse would still be a horse. The lesson is that you should not choose a fund, even an index fund, by its name. Instead, you should carefully check its weighted average book-to-market and market capitalization levels. That is the simplest way to tell the true nature of a fund.

Investors who choose actively managed funds run into another problem we've already met earlier: style drift. Style drift, or the shifting of the fund's asset allocation, leads to out-of-control outcomes. Let's look at the evidence.

A study entitled "Mutual Fund Objective Misclassification" sought to determine whether mutual funds actually adhered to their stated objectives or whether, in pursuit of the Holy Grail of outperformance, they style-drifted.[4] The authors used Morningstar's database for the period 1993–96. Morningstar classifies funds by their *stated* objective. It reviews a fund's prospectus and how the fund is marketed. Morningstar does not then try to "outguess" the fund sponsor. If the fund sponsor calls its fund a growth fund, Morningstar classifies it as such. However, this can be misleading if a fund either style-drifts or tries to "game" its benchmark. For example, a fund might state its objective as low risk and actually pursue a high-risk strategy. Or, it might state its objective as smallcap but purchase large caps if the manager believes that large caps are "hot" and by doing so he can beat his benchmark. To test for style drift, the authors evaluated funds based on many well-established investment criteria, such as P/E and BtM ratios, market capitalization, dividend yield, and so on. They then compared the fund's actual style to its Morningstar classification. Here is what they found:

- Only forty-six percent (484 out of 1,043) had investment attributes that were consistent with the fund's stated objectives; fifty-four percent of funds were misclassified.

- Over one third (353 out of 1,043) of all funds were severely misrepresented. Keep in mind that the Investment Company Act of 1940 states that an investment company will not deviate from its investment policy unless authorized by a majority of shareholders.

- Over the very short period covered by the study, fifty-seven percent of the funds that survived changed their investment style at some point.

- Only twenty-seven percent of funds held constant their investment attributes throughout the period.

- Twenty-three percent of funds were found to be less risky than their stated objectives.

- Thirty-one percent of funds were found to be more risky than their stated objectives.

As an example of style drift, the authors cited the Oppenheimer Main Street Income and Growth Fund. In 1994, it was classified as Income and Growth. However, its average market capitalization of less than $400 million clearly was inconsistent with its stated objective. Jon Fossel, chairman of Oppenheimer, stated: "It's certainly not your conventional growth and income fund." Could it be that the fund classified itself as a more conservative fund so that it might beat its benchmark simply by taking more risk? Let's look at some further evidence.

One study covered 748 stock mutual funds with five-year track records ending October 1995. The authors classified funds into the six categories of aggressive growth; growth; growth and income; income; international; and small capitalization. They found that forty percent of the funds were misclassified—a finding very consistent with the data we saw earlier.[5]

Another study, "Chasing Performance Through Style Drift," found that mutual funds attempt to improve performance by drifting to the style with the highest recent return.[6] George Arrington learned that about one quarter of fund managers shifted style, drifting to the hot asset classes, within most twelve-month periods. Given that there is no evidence of mutual fund outperformance, all the style drifting accomplished was to increase turnover and trading costs, and in all likelihood reduce tax efficiency.

Of great interest are the results of a study called "Mutual Fund Styles," by Stephen J. Brown and William N. Goetzmann.[7] They covered the period 1976 through 1992. The authors were particularly concerned about finding evidence of ex-post (after the fact) changes in style in order to improve relative historical performance. Mutual funds using their self-reported fund objective, *announced ex-post*, may bias performance statistics to minimize poor relative performance. Organizations such as Morningstar, as well as individual investors who simply accept the fund's stated objective, are therefore subject to bias in the reported data. The authors found supporting evidence for the hypothesis that funds might switch to improve their relative historical rankings. There were 237 cases in which equity mutual funds switched their declared objective. For each of these, the authors subtracted the average objective return from the fund return in the year before the switch, using first the old objective and then the new objective. The average *net gain* in benchmarked returns was .098, or 9.8%, with a t-statistic (a measure of statistical significance, with generally any t-stat over two being considered significant) of 5.47, assuming all switches were independent. Magically, relative performance improved. The authors concluded that "While this simple test does not prove that fund managers were switching for strategic (marketing) purposes during this period, the results are certainly consistent with such an interpretation." A skeptic would go much further.

As we have seen, the evidence is very clear that asset allocation determines the vast majority of returns. Therefore, while it is logical that investors should take control over this decision, choosing active managers can lead to the loss of control over a critical issue. To the extent the funds are misclassified, investors are making decisions based on faulty, if not outright misleading, information. The consequences of misclassification are that investors can be misled on four important issues:

- The asset allocation decision,
- How well their portfolio is diversified by asset class,
- Expected return of the portfolio, and
- The risk of the portfolio.

The only way to take control over the risk and expected returns of a portfolio is to use index funds, ETFs, or passively managed funds as the building blocks of a portfolio. And remember that even with index and passively managed funds, it is important to check the fund's vital statistics. If you don't, you may find that a rose by any other name does not smell as sweet.

MISTAKE 26

◆

Do You Believe Active Management Is a Winner's Game in Inefficient Markets?

Even many devotees of active portfolio strategies have conceded that the efficiency of the market for U.S. large-cap stocks is so great that attempting to add value through active management is highly unlikely to produce positive results. They do cling, however, to the idea that active management is likely to add value in less efficient markets. The asset class for which the active management argument is made most strongly is the emerging markets—an "inefficient" asset class if there ever was one. Believers in active management have one problem: there isn't any evidence to support their claim. In fact, we now have substantial evidence supporting the opposite position.

The sharp drop in emerging market equities in 1998 brought down the reputations of many emerging market fund managers. As Richard Oppel, Jr., of *The New York Times* put it: "Another casualty of the [emerging markets] sell-off: the widely held notion that emerging markets are fertile ground for active fund managers."[1] The year 1998 was certainly one in which active managers had plenty of opportunity to add value, either by moving to cash or by choosing the winners (South Korea +110%, Greece +87%, Thailand +27%, and Portugal +26%) and avoiding the losers (Russia −87%, Turkey −51%, Indonesia −45%, Mexico −38%, and Brazil −38%).[2] Let's look at the facts. The 164 actively managed emerging market funds tracked by Morningstar fell 26.9% in 1998, far more than the 18.2% loss by the Vanguard Emerging

Markets Stock Index Fund, the third largest emerging market fund.[3] That is an underperformance of almost nine percent, not including the further expenses of taxes on fund distributions.

To show that 1998's poor performance by active managers was not a fluke, using the Morningstar database I examined the performance of all emerging market funds for the seven-year period 1994–2000. The Morningstar database provides us with a list of sixteen emerging market funds with a seven-year track record. I then compared the performance of the actively managed funds with that of the passively managed DFA Emerging Markets Fund. Even with survivorship bias in the data, the DFA Fund outperformed all but one single fund. Although the DFA Emerging Markets Fund fell 1.1% per annum, it outperformed the average active fund by four percent per annum. The one fund that managed to beat a passive rival did so by just 0.28% per annum. The two Templeton funds provided negative returns of 2.2% and 3.1%. Fidelity's fund returned −11.2% per annum. That is a high price to pay for belief in active management. Other well-known underachievers were the funds of Montgomery, Merrill Lynch, and J. P. Morgan.

Consider this: If you managed to pick the one fund that survived and beat the passive alternative, your belief in active management was rewarded with 0.28% per annum of pretax outperformance. On the other hand, if you were unlucky enough to choose Fidelity's fund, you underperformed by over ten percent per annum. Does this sound like a game you want to play? What is perhaps most disheartening for believers in active management is that since the emerging market returns for the entire period were negative, all an active manager would have to have done to outperform a passive strategy was to hold cash! This certainly undercuts the claim that active managers are best able to protect you in bear markets.

We can draw three conclusions from the data:

1. The emerging markets are not as inefficient as the active managers claim.

2. The costs of operating an emerging market fund, plus the costs of trading in the less liquid markets of these countries, are so great that once other expenses, including taxes, are considered, active managers are unlikely to add value. According to Joshua Feuerman, manager of the State Street Global Advisors Emerging Markets Fund, a round-trip purchase and sale of a block of stock in a typical emerging market costs about 4.5% of the value of the stock. "It's a disgustingly expensive asset class to trade in."[4] Because turnover is much greater in actively managed funds, trading costs hit them harder than passively managed funds.

3. Passive management is most likely to prove to be the winning strategy, whether the asset class is efficient or inefficient.

MISTAKE 27

◆

Do You Believe Hedge Fund Managers Deliver Superior Performance?

Hedge funds, a small and specialized niche within the investment fund arena, attract lots of attention. Hedge funds differ from mutual funds in several ways.

- They are generally available only to high net worth individuals.

- Unlike the typical broadly diversified mutual fund, they generally have highly concentrated large positions in just a few securities.

- They have broad latitude to make large bets, either long or short, on almost any type of asset, be it a commodity, real estate, currency, country debt, stocks, and so on.

- Management generally has a significant stake in the fund.

- Management has strong financial incentives. Fees typically range from one to two percent per annum, plus twenty percent of profits.

- Management has very limited regulatory oversight.

Hedge fund managers seek to outperform market indices such as the S&P 500 by exploiting what they perceive to be market mispricings. Studying their performance would seem to be one way of testing the EMT and the ability of active managers to outperform their respective benchmarks.

Roger Ibbotson, Stephen Brown, and Will Goetzmann investigated hedge fund performance in their study "Offshore Hedge Funds: Survival and Performance 1989–95." Their conclusions were as follows:

- When looking at past returns, there is little evidence of consistently outstanding performance.

- There was no evidence of persistent ability of managers in a particular style classification to earn returns in excess of their style benchmark.

- Of the 108 offshore funds that were listed in a 1989 U.S. Off-Shore Funds Directory, only twenty-five survived the study period. The probability of a fund lasting seven years was very low.

- Most of the funds underperformed the S&P 500 Index.[1]

A *Forbes* article by columnist David Dreman presented a performance index of 2,600 hedge funds (1,500 domestic and 1,100 international) for the period January 1993-October 1998. After deducting for fees, the average annualized returns of the hedge funds was 13.4%, trailing the 19.9% return of the S&P 500 Index.[2]

Very similar results were found in a study by Carl Ackermann, Richard McEnally, and David Ravenscraft.[3] Their study covered 906 hedge funds for the period 1988–95. They concluded:

- Hedge funds provided greater returns than mutual funds but provided no advantage over indexing on a risk-adjusted basis.

- Hedge funds are more volatile than both mutual funds and market indices.

- Survivorship bias was so great that if it had not been taken into account hedge fund returns would have magically improved by three percent per annum.

They also found that while hedge funds did not provide greater net returns to investors, they did provide greater gross returns. This finding conforms to an important part of the EMT: Any excess returns over the market rate of return should equal the cost of that effort (otherwise why undertake the effort). One might conclude that the only ones who benefited from their efforts were the hedge fund managers themselves.

A new study on hedge funds, by hedge fund AQR Capital Management, covered the five-year period ending January 31, 2001. The data for the study came from CSFB/Tremont's database. The study found that the average hedge fund had returned 14.65% per annum, lagging the S&P 500 Index by almost four percent per annum. In addition, the study concluded that many hedge funds were taking on significantly greater risk by investing in highly illiquid securities. Seems that while index funds may be boring, they make better investment vehicles.[4]

The large fees and the incentive based pricing attracts many successful mutual fund managers to the hedge fund arena. Compensation that was in the hundreds of thousands as a mutual fund manager becomes millions as a hedge fund manager. Unfortunately the persistence of performance, just like in the mutual fund arena, doesn't justify the faith of investors. According to Stephen T. Brown, professor at NYU's Stern Business School: "Half of them [ex-mutual fund managers] that survive the first six months are dead two years later."[5] Buried along with them are investor assets.

Hedge fund investing appeals to many investors because of the exclusive nature of the club. It also offers the potential of great rewards. The media conveys instant celebrity status on the latest superstar performer. The few successful ones make for great cocktail party stories. Unfortunately, the evidence is that these fund managers demonstrate no greater ability to deliver above-market returns than do active mutual fund managers. A recent example of a candle that once burned brightly is Julian Robertson's Tiger fund. Its great track record led to huge inflows of funds. The fund hit a peak of $22 billion in 1998. While the S&P 500 Index was up over twenty-one percent in 1999, Tiger Management fell nineteen percent. This led to a huge outflow of cash, and fund assets fell to $7 billion.[6] In early 2000, continued underperformance and fund outflows led to the closing of the fund. The even more famous George Soros was forced to liquidate most of his Quantum Fund to meet redemptions.[7] Yes, a few hedge managers succeed. However, the real tests are: Do more succeed than is randomly expected? Is there persistence in performance? As the historical record suggests that the answers to these questions are no, investors should logically avoid investing in hedge funds.

PART THREE

—————————— ◆ ——————————

Mistakes Made When Planning an Investment Strategy

MISTAKE 28

◆

Do You Treat the Highly Likely as Certain and the Highly Unlikely as Impossible?

Many now have come to believe that the market risk is no longer a realistic consideration while the risk of being under-invested or in cash and missing opportunities exceeds any other.   *—Barron's*, February 3, 1969

It is, of course, the theory that any sharp drop in the market will be cushioned because mutual funds in particular, attracted by all the bargain priced stocks, will immediately start buying and thus shore up the entire market.
      —Dun's Review, September 1968

The only thing that's certain is that after five years of almost uninterrupted prosperity, we're in unchartered territory now. The future isn't bullish, and it isn't bearish. The future is a secret. Perhaps the best advice is: Don't be too sure of anything.
      —Pat Regnier, "How High Is Up?" *Money*,
December 1999

People are commonly biased in several directions: They are optimistic; they overestimate the chances that they will succeed, and they overestimate their degree of knowledge, in the sense that their confidence far exceeds their "hit rate."   —Amos Tversky

One of the biggest and most common mistakes investors make is to treat investment risk as if it isn't really risk. Individuals don't generally make this mistake in other areas of their lives. In fact, when it comes to most non-investment decisions they generally act in a risk-averse manner. The following example illustrates the point. Imagine that you are a thirty-year-old married male, you are the main income earner in your family, and you have two young children. You have recently finished paying off your college debts, have just used most of your savings for the down payment on your dream home, and have a very large monthly mortgage payment. You are a non-smoker, eat a healthy diet, and exercise regularly. You also happen to have good genes—everyone in your family has lived a long life. Your life expectancy is probably something like fifty more years or longer. Given these facts, should you buy life insurance to provide for your family in the event of your early death? Despite the odds of your early death being very low, virtually everyone would make the decision to buy the insurance. The reason is that, while there is a low likelihood of dying early, there is still uncertainty, or risk. In addition, the cost of being wrong (dying uninsured) is very high. The same analogy could be said about purchasing fire insurance. The odds of needing it are very low, yet the cost of being wrong is so high, and individuals are so risk-averse when the cost of being wrong is high (many buy lottery tickets, which is clearly high risk, but the cost of losing is low), that the prudent decision is to buy the insurance. In this case, individuals do not treat the highly unlikely—premature death or the home burning down—as impossible. They also don't treat the highly likely—that they will live a long time or their house will not burn down—as certain. Yet when it comes to investment decisions, this is exactly the type of mistake people often make.

Whenever advisors within my firm sit down with a new client to develop an investment policy statement, one of the many tools we use is the following table. It is designed to help the investor identify his or her tolerance for, or ability to accept, risk.

Maximum Tolerable Loss (%)	Maximum Equity Exposure (%)
5	20
10	30
15	40
20	50
25	60
30	70
35	80
40	90
50	100

We tell investors that the above table is based upon the experience of the 1973–74 bear market, the worst in the postwar era. We then ask them to identify the maximum amount of loss they could tolerate without losing sleep (life is too short not to enjoy it), panicking and selling (probably at the low of the market), or losing the discipline to rebalance (remember if equities fall in value, rebalancing will require you to buy more just when you have experienced a painful loss). We attempt to hammer home the point that just because this was the worst experience of the postwar era, it doesn't mean we cannot experience an even worse one in the future. We want to make sure that investors understand that the reason equities have provided higher returns in the past, and are likely to do so in the future, is that there is risk involved. The risk is that not only can bear markets occur, but it often takes a very long time to be rewarded for accepting the risk of equities. For example, most investors are shocked when you show them the aforementioned data demonstrating that large-cap growth stocks (the ones most investors believe are the safest equity investments) underperformed totally riskless one-month bank certificates of deposit for the twenty-five-year period 1966–90 (8.2% vs. 8.3%). In that twenty-five-year period, risk and reward went unrelated. Actually, what occurred was that the ex-post realized reward was much lower than the expected reward. This is precisely what risk is all about. High risk means a higher likelihood that the realized returns may deviate from the expected, by larger amounts, and over longer periods. Remember, if it were certain that large-cap growth stocks would outperform, there would be no risk premium (the higher *expected* return for the accepting the possibility of a negative outcome).

The majority of today's investors never experienced the pain of the 1973–74 bear market. Or, if they did, they probably had very little invested at the time, as it was early in their investment careers. In addition, it was a long time ago (remember the mistake of "recency"). The only major bear market most baby boomers probably experienced prior to 2000 occurred in October 1987, and it was so short that by the end of the year the market had closed higher than it had begun the year. In addition, the following year the S&P 500 rose almost seventeen percent. The new generation of investors was thus "taught" (or led to believe) that bear markets were an opportunity to buy on any dip in equity prices, as any dip would prove to be very short term (i.e., risk isn't risk). There was even a book, *Dow 36,000*, published in late 1999 (just in time for the 2000 bear market), which claimed that if your investment horizon is long enough (twenty years), stocks are not riskier than bonds. This is the equivalent of believing that there is no risk in the stock market, or of treating risk as if it isn't risk.

The problem this kind of thinking creates is that people begin to treat the highly unlikely—either a 1973-type bear market, or large-cap growth stocks underperforming CDs for twenty-five years—as impossible. Although they might even acknowledge that such events have occurred, they assume that they are so unlikely that they treat the unlikely as if it were really impossible for it to happen again. This in turn causes them to overstate their tolerance for risk, and have too high an equity allocation. This creates the danger that if a bear market arrives, their heavy exposure to equities will cause them more pain than they can withstand. They may then either panic or be forced to sell because they simply cannot accept the possibility of further losses. This is exactly what happened to many investors when the bear markets of the summer of 1998 and the spring of 2000 occurred.

Here are two other examples of treating risk as if it isn't risk:

- From 1998 through early 2000, many investors convinced themselves that the technology revolution was so certain to create great returns that even normally prudent, conservative investors began to invest in very risky Internet companies. They ultimately paid the price for making that mistake.

- From 1963 through 1998, large value stocks outperformed the S&P 500 by 15.6% to 12.6%. Over rolling one-, three-, five-, ten-, and fifteen-year rolling periods they outperformed 69%, 74%, 82%, 93%, and 98% of the time. Academics would explain this outperformance as a risk premium, compensation for accepting the risk of investing in riskier value companies. Instead of building a diversified portfolio including both large-cap value and large-cap growth stocks, some investors, seeing this data, will either heavily tilt their portfolio toward large-cap value, or even own only large-cap value, excluding the S&P 500 from their portfolio. If one truly understands the risky nature of this type of strategy, then it might be an appropriate decision. On the other hand, if the investor interprets the data as "since large value stocks provide higher returns, and do so almost all the time, they really aren't risky," then risk is being treated as if it isn't risk at all. Investors who made this type of decision had their risk tolerance and discipline sorely tested in 1998 and 1999, when the S&P returned almost twenty-five percent per annum while large value stocks returned just over eight percent per annum. The bottom line is: Risk is risk. There is no certainty with investments except with short-term government securities and I-Bonds (even TIPS, Treasury Inflation Protected Securities, have price risk).

You can avoid the mistake of treating the highly likely as certain and the highly unlikely as impossible by remembering the basic economic principle that risk and reward are related. If the investments you are planning to make provide a higher return than riskless short-term government instruments, then there is both risk and uncertainty. The greater the expected difference in returns, the greater the uncertainty and the greater the risk. You should also keep in mind the following advice from Peter Bernstein: "Even the most brilliant of mathematical geniuses will never be able to tell us what the future holds."[1]

MISTAKE 29

◆

Do You Confuse Before-the-Fact Strategy with After-the-Fact Outcome?

You've got to look at the portfolio as a whole, not just position by position. And if you're trying to reduce the volatility or uncertainty of your portfolio as a whole, then you need more than one security obviously, but you also need securities which don't go up and down together.

— Harry Markowitz, Jonathan Burton, *Investment Titans*

I'm a big believer in diversification, because I am totally convinced that forecasts will be wrong. Diversification is the guiding principle. That's the only way you can live through the hard times. It's going to cost you in the short run, because not everything will be going through the roof.

— Paul Samuelson

144

Imagine that you are Phil Jackson, when he was coach of the Chicago Bulls. It is the fifth game of the championship series. Your team is ahead three games to one. Karl Malone has just scored a basket with ten seconds to go, giving the Utah Jazz a 1-point lead. You call a time-out in order to set up the last play. Your star, Michael Jordan, has had a relatively poor game, scoring just 15 points, and he has not shot well. On the other hand, Luc Longley, normally your weakest offense player, has had a career game, scoring 25 points on almost perfect shooting. For whom do you call the last play, Jordan or Longley? Virtually everyone would set the play up for Jordan, possibly the greatest player in history. It would not be rational to ignore career statistics and make a decision based on just one game. Unfortunately, Jordan, being human, misses the shot. In truth, while the decision was clearly the correct one, and we are disappointed by the outcome, we should not be surprised. Given his career statistics we would expect him to make the shot only about fifty percent of the time.

It is now the sixth game, and the same situation arises. Once again you call the play for Jordan. To your great disappointment, he misses again. Again, not too surprising since the probability of his missing both of the last two shots is about twenty-five percent. Amazingly, the same situation arises in the final game. Once again you call on Jordan to hit the big shot. And again he misses. While the outcome was disappointing, surely everyone would agree that the strategy of having your best player take the last shot was clearly the right one. You relied on long-term historical evidence to develop the strategy that would give you the best chance of success. Remember that although you didn't like the outcome, it should not have been entirely unexpected. A career fifty percent shooter will miss (or make) all three shots one out of every eight attempts. If you had made any other choice as to who would take the last shot and they did not succeed, in all likelihood you would have been fired for incompetence.

This example is one of confusing strategy and outcome. Although you didn't like the outcome, because we live in an "ex-ante" (before-the-fact) world without clear crystal balls, the ex-ante strategy was still the correct one. Nissam Nicholas Taleb, the author of *Fooled by Randomness*, had the following to say on confusing strategy and outcome: "One cannot judge a performance in any given field by the results, but by the costs of the alternative (i.e. if history played out in a different way). Such substitute courses of events are called *alternative histories*. Clearly the quality of a decision cannot be solely judged based on its outcome, but such a point seems to be voiced only by people who fail (those who succeed attribute their success to the quality of their decision)."[1] When it comes to investing, our ability to foresee which alternative history will play out is no clearer than it is for a basketball coach. The following example illustrates this point.

Imagine that it is January 1999 and your best friend just inherited $10 million of Exxon stock. Being of modest means up to this point, your friend's inheritance constitutes virtually one hundred percent of her assets. Your friend tells you that she plans on holding the stock as she thinks Exxon is a great company and oil prices will rise in 1999. She then asks your opinion on her strategy. Giving sound counsel, you advise her that putting all her eggs in one basket is a very risky strategy. Your advice is to diversify. Your friend agrees and states that she will sell $5 million of Exxon stock and with the proceeds buy $5 million of Shell Oil. You laugh. You tell her that while owning two companies instead of one is diversification, because both Exxon and Shell are likely to move up and down together (in response to the rising and falling of oil prices), she hasn't achieved effective diversification. Because the price movement of these two stocks is likely to be what statisticians call "highly correlated," in reality she hasn't significantly reduced the risk of her portfolio.

You suggest to your friend that to achieve effective diversification, instead of buying Shell, she should buy something that has "low correlation" to her Exxon stock, something that would benefit if oil prices fell. You therefore recommend that she purchase United Airlines stock. If oil prices rise, Exxon will do well. On the other hand, if oil prices fall, United Airlines will do well, as fuel costs (its largest expense after labor costs) fall. Now, because Exxon and United Airlines have low correlation, the portfolio is effectively diversified—at least against the risk of changing oil prices. The portfolio's risk has certainly been reduced.

Your friend agrees that the strategy is correct and makes her trades the very next day. Fast-forward to the end of the year. Your friend is very angry with you. Why? Oil prices rose dramatically, resulting in Exxon's price rising sharply and United's price falling sharply. You rightly point out that your friend agreed at the beginning with the strategy of protecting against oil price changes. You also point out that at the start of the year, you knew with a virtual certainty that over the next twenty years there would be periods when oil prices did well, with Exxon performing well and United poorly. However, you also knew with a virtual certainty that there would be periods when oil prices would fall, and Exxon would do poorly and United would do well. Since your friend did not have a crystal ball that would allow her to predict oil prices—knowing when to own only Exxon and when only United—the correct strategy (ex-ante) was to diversify. You then point out that the strategy was working exactly as expected. Your friend just didn't like the after-the-fact (ex-post) results. You also point out that she would have been very happy if oil prices had fallen. You proceed to advise your friend to sell some (appreciated) Exxon shares to buy even more of the beaten-down United shares, to again reduce the risk of her overall portfolio through rebalancing.

What can we derive from this story besides keeping your opinions to yourself? Since investors do not have crystal balls, a strategy based on long-term historical evidence and logic is correct ex-ante, whatever the outcome. As proof, do you know of any person who complains at the end of the year that he "wasted" his life insurance premium? Was buying life insurance the wrong strategy? With your investments, diversification is the correct strategy, whatever the outcome.

Confusing ex-ante strategy with ex-post results can lead you to abandon the strategy that is based on the long-term evidence and to chase the latest hot fad (like asking Luc Longley to take the last shot). Let's look at a perfect example that will prove that diversification works, whether you like it or not.

If you could foresee when a particular asset class would perform well, then you would obviously only own that winning asset class. (If you could have foreseen that Michael Jordan would miss those shots, you wouldn't have asked him to take them.) The spectacular failure of active managers should put that idea to rest. If you recognize that your investment crystal ball is a cloudy one, then diversification is clearly the prudent strategy. Knowledgeable investors know that investing is all about achieving the greatest return for the amount of risk taken. They also know that a diversified portfolio makes the taking of risk more acceptable. However, asset allocation is not a panacea—you must be well prepared for the "risk of diversification," or you might lose discipline. In the long run, it is quite possible that the discipline you display in adhering to your asset allocation, and regularly rebalancing, will be more important than the specific asset allocations you choose.

The risks and rewards of diversification can be easily demonstrated by examining the twenty-eight-year period 1973–2000. We can compare the performance of a 60% S&P 500/40% Lehman Brothers Bond Index portfolio with that of a similar (the same 60/40 equity/fixed-income allocation), but globally diversified, portfolio (the kind I recommend building). For the period, the 60% S&P 500/40% Lehman Bond Index portfolio was up 11.6% per annum versus 13% for the diversified portfolio. The diversified portfolio outperformed in seventeen of the twenty-eight years, and thirteen of the first sixteen years. However, let's imagine that you are an investor starting out on January 1, 1989. Having seen the historical evidence and understanding the logic of diversification, you decide to invest in the globally diversified portfolio. Unfortunately, your timing is lousy. The 60% S&P 500/40% Lehman Bond Index portfolio outperforms your globally diversified portfolio in eight of the next ten years. Each dollar you invested in the globally diversified portfolio grew to just $2.15, while each dollar invested in the alternative domestic-only portfolio would have grown to $4.18. After having the discipline to stick with your portfolio for ten years, the disappointing outcome causes you to abandon your carefully thought out strategy. Of course, as soon as you bail out, the globally diversified portfolio once again begins to provide superior returns, outperforming in 1999 by 1.4% and again in 2000 by 3.7%!

The fact that you were unhappy with the outcome of the strategy of diversification doesn't mean that the strategy was incorrect, or even that the outcome was unexpected. Just as Michael Jordan will occasionally miss eight of ten shots, a diversified strategy might underperform for eight out of ten years, or even over much longer periods. Don't make the mistake of confusing strategy with outcome. Exhibit A shows the returns of the two portfolios. Exhibit B demonstrates why diversification is the winning strategy. The table in Exhibit B contains the returns of seven different U.S. and international asset classes, and provides the rank order of the returns of each asset class for the year. See if you can detect any pattern. Obviously, the only pattern is that there is no pattern. Since our crystal balls are quite cloudy, diversification is our insurance policy: it spreads our equity risk across many baskets.

Unfortunately, too many investors have entered what John Bogle calls the "Age of Investment Relativism."[2] Investor satisfaction or unhappiness (and therefore the discipline required to stick with a strategy) to a great degree seems determined by the relative performance of their portfolio to some index—an index which shouldn't even be relevant to an investor who accepts the wisdom of asset allocation and diversification. Relativism, sadly, can best be described as the triumph of emotion over wisdom and experience. The history of financial markets has demonstrated that today's trends are merely "noise" in the context of the long term. Bogle also cited an anonymous portfolio manager who warned: "Relativity worked well for Einstein, but it has no place in investing."[3]

Chasing the latest fad or hot asset class has proven to be a losing strategy—the result of confusing strategy and outcome. It is extremely important for you to understand ahead of time that the individual portions of your investment pie will perform differently over time. This is why we build an investment house with unique and low correlating building blocks (asset classes). Unfortunately, as James Gipson, manager of the Clipper Fund, wrote: "Diversification for investors, like celibacy for teenagers, is a concept both easy to understand and hard to practice."[4] Because of the risk of diversification, it is extremely important for you to determine just how much *tracking error* to major benchmarks you are willing to live with as a trade-off for the benefits of diversification. Tracking error is the amount by which the performance of a portfolio (or fund) differs from the performance of a benchmark (such as the S&P 500 Index).

Diversification means accepting the fact that parts of the portfolio will behave entirely differently from the portfolio itself. Choosing the appropriate level of tolerance for tracking error will help keep you disciplined. The less tracking error you are willing to accept, the more the equity portion of your portfolio should simply look like the S&P 500 Index. On the other hand, if you choose a marketlike portfolio, it will be one that is not very diversified by asset class and will have no international diversification. At least between these two choices (avoiding or accepting tracking error) there is no free lunch. It is almost as important to get this right as it is to determine the appropriate equity/fixed-income allocation. If you have the discipline to stick with a globally diversified passive asset class strategy, you are highly likely to be rewarded for your discipline.

MISTAKE 30

◆

Do You Try to Succeed Even When Success Is Highly Unlikely?

People think of trading as playing tennis against a wall. They can position themselves perfectly, and they can return the ball just right. But when they trade, it is real tennis that they are playing against very skilled players, including professional players.
—Meir Statman, *Wall Street Journal*, November 24, 1998

If picking stocks is a random walk down Wall Street, then picking funds is an obstacle course through Hell's Kitchen.
—Burton Malkiel, as quoted in *BusinessWeek*, December 17, 2001

As we have seen, it is a common human trait to be overconfident of our skills. Even when individuals will admit that a task is difficult, there is still a tendency toward overconfidence. This is certainly true when it comes to identifying active man-

151

agers who will outperform the market in the future. Presented with the evidence on the failure of active managers to outperform, a frequent response is: "The data only represents the average fund. By instituting simple screens you can easily eliminate many losers." Typical suggestions are to eliminate those funds with poor performance, high expenses, and high turnover, or to screen for managers with long tenure. By *carefully* selecting funds, rather than looking at all funds, an investor may feel he can identify funds that will outperform. This approach has a logical appeal, and it will likely improve the results compared to all actively managed funds; however, it is not likely that it will result in market-beating performance. In fact, after reading this section, my hope is that you will agree that it is not logical to think that you can identify the future winners, even with the most logical of approaches.

One of the most respected names in the investment business is Frank Russell (creator of the Russell indices). Russell performs research and due diligence on money managers in its role as a pension plan consultant and chooses the very best to manage funds they sponsor. It would seem logical that if anyone could beat the market by identifying the future great money managers, the Russell organization could. On its Web site (*www.russell.com*) it touts an extensive process, with fifty analysts studying some 1,700 investment managers. These analysts hold over 2,000 meetings a year, during which they grill managers on their investment approach. They use both qualitative and quantitative analysis to narrow those 1,700 to the best 300, and then subject those 300 to further scrutiny. The list is then narrowed down to the very best, before ultimately selecting the very few "superstars" who will have the honor of co-managing one of Russell's funds. Within investment styles (growth and value, small-cap and large-cap, domestic and international), Russell funds use a manager-of-managers approach—selecting and monitoring "many of the most talented money managers in the world." Russell notes that in making the ultimate selection of managers it places the most weight on the investment process used by the manager. The second most important criterion is the strength of the management team. The third, but least important factor, since it is an unreliable predictor, is past performance.

So let's get back on Mr. Peabody's way-back machine and see just how well the Russell approach has performed. To test the process, we can compare the returns of the actively managed Russell manager-of-manager funds with appropriate passive benchmarks. For an appropriate benchmark for each asset class for which Russell has funds, we can use the passively managed asset class funds of DFA (and simulated returns if the funds were not live for the entire period). We will look at both pre- and after-tax performance. A 35% tax rate will be used to calculate after-tax returns. In general, the period we will examine is the ten years from 1991 to 2000. Let's begin by examining the pretax returns for the large-cap asset class:

Russell Equity I	16.9%
Russell Equity Q	18.4%
DFA Large Cap (an S&P 500 Index fund)	17.2%

The average return of the two Russell funds was 17.6%, slightly outperforming a benchmark index fund. However, once taxes are considered, the story is quite different. The Russell funds each lost 2.7% per annum to taxes, about 2% more than the benchmark index fund. Thus, the slight outperformance on a pre-tax basis becomes underperformance of 1.6% on an after-tax basis.

Let's now look at the performance of the large-cap value-oriented Russell Equity III fund. We will look at both five-year data (for which there existed a live DFA Large Value benchmark) and ten-year data that includes two-plus years of simulated returns. The returns are pretax. The first figure covers 1996–2000 and the second covers 1991–2000.

Russell Equity III   12.7%/15.2%
DFA Large Value   14.8%/18.3%

As you can see, the Russell fund clearly underperformed even before taxes are considered. For the live five-year period, the Russell fund lost 3.1% per annum to taxes, 0.4% more than did the similar DFA fund. It is also worth noting that DFA has introduced a *tax-managed* large-cap value fund that should significantly reduce the drag from the negative impact of taxes on returns. In its first two years this fund lost an average of only 0.52% to taxes.

Let's now turn to smallcaps for which Russell has the Equity II Fund. We can compare its performance to the DFA Micro Cap Fund and the DFA Small Cap Fund (simulated data prior to March 1992). We will look at the ten-year pretax returns.

Russell Equity II   17.1%
DFA Micro Cap   17.5%
DFA Small Cap   19.9%

It appears that in this small-cap asset class, which is supposedly inefficient (thus allowing active managers to exploit the market's pricing mistakes), Russell failed at its goal, even on a pretax basis. Unfortunately for Russell, the story doesn't get any better on an after-tax basis. The Russell fund lost 2.4% per annum to taxes, while the DFA Micro Cap Fund lost slightly less (2.1%). Over its life the DFA Small Cap Fund had similar tax efficiency experience to that of its sister fund. Once again, note that DFA now has created a tax-managed small-cap fund that should significantly reduce the negative tax impact on returns. In its first two years the fund lost only 0.13% on average to taxes.*

Let's now examine the ten-year performance of the Russell Real Estate Fund as compared to that of the DFA Real Estate Fund (simulated data prior to 1993):

Russell Real Estate   14.9%
DFA Real Estate   15.8%

Once again we see no evidence of outperformance. The Russell fund has also been a bit less tax efficient than the DFA fund, losing about 2.7% per annum to taxes versus 2.3%.

Moving on to the asset class of international stocks, we can compare the performance of the Russell International Fund with that of the DFA Large-Cap International Fund that basically conforms to the EAFE Index. We will examine the ten-year period ending 2000. The DFA Fund was live for all but the first six months, for which we will use simulated data:

Russell International Fund   9.2%
DFA Large-Cap International Fund   8.8%

The Russell International Fund did manage to outperform by 0.4% per annum. However, the Russell fund lost just over 1.5% per annum to taxes, about 0.8% more than did the similar DFA Fund, more than wiping the pretax advantage. One note of caution—when looking at the performance of active managers against broad market cap weighted international indices such as EAFE, we have to be careful of the "Japan" effect. Leading up to 1989, the Japanese market had so far outperformed other markets that Japan represented almost seventy percent of the EAFE index.

---

*While tax management strategies should produce greater tax efficiency, the newness of the funds in all likelihood overstates their long-term tax efficiency. A simulated study by Kenneth French, depending on the assumptions made about growth of assets under management and investment horizon, indicated improved long-term, after-tax returns of approximately one to two percent per annum.

Most active managers were unwilling to hold such a heavy weighting in one country. The result was massive underperformance by active managers throughout the 1970s and 1980s. Since 1989, however, Japanese stocks have underperformed by so much that their weighting is now only about one third of what it was at the peak. The performance during the 1990s gave the "advantage" to active managers, who were able to outperform (just as they had underperformed earlier) simply by underweighting Japan as a diversification strategy. Thus, one must be careful in interpreting the data. The underperformance of Japan in the 1990s has restored a more balanced weighting, and so the Japan issue, at least for now, should not have as much of an impact.

We will conclude our analysis by comparing the performance of the Russell Emerging Markets Fund with that of the DFA Emerging Markets Fund. We will compare the pretax performance of the funds for the period five-year period 1996–2000:

Russell Emerging Markets   −4.1%
DFA Emerging Markets   −0.1%

In what is supposedly the most inefficient asset class in the world (where active managers claim to be able to add the most value), we actually find the worst performance, with Russell underperforming its benchmark by four percent per annum pretax. It should be noted that with the low level of absolute returns, neither fund was impacted much by taxes (the tax impact for the Russell fund was 0.3% per annum and for the DFA fund it was 0.5% per annum).

To summarize, it is very hard to see any evidence of the ability of Frank Russell to add value, especially on an after-tax basis.

Here is further piece of evidence against the likelihood and wisdom of trying to find the *future* great investment managers. It would seem logical to believe that if anyone could beat the market, it would be the pension funds of the largest U.S. companies. They have access to the best and brightest portfolio managers, all clamoring to manage the billions of dollars in these plans. Presumably, these pension funds rely on the excellent track records of the "experts" they eventually choose to manage their portfolios. It seems unlikely that they would ever choose fund managers with poor past performance. In addition, the pension plans often hire professional advisors such as Frank Russell, SEI, and Goldman Sachs to help them perform due diligence in interviewing, screening, and ultimately selecting the very best of the best. As individuals, we don't have access to many of these great managers since we would not meet their investment minimums. We also don't have the luxury of being able to personally interview the firms and perform a thorough due diligence. And we don't have professionals helping us to avoid mistakes in the process.

Piscataqua Research, in a study covering the period 1987–96, found that only 10 out of 145 major pension funds, or just seven percent, outperformed a portfolio consisting of a simple 60%/40% mix of the S&P 500 Index and the Lehman Bond Index, respectively.[1] A 60% equity/40% fixed-income allocation was used, since that is estimated to be the average allocation of all pension plans. The Piscataqua Research study provides evidence against not only the strategy of choosing managers based on past performance, but the use of active managers in general.

Another study of pension fund managers found very similar results. T. Daniel Coggin and Charles A. Trzcinka studied the performance of 292 pension plans with twelve quarters of data up to the second quarter of 1993.[2] Here is a summary of their findings:

- It is very difficult to find investment managers who consistently add value relative to appropriate benchmarks.

157

- There was no correlation found between relative performance in one period and future periods.

- There was no evidence that the number of managers beating their benchmarks was greater than pure chance.

The authors concluded: "Those relying on historical data on returns are likely to be disappointed."

Also insightful on the likelihood of finding managers who will beat their benchmark is the experience of the chief investment officer of the State Universities Retirement System of Illinois, John R. Krimmel. His comments on the firings of the two active fund managers the system had employed can be summarized as:

- It's a tough area in which to add value.

- The academic research bears that out, and our experience shows that as well.

- Over the long haul we've just about broken even (with the benchmark) but with slightly higher volatility.[3]

Returning to our starting point: Is it logical for you to believe that you can predict which actively managed funds will outperform, or are you overconfident of your skills? If you are trying to find the great fund managers who will outperform in the future, ask yourself: What am I going to do differently, in terms of identifying the future winning fund managers, than did the pension plans and their advisors? Surely these organizations have thought of eliminating from consideration the poorly performing funds and the high-cost funds? And, if you are not going to do something different, what logic is there in playing a game at which others with superior resources have consistently failed? Or is it that you believe that you can interpret the data more correctly than have others with far more resources?

By seriously considering these questions you can avoid the

mistake of trying to find the future great fund managers. Yes, it is possible that you will succeed. However, both the evidence and the logic suggest that the odds against success make this a game you are better off not playing. Think about it: Of the 355 equity funds that existed in 1970, only 169 were left standing as of June 2001. Of the survivors, just nine managed to outperform the S&P 500 Index.[4] Daniel Kahneman, professor of psychology and public affairs at Princeton University, put it this way: "What's really quite remarkable in the investment world is that people are playing a game which, in some sense, cannot be played. There are so many people out there in the market; the idea that any single individual without extra information or extra market power can beat the market is extraordinarily unlikely. Yet the market is full of people who think they can do it and full of other people who believe them. This is one of the great mysteries of finance: Why do people believe they can do the impossible? And why do other people believe them?"[4]

MISTAKE 31

◆

Do You Fail to Understand the Importance of Saving Early in Life?

There are two reasons why the best time to invest is when you have funds available to do so. First, there is a substantial body of evidence which suggests that efforts to time investments are nonproductive. Second, but more significant, is the importance of compounding. The following examples of investors Sally, Sam, Jane, and John will illustrate the powerful effects of compounding.

Sally begins to save $5,000 a year at age twenty-five. She continues to save this amount for ten years, until age thirty-four, at which point she stops saving. Sam, on the other hand, waits until age thirty-five to start saving. He then saves $5,000 a year for the next thirty years. At the end of ten years, Sally will have invested a total of $50,000. At the end of Sam's thirty-year program, he will have invested a total of $150,000, or three times as much as Sally. But this is not the end of the story.

Assuming a ten percent per annum compound rate of return, at age sixty-five, Sally will have generated a portfolio of about $1.4 million. Despite having saved and invested three times as many dollars, Sam's portfolio will have grown to only $820,000, forty percent less than Sally's. When Sam and Sally are seventy-five, their two portfolios will have grown to $3.6 million and $2.2 million, respectively.

If Jane waits until age forty-five to begin investing, she must save $24,000 each year for the next twenty years to achieve the same portfolio as Sally. Remember, Sally only had to put aside $5,000 for ten years. If John waits until age fifty-five to begin an investment program, he will have to save $87,000 a year for ten years to reach the same goal. This illustrates the powerful roles that time and compounding play in investment outcomes. The moral is simple: If you can put off buying those desirable consumables in your early investing years, and instead put a reasonable amount into a passively invested diversified asset class portfolio, you should be able to acquire a whole lot of those desirable consumables later in life.

MISTAKE 32

◆

Do You Fail to Evaluate the Real Cost of an Expenditure?

I have a good friend we shall call Louis. During the process of discussing his overall financial plans, I brought up the subject of the expense of the private school education he was providing for his child. Louis also has a second child who will soon be starting school, and a third child is on the way. When I asked Louis what the cost of a private school education was, he stated that it was about $10,000 per annum (before considering all the requests for donations). I pointed out to Louis that although the $10,000 was the current outlay, he was vastly underestimating the true cost and implication of this expenditure. Let me explain.

Louis had the choice of either paying $10,000 for the private school education or sending his child to the local public school. Louis and his wife decided that the $10,000 additional cost was a good *investment*. I then offered Louis an alternative perspective on how to evaluate the cost of the expenditure.

I pointed out that had Louis chosen to send his child to the public school, he would have had $10,000 additional funds available to invest each year for the next twelve years. The dollars invested would then be available in his retirement. The next logical question was the amount of retirement income Louis was sacrificing to provide the private school education. Here are the assumptions used in presenting the answer:

- Louis is thirty-five years old and wishes to retire and begin to withdraw funds from his retirement account at age sixty-five.

- Private school cost is $10,000, increasing at an assumed inflation rate of 3% per annum.
- Twelve years of private education will be required.
- Return on investment will be ten percent per annum.
- Upon retirement, Louis will withdraw a very conservative four percent of the portfolio, adjusted for inflation, each year.

Using these assumptions, Louis would have an additional portfolio of $1,645,996 at age sixty-five. This would allow him to withdraw an additional $65,840 the first year, and then adjust upward for inflation thereafter. In today's dollars that equated to $26,335 per annum in additional buying power. These figures were just for the first child; the costs for the other children would be somewhat less as the time horizon for the assets to grow would be less.

The point of the exercise was not to convince Louis to send his children to a public school, but to help him understand the true cost of that private education: Louis was likely to have $26,335 less per annum in today's dollars to spend in retirement. The question of whether or not to send the children to a public or private school should not be decided on a purely economic basis. However, one should understand the true implications of any expenditure decision. This type of analysis should be done for any major expenditure in order to properly evaluate the full implications of the decision.

MISTAKE 33

◆

Do You Believe Diversification Is the Right Strategy Only If the Investment Horizon Is Long?

On one of the investment electronic bulletin boards I frequent on the Internet, there was a discussion about the benefits of diversification. One poster suggested that since his investment horizon was relatively short (ten years), he did not want to take the chance of investing in such risky asset classes as international equities, emerging markets, small caps, and value stocks. While agreeing that the poster's investment horizon should affect his asset allocation decision, I suggest that he came to the wrong conclusion. In fact, as I hope you will agree, the shorter your investment horizon, the greater the need for diversification across asset classes.

The length of the investment horizon should affect your equity/fixed-income asset allocation decision. The longer the horizon, the more likely it is that equities will outperform fixed-income instruments. Also, the longer the horizon, the greater the ability to wait out a bear market. With that in mind, you might use the following table to help you decide on an equity/fixed-income allocation:

Investment Horizon	Maximum Equity Allocation (%)
0–3 years	0
4 years	10

(continued)

Investment Horizon	Maximum Equity Allocation (%)
5 years	20
6 years	30
7 years	40
8 years	50
9 years	60
10 years	70
11–14 years	80
15–19 years	90
20 years or longer	100

Because most investors are generally not risk-neutral, and are in fact risk-averse, the table is probably more conservative than historical evidence would require. Accordingly, investors with a high tolerance for risk might want to be more aggressive. It is also important to keep in mind that the ability to take risk (length of investment horizon) is only one consideration in developing a portfolio. Among the other considerations are the willingness and the need to take risk.

Once we have determined the equity/fixed-income allocation, we then must decide on the specific allocation we desire between the various equity asset classes. However, broad global diversification is the winning strategy in a world where investors do not have clear crystal balls. For example, with the freedom of capital to move around the globe with ease in the search for the highest risk-adjusted returns, it is logical to believe that the equity markets of the developed countries will produce very similar returns to those of the United States, over the long run. If investors believed that the United States offered better prospects, then that information would already be incorporated into prices. If we compare the returns of the EAFE Index with the returns of the S&P 500 (both indices dominated by large-cap growth stocks) over the thirty-one-year period 1969–1999, we find virtually identical returns. The difference in returns was a mere 0.09%, with the S&P 500 outperforming by 12.93% to 12.84%. An investor looking at the data might conclude that since she doesn't have thirty-one years to wait, she shouldn't take the risk of owning international equities. This line of thinking is incorrect since the future may not look like the past. No matter how clear the future might appear, we have no way of knowing exactly what the outcomes will be. If you doubt this, just look back to 1989 and compare the returns of Japanese stocks to U.S. stocks since then. In addition, the whole line of thinking is backwards. Here is why.

Over very long periods, various equity asset classes have had similar returns. We just reviewed the evidence on U.S. large caps and international large caps. Let's now compare the returns of various U.S. asset classes over the period 1928–2000:

Small value	14.5%
Large value	12.7%
Small caps (CRSP 6–10)	11.9%
Large caps (S&P 500)	10.7%
Small growth	10.6%
Large growth	9.9%

Two observations can be made. First, risk and reward were related. Riskier small and value stocks outperformed less risky large and growth stocks. Second, the difference between the highest returning and lowest returning asset class was *just* 4.6% per annum. Of course, small differences in annual returns become magnified when compounded over long periods.

As we have seen, there is not a great difference in returns between asset classes, both domestically and internationally, over very long periods. However, when the investment horizon is still long, though somewhat shorter than thirty years, there have been huge differences in returns. Let's look at a few examples, beginning with the EAFE and S&P 500 indices. For the eighteen-year period 1971–88, the S&P 500 Index underperformed the EAFE Index by 6.2% per annum (17.2% to 11.0%). Now, imagine yourself as a U.S. investor who in 1971 had *only* an eighteen-year horizon and therefore didn't want to take the risk of owning international stocks. Then, from 1989 through 2000, the S&P 500 Index outperformed the EAFE Index by 11.4% per annum (16.7% to 5.3%). Now imagine yourself as a foreign investor in 1989 with just an eleven-year horizon and thus unwilling to take the risk of owning U.S. stocks.

Next, let's look at a few U.S. examples. While large-cap growth stocks have underperformed small-cap growth stocks by just 0.7% per annum over the long term, there have been fairly long periods of great divergence in performance. For example, for the nine-year period 1975–83, small-cap growth stocks outperformed large-cap growth stocks by 16.9% per annum (30.6% to 13.7%). Now imagine yourself as a U.S. investor in 1975 with just a nine-year investment horizon; you therefore decide that you don't want to take the risk of owning small-cap stocks. Of course there were periods where the reverse was true. For example, from 1994 to 1999, large-cap growth outperformed small-cap growth by 8.4% per annum (24.8% to 16.4%). Here is another dramatic example. Although small value stocks outperformed large growth stocks by 4.6% per annum over the entire seventy-three-year period from 1928–2000, for the twenty-three-year period 1966–88 they outperformed by 9.3% per annum (16.9% to 7.6%). Imagine yourself in 1966 with *just* a twenty-three-year horizon and therefore not wanting to take the risk of owning simple value stocks.

Although diversification across non-highly correlating asset classes is the winning strategy no matter what the investment horizon, you should note that diversification across equity asset classes is actually more important as the investment horizon shortens. This is because any one asset class can underperform by very large amounts over even fairly long horizons, let alone relatively short ones. If your investment horizon is very short, then the way to control risk is to increase your allocation to short-term fixed-income assets, not to increase your allocation to any one equity asset class, no matter how safe you think it to be.

MISTAKE 34

◆

Do You Believe that This Time It's Different?

Apparently there has been a fundamental change in criteria for judging security values. Widespread education of the public in the worth of equity securities has created a new demand.
    —*The Outlook & Independent Magazine*, May 15, 1929

It has seemed to be taken for granted in speculative circles that this is a market of "manifest destiny," and that destiny is to go continuously forward.
    —*New York Times*, September 1929

The United States has entered a new investment era to which the old guidelines no longer apply.
    —*Barron's*, February 3, 1969

Those who cannot remember the past are condemned to repeat it.   —George Santayana

With the dramatic changes in our economy fostered by the Internet and biotechnology revolutions, along with the spectacular performance of the heavily technology-weighted NASDAQ (at least up until March 2000), came the clarion call: "It's a different investment world." All the old rules about valuations and risk and reward were said to no longer be applicable. It no longer mattered what price you paid for a great company— ultimately you would be rewarded. All rational arguments against this line of thinking were dismissed with the claim: *This time things are different*. The following is a summary of the new era investing strategy.

It's a new world order. It's the new new thing. Investors should own great companies at any price. Never discard the right company just because the price is too high. It's different this time. The Internet is changing the world. It's a great revolution, supercharging the economy. The United States clearly is the leader in technology and productivity is growing at the fastest rate ever. We dominate the Internet, biotech, and financial services sectors. That is where the future is. Besides, the U.S. free enterprise system has proven it's the best model. Others have to now catch up. Just look at returns over the last few years. The opportunity is enormous. You can't afford to miss out. The future for New Age companies like AOL, Amazon, Cisco, Priceline, and the like is so bright and obvious, how can you possibly go wrong?

Mutual funds that jumped on the technology bandwagon provided spectacular returns for the early investors in this new era. New funds and new products such as QQQ (an exchange traded fund designed to replicate the performance of the tech-heavy NASDAQ 100) were created at breakneck speed as investors stampeded into this New-Age "gold rush."

For students of financial history, there is a great amount of similarity between today's New Age investing and the go-go era of the early 1960s. Investors in that era heard the same clarion calls as we then entered the computer revolution. At that time there was a group of stocks called the "nifty fifty." They were known as "one-decision" stocks—stocks that should be bought no matter the price and simply held forever (hence the term "one-decision"). Let's go to the videotape to see the results of that last "This time things are different" era.

From 1963 through 1968, five leading go-go funds (Enterprise Fund, Fidelity Capital, Fidelity Trend, T. Rowe Price New Horizons, and Ivest) provided cumulative Internet-like returns of 344%, nearly three and a-half times the return of the S&P 500. The assets of the five funds increased an astounding seventeen times, from $200 million to $3.4 billion. Over the next five years, however, the story was quite different. Those same funds fell a cumulative 45%, about two and a-half times as much as the 19% fall for the S&P 500.[1] When thinking about these figures, keep the following points in mind. First, a drop of 45% has a much greater impact than an increase of the same percentage. For example, if you start with an investment of $100 and it rises 90% in the first year, and falls 45% in the second, while your average annual return is +22.5%, your annualized return is only about 2% per annum. Second, many individuals invested in the funds after some or much of the gains were already achieved. Thus many, if not most, investors earned nothing like those 344% cumulative returns. On the other hand, the funds did have $3.4 billion under management when the bubble burst. It is quite possible, perhaps even likely, that the average investor in the five funds not only would have underperformed the S&P 500 during the full twelve-year period but might actually have lost money.

Returning to our go-go, nifty fifty era, it is also worth noting that not a single stock from that nifty fifty group, those "one-decision, can't miss, buy at any price" companies, that ever traded at a P/E of over fifty, managed to outperform the S&P 500 over the next quarter century.[2]

If we had a videotape playing back for us the wisdom of the

investment gurus of the new era 1960s, it would sound remarkably similar to the new wisdom of the twenty-first century. In the Sixties it was the same technology revolution story. Many companies eventually succeeded, and many failed. But most failed to justify the valuations placed on them. Here is a sampling of the hot technology stocks of 1968, and what happened to them when that bubble burst.

Hot Tech Stocks of 1968

Company	1968 High	1970 Low	% Drop	P/E at High
Fairchild Camera	102	18	−82	443
Teledyne	72	13	−82	42
Control Data	163	28	−83	54
Mohawk Data	111	18	−84	285
Electronic Data	162	24	−85	352
Optical Scanning	146	16	−89	200
Itek	172	17	−90	71
University Computing	186	13	−93	118

Source: *Dun's* magazine (1971); itulip.com

Note the P/E ratios of those once high flyers and the size of their eventual collapse in price. Note too the similarity between what happened to 1968's hot stocks and what happened in 2000 to the new era tech stocks, especially the dot.coms.

There is really no reason to think that the latest technology revolution will have any bigger impact than the previous society-changing inventions such as the automobile, air travel, TV and radio (RCA hit 114 in 1929 and it took almost sixty years for it to recover to that level—how's that for a sure thing?), or the electronics and computer revolution.

Remember that technology benefits everyone. In fact, it often benefits the users more than the inventors and eventual industry winners—even if you can somehow identify them ahead of time. Besides, even if you are right about technology's great future, are you the only one who knows this? If not, the market has already incorporated this great future into current prices (remember that is how prices reach lofty levels). The only way to outperform the market is to exploit pricing mistakes by others. With investment professionals determining prices (they do about eighty percent of all dollar-weighted trading), are you really sure they have undervalued these technology stocks? Bear in mind, the evidence is very clear that great earnings do not necessarily translate into great returns. Low-earning value companies have historically provided much higher investment returns (as compensation for their greater risk) than high-earning growth companies.

You can avoid the mistake of thinking this time it's different by studying financial history. You will learn that there is nothing new or different, only the financial history you don't know. As Alan Greenspan noted in his address to Congress on February 26, 1997: "Regrettably, history is strewn with visions of such 'new eras' that, in the end, have proven to be a mirage."

MISTAKE 35

◆

Do You Fail to Tax Manage Your Portfolio Throughout the Year?

Even investors who are tax wise make the mistake of not tax managing their portfolios throughout the year. Just as there are tax management strategies that mutual funds can employ to improve their tax efficiency, there are similar strategies that you can use. Let's quickly review the strategies that a tax-wise fund uses.

- Strategically harvest losses—selling stocks that are trading below their cost basis. The losses can be used to offset realized gains in order to minimize taxes.

- Choose highest cost basis purchases to sell first to minimize gains and maximize losses. This involves a fund keeping track of the cost basis of each share it purchases. When selling a portion of the shares owned, the fund designates those to be sold to be the shares with the highest cost basis, minimizing taxes.

- Never willingly realize short-term gains. Not selling any shares until the holding period is sufficient to qualify for the lower long-term capital gains rate.

- Trade around dividend dates, because dividends are highly tax-inefficient. Not buying shares of a company's stock just prior to the date of record for dividend payments to shareholders. Note that the ex-dividend date is not the same as the date of record. The ex-dividend date is the date after the record date when the dividend is "separated" from the stock. The stock then trades at a lower price, net of dividends.

- For passive asset class funds: expanding the buy and hold ranges. For example, DFA's Small Cap Fund buys stocks whose market cap places them within the smallest eight percent (a market cap of approximately $1.3 billion). However, to minimize trading costs and taxes, it will not sell such a stock until its market cap exceeds that of the smallest ten percent of stocks (approximately $1.7 billion). This is in contrast to an index fund that generally will sell a stock as soon as it leaves the benchmark index.

By mimicking those strategies, in conjunction with other techniques, you can improve your after-tax returns. Tax-wise investors know that they should check their portfolios at the end of the year to see if there are losses that can be harvested to offset other gains. To maximize the benefit of harvesting losses, the specific lot identification method should be used. By doing so, an investor would be selling the lot with the highest cost basis, thus maximizing the current loss and the current deduction. However, it is a mistake to wait to harvest losses until the end of the year. Harvesting is a full-time job. One reason is that a fund might have a loss that can be harvested during the year, but by year end the loss might have been recouped. In that case, the opportunity to tax-loss harvest would have been lost. In addition, it is important to take any short-term loss before it becomes long term. Short-term losses are deductible at the higher ordinary income tax rates, while long-term losses are deductible at the lower long-term rate. An investor who tax-loss harvests resets his cost basis to a new lower level. The tax rate differential then provides the opportunity to arbitrage the tax system. Let's see how that might work.

Assume an investor buys a fund at $100 on January 1, 2000. On March 1, 2000, it is trading at $50. The investor sells the fund. The loss is characterized as short-term since the fund was held for less than one year. If we assume a 40% ordinary federal income tax rate (the example gets better if state taxes are involved), the investor will have a $20 deduction. The net loss is $30. (Note that the deduction of losses at the higher ordinary income tax rates is limited to offsets against short-term capital gains and the $3,000 short-term loss limitation, though excess losses can be carried forward. If there are net long-term gains in a given year, any short-term losses must be applied against those gains, reducing the value of the deduction to the lower long-term capital gains rate.) Since the investor does not wish to be out of the market for thirty days (time needed to avoid the previously described "wash sale" rule), he immediately purchases a very similar fund with the $50 proceeds of the sale. For example, if an investor had sold a

Russell 2000 fund, he might purchase a mutual fund or ETF that replicates the S&P 600. The two funds would be very similar in their exposures to the risk factors of size and value, and thus should have very similar returns going forward.

Let's jump forward to March 2, 2001 (one year and a day). Both the fund we sold and the one we purchased has each risen to $100. If we simply held the first fund we would have had no gain or loss, and would have had no tax deduction in the prior year. On the other hand, if we harvested the loss and replaced the original fund with the similar fund, we would now have a gain of $50 on which we would have to pay taxes at the long-term capital gains rate. Let's assume that it is 20%. Thus we owe taxes of $10, and have a net gain of $40. Not only did we pick up a $10 arbitrage of the tax system (received $20 deduction and paid only $10, or had net loss of $30 and net gain of $40) but we also gained the time value of the tax deduction for a full year. Note that the investor in our example did not have to sell the fund in March 2001. If he continued to hold it, the tax on the unrealized gain would be deferred until the fund was sold.

When realizing a loss, an investor has the choice of reinvesting immediately in a similar fund (assuming one is available) or waiting out the required thirty-one days necessary to avoid the wash sale rule. Which is the winning strategy? The evidence is clear that the vast majority of returns occur over very short periods. For example, according to an analysis by Sanford Bernstein & Co., the best sixty months (seven percent of the months) of the period 1926–93 provided virtually all of the returns; the remaining 756 months provided an average return of just one basis point.[1] Given the evidence, you should strongly consider not waiting to reinvest. Instead, at the time that you sell, buy a similar fund. Keep in mind that if there is another loss thirty-one days later you can swap back and get another deduction, and again reset your basis.

There are many funds and/or ETFs that make good substitutes for one another. Also keep in mind, however, that to avoid the wash sale rule, you cannot sell and buy two instruments that are substantially identical in nature. It is likely that the IRS would disallow the deduction. So you should be careful in your choice of alternatives.

There is another important tax strategy of which you should be aware. If you have held a fund for more than a year, you should always check to see what estimated distributions the fund plans to make during the year—specifically focusing on the amounts that will be ordinary income, short-term capital gains, and long-term capital gains. Most funds make distributions once a year, usually near the end of the year; but some make them more frequently, and sometimes funds make special distributions. You can usually obtain this information from your fund prior to the effective distribution date (not the distribution date itself, but what is known as the ex-dividend date). It is important to check to see if there are going to be large distributions that will be treated as either ordinary income or short-term gains. If this is true, then you might benefit from selling the fund before the ex-dividend date. By doing so, the increase in the net asset value will be treated as long-term capital gains, and taxes will be at the lower long-term rate. If the fund making the large payout is selling for less than your tax basis, you certainly should consider selling the fund prior to the distribution. Otherwise you will have to pay taxes on the distribution, despite having an unrealized loss on the fund—a tax hell for an investor if ever there were one.

Just as a tax-managed fund trades around dividend dates (i.e., they avoid purchasing a stock that is about to go ex-dividend), it is also important for you to avoid making purchases of mutual funds just prior to the ex-dividend date. You will be taxed on income you didn't really earn. Depending on the size of the distribution that is expected, you should not consider buying within thirty to sixty days of the ex-dividend date.

Finally, just like tax-managed funds, you should generally avoid intentionally taking any short-term gains (simply wait until the long-term holding period is achieved); that way you can expand your "hold" ranges. For individuals, this last point refers to the rebalancing table you should create. Rebalancing is important as it allows you to control your portfolio's asset allocation. Without it, market movements will cause style drift. However, because rebalancing in taxable accounts generally involves paying taxes (since you are selling winners to buy losers), it should be done only when significant style drift has occurred. This is why you should consider using a 5/25 rule to determine when to rebalance, rebalancing only when an asset (or asset class) has drifted either an absolute 5% from its target, or a relative 25%. Either of these two measures can trigger the need to rebalance. For example, if an asset class has a target of 30%, rebalancing should occur any time the actual allocation falls below 25% or rises above 35% (the absolute 5% rule is the determining factor). If an asset class has a target of 10%, the rebalancing would be triggered at either 7.5% or 12.5% (the relative 25% rule is the determining factor). By allowing a bit of drift to occur, you can minimize the impact of taxes without losing control over the risks and rewards of your portfolio.

Tax-managing a portfolio is a very important part of the winning strategy. It is also a full-time job. By waiting until year end to do tax planning, opportunities to tax-manage might be lost.

MISTAKE 36

◆

Do You Let Taxes Dominate Your Decisions?

Minimizing the impact of taxes on returns is an important part of the winning strategy. However, many investors make the mistake of letting the avoidance of taxes drive investment decisions, often with disastrous results. The following example will illustrate the point.

Let's assume an investor decides to buy 1,000 shares of Qualcomm at 20. The $20,000 investment represents five percent of his $400,000 portfolio. Qualcomm then proceeds to skyrocket to 200, so his investment is now worth $200,000, and represents about one third of his portfolio, which has grown to $600,000. The investor recognizes that having as much as one third of his portfolio in a single stock is highly risky. However, he is reluctant to sell because if he sold, the $180,000 realized gain would result in a federal capital gains tax of $36,000. Despite the risk of owning this very highly priced stock that now makes up almost a third of his portfolio, he refuses to sell, letting the unwillingness to pay the tax drive his decision. The stock eventually falls to $43, at which point our investor finally sells. A sale at $200,000 would have produced net cash of $164,000. The sale at $43 produced only about $38,000 ($4,600 in taxes would be due on the $23,000 gain). Trying to avoid the $36,000 capital gains tax bill cost our investor about $126,000. Or imagine an investor who bought Cisco at 5 and could have sold it at 80, but watched it drop all the way to about 13. Many other examples of this type of behavior could be cited.

Investors who have a very low basis in a stock often let the tax situation drive their decisions, forgetting that they are taking large risks. When evaluating the sell decision, they may not only become trapped by the tax situation; they may also make other mistakes we analyzed earlier.

- They have too many eggs in one basket.
- They are overconfident of their stock selection skills.
- They treat the highly unlikely as impossible (Qualcomm/ Cisco is a great company. What could possibly go wrong?).
- They are subject to recency and extrapolate the rapid rise in price into the future.
- They are subject to the herd mentality.

Obviously, with hindsight, faced with the prospect of having to pay such large capital gains, the investor in our example would have been better off selling the stock and paying the tax. However, no hindsight is needed to prevent this type of mistake from occurring: Two things are required. The first is a written investment policy statement (IPS) with a rebalancing table. The second is the discipline to adhere to the plan. An IPS should have targets and limits on the allocation that any one stock or asset class is allowed within the portfolio. For example, our Qualcomm investor might have established a maximum buy limit for any one stock of ten percent of the total portfolio. The maximum hold range might be set at fifteen percent. If a stock exceeds fifteen percent, the investor would sell enough shares to return the stock's position within the portfolio to the maximum fifteen percent level, or even to the target ten percent (depending on what rules the investor establishes).

There is one other way you can avoid the mistake of being trapped by taxes: Remember that the only thing worse than having to pay taxes is to not have to pay them.

MISTAKE 37

◆

Do You Confuse Speculating
with Investing?

One of the most frequent theories I hear about investing goes like this:

- It is *obvious* that technology companies will experience much faster growth rates than the economy in general.

- The *obvious* result is that technology companies will experience much greater growth in earnings than will firms in other sectors.

- Thus technology stocks should be overweighted in a portfolio.

- Investors can accomplish this overweighting by purchasing either individual technology stocks or a technology sector fund.

The argument for overweighting a fast-growing sector such as technology (or biotechnology, or health care, or whatever sector is the flavor of the moment) is really just another version of the argument that growth stocks will outperform value stocks because of their superior sales and earnings performance. Unfortunately for those "betting" on technology, or growth stocks in general, there is no logical or factual support for this view.

The most important tenet of modern portfolio theory is that the market is highly efficient in processing information. The result is that current market prices reflect the total knowledge and expectations of all investors in a free market and no one investor can know more than the market does collectively. Given the highly efficient flow of information that exists in the U.S. capital markets, it seems illogical to believe in the proposition that if technology companies are indeed expected to produce much higher earnings growth, their stocks don't already reflect those great prospects. For technology stocks to be "undervalued" (giving an investor a reason to buy them), the market must be unaware of their great prospects relative to companies in other sectors of the economy. That doesn't seem like a logical proposition. Yet for investors to buy either technology stocks or a technology fund, that is exactly what they must believe.

Even if we know with certainty that technology companies will produce superior earnings, it does not guarantee that the stocks of those companies will provide superior investment returns. In fact, the evidence suggests just the opposite. For example, from 1964 to 2000, while large-cap growth stocks produced annual returns of 11.1% per annum, the S&P 500 stocks returned 11.9% per annum, and large-cap value stocks returned 14.7% per annum. For small stocks, the evidence is even more compelling. Small growth stocks returned just 11.9% per annum, compared to the return of 17.4% per annum for small value stocks. These historical return figures demonstrate that earnings growth rates are not the major determinant of investment returns of either individual stocks or economic sectors. Instead, it is the exposure to the risk factor of value (and/or size—small companies are perceived as riskier than large companies) that is the major determinant of returns.

Let's look at the specific evidence on technology funds. Using the Morningstar database, there are just seven technology funds that survived the fifteen-year period ending June 1999. The average *pretax* return for those seven funds was just 0.5% greater than the 19.2% return of the S&P 500 Index. From a statistical viewpoint, this is not a very significant difference. It is also probably far less than the average investor would have guessed. If we go back just a bit further and examine the nineteen-year period ending December 1998, of the three technology sector funds that survived the period, not one outperformed the 16.94% return of the S&P 500 Index. The average underperformance was over two percent per annum. In addition, despite investor perception of the superior recent performance of tech stocks, the fact is that for the three-year period ending December 1998 the S&P 500 was up over twenty-eight percent per annum while the thirty-seven tech sector funds in the Micropal universe returned just over twenty-three percent per annum. Once again, these figures are pretax returns. Since the average actively managed fund is far less tax efficient than a passively managed index fund (because of greater turnover and the resulting distributions of realized gains), it is highly likely that the relative after-tax performance of the technology funds would have looked even worse. In addition, the Morningstar and Micropal databases suffer from survivorship bias. Despite this evidence, or likely because they were unaware of it, investors continued pouring money into tech stocks and tech funds right through 2000.

There is another often overlooked bit of logic on why tech stocks should not be expected to outperform the overall market: Technology doesn't just benefit the inventors any more than the invention of the telephone or electricity benefited just their inventors. The benefits of technology flow throughout the economy. For example, one reason that Wal-Mart has achieved its superior results is the way it benefited from its implementation of computerized inventory systems. Over the past twenty years, for example, Wal-Mart's stock has far outperformed the stock of Intel, the maker of the chip inside many computers. And Intel has been one of the best performing stocks over the past twenty years.

Jane Bryant Quinn, in her Newsweek column of April 24, 2000, cited a study by the investment firm of Sanford Bernstein that provided more evidence against the "Technology is king" myth. The study found that of the thirty-four leading tech stocks back in 1980 only one—Intel—emerged a winner. Of the rest, twenty-two were no longer trading, and the other eleven trailed the S&P 500 Index.

There is another reason why investors should think twice before overweighting any economic sector, be it technology or possibly health care, especially given the magnitude of the aging population. When an investor overweights a sector, he or she is *speculating* (not investing) that that sector will outperform. In return for the hope of outperformance, investors must also acknowledge that they are accepting the risk that the sector they have chosen to *over*weight will *under*perform. Logical investors only accept risk if they expect to be compensated with greater returns. The evidence suggests that there is no logical reason to expect those greater returns. Investors, however, seem to find it difficult to ignore the siren call of the next great innovation and the potential to find the next Cisco or Microsoft. Unfortunately, all too often they end up with the next Priceline, E-loan, or dot.bomb. The story that follows is a sobering reminder of the pitfalls of falling prey to such siren calls.

At the annual 2001 MacWorld Exhibition in San Francisco, Apple Computer introduced several new hardware and software products. CEO Steve Jobs proclaimed that the PC industry was on the verge of a third golden age of innovative growth. Let's use our videotape machine to see just how well the two previous golden ages had rewarded investors lucky enough to be allocated shares in Apple's initial public offering. Unfortunately, the returns were anything but golden. Investors in Apple's hot-issue IPO in December 1980 earned a 5.6% annualized return for the next two decades.[1] While taking all the risk of equity investing (including non-diversification of risk), investors lucky enough to own the IPO earned about one percent less than the rate provided by riskless one-month Treasury bills. It is worth noting that Apple at least survived the two previous golden ages; there were many once golden companies an investor could have owned that didn't even survive—among them such companies as Wang Laboratories, Atari, and Data General. At one time all were industry leaders and "certain" winners. Ready for that third golden age?

Investing in individual stocks or market sectors is speculating, not investing. It is speculation in that you are making a bet that the stock or the sector you choose will outperform the rest of the market. You are betting that somehow the market has *mispriced* the investment on which you are gambling. Making such a bet does provide you with the hope of outperformance. You might for example have bought Cisco instead of Apple. Unfortunately, you also must accept the possibility, if not probability, of underperformance. This might be acceptable if there was a logical expectation for higher returns to compensate for the risks of underperformance. Unfortunately, there is a great body of evidence which suggests that after expenses you are far more likely to underperform than outperform.

You can avoid this type of mistake by building a portfolio that is diversified across many asset classes. By doing so, you will have exposure to all sectors of the economy. If some guru then tells you that you should buy technology stocks, or health care stocks, or stocks or funds in any other particular sector, you can just tell yourself that you already own them.

MISTAKE 38

◆

Do You Try to Time the Market?

It must be apparent to intelligent investors who if anyone possessed the ability to do so [forecast the immediate trend of stock prices] consistently and accurately he would become a billionaire so quickly he would not find it necessary to sell his stock market guesses to the general public.
>—Weekly staff letter, August 27, 1951, David L. Babson & Company, quoted in Charles Ellis, *The Investor's Anthology*

Market timing is impossible to perfect.
>—Mark Rieppe, vice president, Charles Schwab Center for Investment Research, November 27, 1998

Investors would do well to learn from deer hunters and fishermen who know the importance of "being there" and using patient persistence—so they are there when opportunity knocks. —Charles Ellis, *Investment Policy*

One bit of *conventional wisdom* held by investors is that there are smart people who can somehow be invested when the market is in its bull phase and yet manage to hibernate when the historically inevitable bear market arrives. The airwaves and publications are filled with recommendations on which direction the market is headed. And market timing is the endeavor to which many investors devote most of their efforts, despite the fact that many academic studies have all come to the same conclusion: Market timing (as well as stock selection) has almost no impact on the returns of a portfolio. Here is what the legendary investor Bernard Baruch said about market timing: "Only liars manage to always be out during bad times and in during good times." And here is what John Bogle, Vanguard's legendary founder, had to say on the matter: "The idea that a bell rings to signal when investors should get into or out of the stock market is simply not credible. After nearly fifty years in this business, I do not know of anybody who has done it [market timing] successfully and consistently. I don't even know anybody who *knows* anybody who has done it successfully and consistently.[1] Yet market timing appears to be increasingly embraced by mutual fund investors and the professional managers of fund portfolios alike." These legendary investors believe so strongly that market timing is likely to produce negative results not only because of their own experiences but also because the historical evidence is so powerful. By going to our videotape we can discover just how great are the odds a market timer must overcome in order to be successful in his or her effort to outperform.

One study, "A Market Timing Myth," covered the period 1991–98 and examined the market returns for the period when eliminating the best and worst ten, twenty, thirty, and forty days of market performance out of the entire 2,023 trading days.[2] The author, John D. Stowe, calculated the returns of such a successful strategy, after expenses (though not after taxes). He also calculated the odds of such a successful effort. The return of the market for the entire period was 19.87%. Because an active strategy has costs, those costs must be considered. Stowe assumed a one percent cost of a round-trip buy and sell trade. The implication for returns was astounding. The return figures are annualized returns, first before and then after expenses (though not taxes). In summary, here is what he found.

- If you missed the best ten days (0.5% of the trading days), your return dropped to 15.06% before expenses/13.62% after expenses. Thus if you missed out on the best ten days you missed out on 24%/32% of the available returns.

- If you missed the best twenty days (1% of the trading days), your return dropped to 11.98%/9.2%, and you missed out on 40%/54% of the available returns.

- If you missed the best thirty days (1.5% of the trading days), your return dropped to 9.4%/5.35% and you missed out on 53%/73% of the available returns.

- If you missed the best forty days (2% of the trading days), your return dropped to just 7.15%/1.9%, and you missed out on 64%/90% of the available returns.

Stowe also looked at the impact on returns if you somehow were able to avoid the worst market days.

- If you missed out on the ten worst days, your return improved to 25.85%/24.28%. However, 26% of the improvement in returns was eaten up by the expense of the effort.

- If you missed out on the twenty worst days, your return improved to 29.56%/26.35%. However, 33% of the improvement in returns was eaten up by the expense of the effort.

- If you missed out on the thirty worst days, your return improved to 32.76%/27.85%. However, 38% of the improvement in returns was eaten up by the expense of the effort.

- If you missed out on the forty worst days, your return improved to 35.74%/29.09%. However, 42% of the improvement in returns was eaten up by the expense of the effort.

Since a market timing strategy, at least for taxable investors, would likely convert most of the market's gain from long term to short term, such a strategy would have a very significant negative impact on any potential value added.

Stowe then calculated the odds of success of any such market timing strategy. Here is what he found.

- The odds of being able to avoid the ten worst days are $1{:}3.094 \times 10^{26}$.

- The odds of being able to avoid the twenty worst days are $1{:}4.93 \times 10^{47}$.

- The odds of being able to avoid the thirty worst days are $1{:}4.596 \times 10^{66}$.

- The odds of being able to avoid the forty worst days are $1{:}1.444 \times 10^{84}$.

Stowe noted that the odds of winning a state lottery are far better.

Here is some further evidence that the most likely winning strategy is passive investing. Legendary investor Peter Lynch pointed out that an investor who stayed fully invested in the S&P 500 over the forty-year period beginning in 1954 would have achieved an 11.4% rate of return. If that investor missed just the best ten months (two percent), the return dropped (by twenty-seven percent) to 8.3%. If the investor missed the best twenty months (four percent), the return dropped (by fifty-four percent) to 6.1%. Finally, if the investor missed the best forty months (eight percent), the return dropped (by seventy-six percent) all the way to 2.7%.[3]

Let's take a look at the results of market timing "experts." Mark Hulbert, publisher of *Hulbert's Financial Digest*, studied the performance of thirty-two of the portfolios of market timing newsletters for the ten years ending in 1997.[4] During this period, the S&P 500 Index was up over 18% per annum. Here is what he found:

- The timers' annual average returns ranged from 5.84% to 16.9%.

- The average return was 10.09%.

- *None of the market timers beat the market.*

MoniResearch studied the performance of eighty-five managers with a total of $10 billion under management.[5] Here is what they found:

- The timers' annual average return ranged from 4.4% to 16.9%.

- The average return was 11.04%.

- *None of the market timers beat the market.*

Two researchers, from Duke University and the University of Utah, respectively, collaborated on a study examining the performance of the stock selections of 237 market timing newsletters over the 12.5-year period June 1980-December 1992.[6] They used a database supplied by Mark Hulbert. If an investor held an equally weighted portfolio of all the newsletters, he or she would have earned an 11.3% rate of return. This compared to the rate of return of 15.8% earned by an S&P 500 Index fund. If we considered the costs associated with the trading recommendations of these financial tout sheets, the results would look even worse:

- Transaction costs would have to be subtracted.

- The negative impact of the taxes generated by all of the trading activity must be considered.

- Adding insult to injury, the cost of the newsletters themselves would have to be subtracted from returns.

- Perhaps most telling is that only 5.5% (13 of 237) of the newsletters survived the entire 12.5-year period. How would an investor, at the start of the period, have known which thirteen would survive?[7]

Another study, by Andrew Metrick, found similar results. Metrick studied the equity portfolio recommendations of 153 newsletters covering the seventeen-year period ending December 1996. His conclusions:

- There was no evidence of stock-picking ability.

- There was no evidence of abnormal short-run performance persistence ("hot hands" didn't stay hot).

Metrick noted that there were over two million subscribers to over 500 newsletters. He also noted that while the publishers were making millions for themselves they weren't adding any real value for their readers.[9]

Another study by Mark Hulbert examined the performance of twenty-seven mutual fund portfolios for which he had ten years of data. During that time, only one of the twenty-seven (3.7%) was able to beat the market as measured by the Wilshire 5000 Index, through June 1996. When he studied 106 newsletter portfolios with at least five years of data, he found that just twelve (11.3%) had managed to outperform the Wilshire 5000 Index. Not surprisingly, the longer the time frame covered by Hulbert's study, the lower the percentage of newsletters that were able to beat a market benchmark.[9]

Let's look at another form of market timing, tactical asset allocation (TAA). TAA is an investment strategy that gained great popularity in the 1980s and 1990s. The objective of TAA is to provide better-than-benchmark returns with (possibly) lower volatility. This would be accomplished by forecasting returns of two or more asset classes and varying the exposure (percent allocation) accordingly. The varying exposure to various asset classes that TAA depends on is based on economic and market (technical) indicators. A TAA fund would then be measured against their benchmark. Although the benchmark might be 60% S&P 500 Index and 40% Lehman Bond Index, the manager might be allowed to have his or her allocations range from 50% to 5% for equities, 20% to 50% for bonds, and 0% to 45% for cash.

In reality, TAA is just a fancy name for market timing. By giving it a fancy name, however, Wall Street seems able to charge high fees. Let's see if the high fees are worth the price of admission. For the twelve years ending 1997, while the S&P 500 on a total return basis rose 734%, the average equity fund returned just 589%, but the average return for 186 TAA funds was a mere 384%, about half the return of the S&P 500 Index.[10] One more myth debunked.

One last point on market timing. Market timing, like any active strategy, entails increased costs. Those costs will come in the form of trading expenses (bid-offer spreads, commissions, and market impact) and capital gains taxes. Research suggests that once expenses are considered, simply to match a buy-and-hold strategy a market timer would have to be right about seventy percent of the time.[11] Having seen the evidence on the odds against such a success rate, you might logically conclude that stock market forecasts have about as much value as George Carlin's Hippy Dippy Weatherman's forecast: "Tonight's weather is dark, followed by widely scattered light in the morning."

You can avoid the mistake of trying to time the market by developing an investment policy statement and having the discipline to ignore forecasts that have no value, other than possibly for entertainment. You will be well served by keeping in mind Peter Lynch's admonition: "Far more money has been lost by investors in preparing for corrections, or anticipating corrections, than has been lost in the corrections themselves."[12] As Woody Allen said: "Most of success in life is in just showing up."[13]

MISTAKE 39

◆

Do You Rely on Market Gurus?

An out-of-town visitor was being shown the wonders of the New York financial district. When the party arrived at the Battery, one of his guides indicated some handsome ships riding at anchor. He said, "Look, those are the bankers' and brokers' yachts." The naïve customer asked: "Where are the customers' yachts?"
 —Fred Schwed, Jr., *"Where Are the Customers' Yachts?"*

An economist is an expert who will know tomorrow why the things he predicted yesterday didn't happen today.
         —Laurence J. Peter

Pundits can't predict the future to save their lives, but when it comes to explaining the past, nobody does it better.
—Caroline Baum, "Punditry Is Always and Everywhere the
 Same," *Bloomberg*, February 23, 2000

My peer group has enough trouble trying to predict the next six months. Trying to predict over the next five-year period is virtually anyone's guess. It is generally a meaningless, throwaway number for most analysts.
   —Lehman Brothers technology analyst Karl Keirstead,
        Wall Street Journal, January 24, 2001

For professional investors like myself, a sense of humor is essential. We are very aware that we are competing not only against the market averages but also against one another. It's an intense rivalry. We are each claiming, "The stocks in my fund today will perform better than what you own in your fund." That implies we think we can predict the future, which is the occupation of charlatans. If you believe you or anyone else has a system that can predict the future of the stock market, the joke is on you.
    —Ralph Wanger, *A Zebra in Lion Country*

I'd compare stock pickers to astrologers, but I don't want to bad-mouth astrologers.
—Professor Eugene F. Fama, *Fortune*, July 6, 1998

We tend to think that traders make money because they are good. Perhaps we have turned the causality on its head; we consider them good just because they make money. One can make money in the financial markets totally out of randomness. —Nassim Nicholas Taleb, *Fooled by Randomness*, p. 80.

There is probably no arena for predictions where the payoff for being correct is more rewarding than the stock market. Therefore, it should not be surprising that a great amount of effort (and investor dollars) is expended in trying to predict the market's future direction. The question for investors is whether or not they should rely on the forecasts of industry professionals. The evidence suggests that the answer is an emphatic, "No!"

Despite all the innovations in information technology and all the academic research, forecasting stock market prices with any consistency or accuracy remains an elusive goal. William Sherden, author of *The Fortune Sellers*, was inspired by the following incident to write his book. In 1985, when preparing testimony as an expert witness, he analyzed the track records of inflation projections by different forecasting methods. He then compared those forecasts to what is called the "naive" forecast—simply projecting today's inflation rate into the future. He was surprised to learn that the simple naive forecast proved to be the most accurate, beating the forecasts of the most prestigious economic forecasting firms equipped with their Ph.D.s from leading universities and thousand-equation computer models.

Sherden reviewed the leading research on forecasting accuracy from 1979 from 1995 and covering forecasts made from 1970 to 1995. He concluded that:

- *Economists cannot predict the turning points in the economy.* He found that of the forty-eight predictions made by economists, forty-six missed the turning points.

- *Economists' forecasting skill is about as good as guessing.* Even the economists that directly or indirectly run the economy (the Federal Reserve, the Council of Economic Advisors, and the Congressional Budget Office) had forecasting records that were worse than pure chance.

- *There are no economic forecasters who consistently lead the pack in forecasting accuracy.*

- *There are no economic ideologies that produce superior forecasts.*

- *Increased sophistication provided no improvement in forecasting accuracy.*

- *Consensus forecasts do not improve accuracy.*

- *Forecasts may be affected by psychological bias.* Some economists are perpetually optimistic and others perpetually pessimistic.[1]

Perhaps our most famous economist, Nobel Laureate Paul Samuelson, observed: "I don't believe we're converging on ever improving forecasting accuracy. It's almost as if there is a Heisenberg [uncertainty] Principle."[2] Michael Evans, founder of Chase Econometrics, confessed: "The problem with macro [economic] forecasting is that no one can do it."[3]

Since the underlying basis of most stock market forecasts is an economic forecast, the evidence suggests that stock market strategists who predict bull and bear markets will have no greater success than do the economists. Clear evidence against the ability of professional fund managers to predict the market is seen in the results of a study by Goldman Sachs that examined mutual fund cash holdings from 1970 to 1989. In their efforts to time the market, fund managers raise their cash holdings when they believe the market will decline and lower their cash holdings when they become bullish. The study found that mutual fund managers miscalled *all* nine major turning points.[4]

The year 2000 provided further evidence that simply because something is generally regarded as conventional wisdom—market strategists can accurately forecast the market—does not make it correct. In other words, if millions of people believe a foolish thing, it doesn't make it any less foolish. At year-end 1999, the *Wall Street Journal* polled the market strategists from eleven of the top investment banking firms on their forecast for the S&P 500 Index at year-end 2000.[5] The index had closed 1999 at 1469.25. The average forecast of the eleven strategists called for the S&P 500 to close at 1579. This translates into a projected gain of 7.5%. It is worth noting that with the benefit of further information one analyst, Goldman Sachs's highly regarded Abby Joseph Cohen, in March actually raised her forecast by fifty points from 1525 to 1575. The S&P 500 Index managed to close the year 2000 at 1320, a loss of just over ten percent. The Index would then have to rise twenty percent from its year-end closing levels to reach the average projected forecast. The superstar forecasters not only dramatically missed their target; only one sole analyst even managed to get the direction correct. When the market is rising, it really makes no difference how bullish a market strategist is. The real value of any forecaster is her ability to call the market turns correctly. The year 2000 handed those investors with faith in any such ability a very large tuition bill.

Here is a further bit of evidence against relying on the forecasts of investment experts. Zacks Investment Research studied the performance of the "best picks" of the analysts they cover. In 1998, while the S&P 500 rose 28% and the Russell 2000 (a small-cap benchmark) fell just 8.2%, the "best picks" fell 11.5%. In 1999, while the S&P 500 rose 21% and the Russell 2000 rose 7.6%, the "best picks" again fell, this time by 12%.[6]

I couldn't resist including the following amusing bits of anecdotal evidence against the wisdom of relying on market experts. The first involves a stock-picking contest held every six months by the *St. Louis Post-Dispatch*. The contest always includes three "experts" from the investment community. Let's see how investors would have fared if they purchased the *single best* stock selection for the second half of 2000 of each of the three so-called experts.[7]

As a benchmark for the experts' picks, we can use the performance of the S&P 500 Index, which was down 8.6% from July 1, 2000, through year end. The "winner" of the contest was Mike Brown, backed by the superior research of the firm for which he works, PaineWebber. Mike also has his own radio show on which he dispenses investment advice. Just how well did Mike do? His stock selection for the single best performing stock was Microsoft. The stock fell forty-six percent during the period, underperforming the benchmark by thirty-seven percent. Remember, this was the *winner* of the experts' contest! How did the losers do? Tom Grady of Pines Financial chose Vishay Intertechnology. It fell sixty percent, underperforming the benchmark by fifty-one percent. The loser was Roger Drone, director of research at Forsyth Securities, Inc. His selection, LSI Logic, fell sixty-eight percent, underperforming the benchmark by only fifty-nine percent. The real losers of course were not the contest's participants. Instead, the real losers were the individual investors who placed confidence in the ability of professionals to know which stocks would outperform.

The second bit of anecdotal evidence against the wisdom of relying on market experts was provided by *USA TODAY*.[8] At the start of the year, the paper polled ten top strategists for their best picks. The average year-to-date return was a negative twenty-two percent. Of the fifty stocks recommended, forty-three were down for the year, eleven had fallen more than fifty percent, and four fell at least seventy-five percent. Contrast this performance with the year-to-date returns of such passive investment alternatives as the S&P 500 that had fallen less than seven percent, and DFA's passive asset class funds of Micro Cap, Small Value, and Large Value that had risen by 22.7%, 23.3%, and 9.3%, respectively. Obviously, if the strategists really had insights into the market they could have easily outperformed a market benchmark such as the S&P 500 by simply buying small caps, and small and large value stocks, or the index funds that represent those asset classes.

These experts aren't alone in their misery. Several decades ago, *Institutional Investor* magazine created an All-Star team consisting of the "top" analysts in each industry. These analysts are chosen based on a poll of hundreds of institutional investors. Each year the magazine puts its All-Star team on the cover of its publication. A while back, *Financial World* set out to measure the performance of these All-Stars. They stated that it was not an easy task to get the brokerage houses to release the forecasts. We shall see why. After months of digging, the magazine managed to come up with the recommendations of twenty superstars. For the period in question, while the market rose 14.1%, following the recommendations of the All-Stars would have provided a return of just 9.3%. And it is likely that there is survivorship bias in the data—the firms that wouldn't release their analysts' forecasts probably had even worse results. Surely they would have been happy to publish superior returns.[9]

Further evidence on relying on such forecasts was provided by a study done by David Dreman and Michael Berry. They examined approximately 500,000 quarterly earnings forecasts from brokerage analysts for the period 1973–91. The average forecasting error was a whopping forty-four percent. Also of note was that in recent years the average error got worse—in the last eight years of the study, the average error was fifty percent. When even small errors in forecasts can lead to huge losses, it seems that relying on forecasts of analysts is not a prescription for success.[10] Let's look at one more example.

Each year *Fortune* selects its All-Star team of security analysts—the very best of the gurus. How did the stock recommendations the year 2000's All-Stars made in July of that year perform? While the S&P 500 Index was falling nine percent, their stock picks were falling twenty-two percent through the end of May 2001.[11]

Unfortunately for investors who rely on the forecasts of market analysts and strategists, such forecasts are only likely to produce yachts for the forecasters themselves, not for their clients. Steve Forbes, publisher of the magazine that bears his name, obviously agrees, quoting his grandfather, who founded the magazine eighty years ago: "You make more money selling the advice than following it."[12] I agree with Peter Lynch's conclusion: "To the rash and impetuous stockpicker who chases hot tips and rushes in and out his of equities, an 'investment' in stocks is no more reliable than throwing away paychecks on the horses with the prettiest names, or the jockey with the purple silks . . . [But] when you lose [at the racetrack, at least] you'll be able to say you had a great time doing it."[13] The story that follows is evidence of the wisdom of both Forbes's and Peter Lynch's advice.

Michael Murphy is the publisher of the *California Technology Stock Letter* and the author of *Every Investor's Guide to High-Tech Stocks and Mutual Funds*. He also runs a mutual fund. Both Murphy's newsletter and his book, which is now in its third edition, are quite popular. One has to wonder, however, if they would be quite as popular if investors knew the facts on the returns achieved by investors in Murphy's fund, the Murphy New World Technology Fund. The fund's first full year of operation was 1994. Here are the returns for the first seven full years of the fund's life, compared to the returns of the benchmark S&P 500 Index.

Year	Murphy New World Technology Fund (%)	S&P 500 Index (%)
1994	-5.7	1.3
1995	29.8	37.4
1996	10.5	23.1
1997	-17.3	33.4
1998	-8.2	28.6
1999	97.8	21.0
2000	-58.6	-9.1
Growth of $1 invested	$0.84	$3.24

We should also note that based on Morningstar data for the last five years (for which data is available), Mr. Murphy's tech fund underperformed Vanguard's S&P 500 Index Fund on an after-tax basis by 17.5% to −8.0%. That is an underperformance of over 25% per annum for five full years.

Michael Murphy attempts to dazzle investors with marketing material touting his "growth flow" strategy of identifying the future market winners. What is amazing is that despite the dismal performance, Murphy continues to sell his newsletter and continues to successfully sell books based on his theories. Either investors are unaware of the poor performance, or we have an example of the triumph of hope over experience.

One last story on the wisdom of following the advice of gurus. In 1997, Clayton Christensen's book, *The Innovator's Dilemma: The Revolutionary National Bestseller That Changed the Way We*

Do Business was published. Amazon.com's Web site review stated that the book shows how such products as the Honda Supercub, Intel's 8088 processor, and hydraulic excavators were disruptive technologies that helped to redefine the competitive landscape of their respective markets. The review described, "These products did not come about as the result of successful companies carrying out sound business practices in established markets . . . These and other products cut into the low end of the marketplace and eventually evolved to displace high-end competitors and their reigning technologies." Amazon's review went on to highly recommend this "important" book.

According to *BusinessWeek*, Clayton Christensen is not only a Harvard Business School professor, he is also a "Management Guru," a "rising star of the New Economy," and "the most innovative business thinker in the world today." In March 2000, Mr. Christensen, along with St. Louis brokerage owner Neil Eisner, opened the Disruptive Growth Fund. Given his reputation, the financial world and investors had great expectations for the fund.[14]

Christensen chose stocks based on his theory that companies that develop innovative products—"disruptive technologies"—can topple market leaders. Before even reaching its first anniversary, the fund was liquidated—but not before it had lost sixty-four percent of its value. The only thing disruptive about the fund was that it disrupted the financial health of its investors.[15]

William Sherden offers the following advice to investors in *The Fortune Sellers*: "Avoid market timers, for they promise something they cannot deliver. Cancel your subscription to market timing newsletters. Tell the investment advisers selling the latest market-timing scheme to buzz off. Ignore news media predictions, since they haven't a clue . . . Stop asking yourself, and everyone you know, What's the market going to do? It is an irrelevant question, because it cannot be answered."[16]

To conclude on an amusing note, it seems that weather forecasters have wrongly borne the brunt of criticism on their inability to make accurate forecasts. In addition to studying the predictive ability of investment experts, Sherden studied the performance of six other forecasting professions: meteorology, technology assessment, demography, futurology, organizational planning, and economics. He concluded that while none of the experts were very expert, the folks we most often make jokes about—weathermen—actually had the best predictive powers.

You can avoid the mistake of relying on the forecasts of "market gurus" by remembering that there are only three types of market forecasters: those who don't know; those who don't know they don't know; and those who know they don't know but get paid a lot of money to pretend that they do.

MISTAKE 40
◆

Do You Use Margin to Boost Investment Returns?

Many investors, often with encouragement from the brokerage community, use margin in an attempt to generate increased investment returns. Margin is the use of leverage (borrowed funds) to increase the amount available to invest. When borrowing from a brokerage firm to increase equity exposure, the firm will typically lend an investor up to an amount equal to their initial equity investment. Let's look at an example of how margin (leverage) works.

If an investor owned $100,000 of stock, a brokerage firm (or bank) would be willing to lend an additional $100,000, assuming the funds were used to buy more equities (with the total equity holdings used as collateral for the debt). The investor would have $200,000 of equity holdings and $100,000 (fifty percent) margin. The firm will allow the investor to maintain that debt as long as margin does not exceed seventy percent of the equity holdings. In our example, the value of the equity holdings would have to be maintained at a minimum of about $143,000 (100,000 is seventy percent of 143,000). If the value fell below that level a "margin call" would be made. At that point, the investor would have to either pay down the debt to bring it back to the seventy percent level, or put up more collateral.

Why would an investor use margin? The answer is simple, to enhance total returns. From 1964 through 2000 the S&P 500 returned approximately twelve percent per annum. During the same time frame one-month treasury bills returned approximately six percent. Thus the equity risk premium was six percent. Investors seek to capture that risk premium. During this time period the standard deviation of the S&P 500 was about sixteen percent. The Sharpe ratio (measure of how much return was earned above the treasury bill rate relative to the risk taken, with risk defined as standard deviation of returns) was thus about 0.4 (six divided by sixteen).

Let's now look at the returns relative to the risk that a margin investor earned. It is important to note that investors cannot borrow at the risk-free rate. Margin costs are typically between 1.5% and 3% above the one-month LIBOR rate (London Interbank Offering Rate—the rate at which banks lend to each other). The size of the spread depends on the depth (profitability) of the relationship with the investor. For illustration purposes we will assume a spread of two percent. Brokerage firms love margin business as it is almost (but not quite) riskless lending (they hold the collateral, and the loan is overcollateralized) at high spreads.

In addition, the firm will make incremental profits from the commissions/loads it is likely to earn from the incremental investments made. Historically, the average spread between LIBOR and one-month Treasury bills has been about 0.5%.

We can now calculate the Sharpe ratio for the funds invested using margin. The investor would still have earned twelve percent per annum on his holdings. The cost of the debt would have been 6% + 0.5% +2%, or 8.5%. The investor would, of course, have experienced the same 16% volatility. Thus the Sharpe ratio for the leveraged portion of the portfolio would have been just 0.2, or about one-half of the Sharpe ratio of the non-leveraged investor. While the investor was taking the same risk (with volatility being our measure of risk), he or she received much lower returns. Rational investors only accept lower returns if they are accompanied by lower risk.

In a taxable account, margin interest can be deducted against investment gains (dividends and realized gains). The deduction will be at the higher ordinary income tax rate, while a potential gain might be taxed at the lower long-term capital gains rate. In addition, the investor can deduct the interest expense currently, while the capital gains tax can be deferred until realized. However, even with the benefit of the "tax arbitrage", the Sharpe ratio of the margined part of the investment is still lower. In addition, there is also the risk that a margin call might occur, with no long-term gain ever being achieved. Thus no tax arbitrage is accomplished.

Unfortunately, this is not the end of our tale. While non-leveraged investors can wait out bear markets (assuming they have the discipline to do so), as indicated earlier, margin investors also accept the risk of a margin call. If a fall in value causes the margin loan to exceed seventy percent of the collateral, the firm will call the loan. If the investor cannot come up with incremental collateral, or pay down the debt to the required seventy percent level, then the firm has the right to sell the collateral (and will in all likelihood do so) to pay the debt down to the required level. Thus an investor might be forced to sell their holdings. Forced margin calls are a frequent occurrence in severe bear markets—like the ones experienced in 2000 and 2001. Having their investments liquidated, the investor would then not be able to benefit from any future rise in value. They might never have earned the twelve percent returns earned by the non-leveraged investor.

Thus we can conclude that the use of margin for investing purposes is an inefficient use of one's capital. The rewards are simply not commensurate with the risk. If an investor wishes to increase the expected return of a portfolio the more prudent approach is to increase the exposure to the riskier asset classes of small and value stocks. At least by doing so the increased risk is accompanied by higher expected returns. In addition, the investor does not run the risk of a margin call occurring.

MISTAKE 41

◆

Do You Work with Commissioned Advisors?

It has been a problem since the dawn of the retail brokerage business. Brokers have a strong incentive to get customers to trade when it might be in clients' interests to do nothing.
                                        —*BusinessWeek*, July 14, 1997

Definition of a stockbroker: Someone whose objective it is to transfer assets from your account to their account.
                                        —Anonymous

If you begin your investment journey dealing with a stock-broker, there is a good chance you'll end it dealing with another kind of broker, the pawn kind.   —Anonymous

Unless you are a do-it-yourself investor, you are working with an investment advisor of some kind. That person is typically either a stockbroker or a registered financial advisor. It is my strong advice that you should only work with advisors who are fee-only, not commission-based.

A fee-only relationship is the only way in which you can be sure that the advisor's interests are aligned with yours. The only thing they are selling is their advice. No one else is providing them with any compensation. Most fee-only advisors work on a fee that is based on a percentage of assets under management, in which case there is total alignment of interests. The more your portfolio is worth, the greater their compensation. Their only incentive is to help you grow the value of your portfolio. If you work with an advisor who is paid on a commission basis, there is no guarantee the person selling you a product is not suggesting that particular product because they get a large commission upon sale, even though there might be a better alternative for you. Remember, commissioned-based advisors are not just selling advice, but also products.

The worst example of this conflict of interest is that investors in profit-sharing plans and other tax-deferred accounts have been sold expensive variable annuities. (It should be noted that, by law, under the "old" 403(b) plans, an individual could only hold variable annuities. When the new 403(b)–7 was added, that changed.) Considering that the only valuable benefit of a variable annuity is the tax deferral, there is virtually no reason anyone should be paying the expensive charges of a variable annuity when the account structure already provides the benefit of the tax deferral. Of course the salesperson will have received a commission of as much as eight percent. It is also worth noting that no-load, no surrender charge, and low-expense variable annuities are available. Therefore, there is no reason to buy a high-expense, load annuity with heavy surrender charges.

Commission-based advisors most likely will also push for expensive and tax inefficient actively managed funds over index funds. The likely reason is not that they believe that the actively managed funds will provide better performance, but that they will be paid a load and/or receive a trailing fee as long as you hold the fund. Of course, it is possible that they might actually believe, despite all evidence to the contrary, that somehow they can identify the few active managers who will beat their benchmarks in the future. But you could not be certain of their motives unless they were a fee-only advisor whose interests were aligned with yours. Consider the following memo which was sent in response to requests from a brokerage firm's sales force for the firm to offer index funds. The sales force was simply responding to similar requests from clients who had heard about the superior performance of these passively managed funds.

> Index funds are passively managed mutual funds. They simply buy and hold all the stocks of a popular index such as the Standard and Poor's 500. Because their turnover is low and they don't require large research staffs, most have low operating expenses . . . The performance of an index fund is a function of two factors; the performance of the index itself, and the fees to operate and DISTRIBUTE the fund. For a fund to be successful in the brokerage community it must adequately compensate brokers through either an up front commission or an ongoing service fee. As a result, a broker sold index fund would underperform no-load index funds. This is why most index funds are offered by no-load fund groups" (emphasis mine).

The reason that brokers do not sell index funds is not because these funds do not perform well; they don't sell them because investors can buy them cheaper elsewhere. In addition, there is just not enough revenue available to compensate the broker, whose first priority is generating fees, not obtaining the best possible results for clients. Mutual fund sponsors avoid indexing because, while the record proves that it is the winning strategy for investors, it is not very profitable for fund sponsors. They see indexing as the losing business strategy. This is clearly a conflict of interest.

The same thing is true when it comes to individual stocks. Commission-driven compensation requires investors to trade in order to generate profits, both from commissions and market-making activities (they can earn the bid-offer spread if they make a market in the particular stock being traded). Thus, there is an incentive to have the investor actively trade an account, when doing nothing might be in the investor's best interests. The activity known as "churning" has been the cause of filing of many investor lawsuits.

There is one other issue related to dealing with brokerage firms as advisors that has nothing to do with the form of compensation. A conflict of interest may arise when an investor wants to purchase bonds. A brokerage firm might be holding inventory of bonds that it wants to dispose of. The firm will typically incent its brokers to dump these bonds on unsuspecting clients by offering them larger commissions. An investor then might end up being sold a bond that might not be the most appropriate one for her based on her desired maturity and credit risk. In addition, although commissions will generally appear on a purchase statement, the firm may mark up its bond inventory so that the investor ends up paying an above-market price, without the client's knowledge of this occurring. Investors are particularly vulnerable to this with municipal bonds, as prices for municipal bonds are not generally posted as they are for stocks. Therefore, while you might see a commission charge, there might also have been a mark up of one percent, or even more. The investor will never see this cost, except of course through lower returns. This can be avoided by requiring that the advisor shop several wholesale market makers for the best price.

Citing from the National Association of Securities Dealers (NASD) dispute resolution Web site, *www.nasdadr.com*, Dan Solin, a securities attorney, told me that the types of controversies which cause complaints to be filed against brokers fit into the following categories, listed in order as reported for 2000: breach of fiduciary duty, negligence, misrepresentation, failure to supervise, unsuitability, unauthorized trading, omission of facts, churning, margin calls and on-line trading. Dan added that, in general, brokers sell whatever the client will buy. Many brokers make little or no effort to diversify or to contain transaction costs. To the contrary, these costs are often the prime motivation behind the sale. He told me of a case in which he represented a client against two major firms where the turnover was around 150% a month. It was estimated that the portfolio would have had to earn thirty percent a year to break even!

Dan explained to me that in his experience most clients have no idea how often their accounts are being turned over, how much they have lost in their accounts, or how risky are their portfolios. The concept of diversification means to most of them that they should not be invested 100% in tech stocks—and this has been only a recent revelation. To his surprise, unauthorized trading is far more frequent than one would imagine. The broker believes that if the stock goes up, the client will not complain. If it goes down, he will offer to waive the commissions or to give the client a shot at an IPO. Dan added that "The number of outright crooks in the securities business is alarming. These include 'pump and dump' operations, boiler rooms, and firms infiltrated by organized crime. Many firms are financially irresponsible, or unscrupulous, or both. The number of investors willing to deal with such firms (without any prudent investigation) is mind-boggling. These are the firms that go out of business and do not pay awards." Dan provided me with the following data, again from www.nasdadr.com, as well as from his insights on arbitration awards:

- In 2000, there were 5,558 new matters filed with the NASD and approximately 600 new matters filed with the NYSE. Given the number of investors, and the ethics of brokers, it is apparent to me that most investors (and their advisors) do not know that they may have claims against their brokers.

- Recently, there has been an increase in the number of claims filed with the NASD. Total filings for 2001 are projected to be over 6,700. This is still far less than the number of investors who have claims.

- Investors prevail at the NASD in approximately fifty-four percent of the time. This number drops to forty-five percent for cases before the NYSE.

- When investors are not represented by attorneys, the odds of prevailing drop by twenty-seven percent.

- It takes an average of 519 days from the date of filing for the NASD to decide a claim. The NYSE completes the process in 311 days, on average.

- The NYSE awarded $161 million to investors in 1998. In my opinion, if investors knew their rights, this number would be over $1 billion.

- Surprisingly, forty-nine percent of these awards were not paid, because many of the guilty brokers left the industry.

- Most of the relatively few attorneys who specialize in these matters will not take a case unless the losses are at least

$100,000. These cases are typically done on a contingent fee basis, with the lawyer's fee ranging from 33.3% to 40%. The client pays expenses, which typically run at $5000–$15,000, mostly for outside experts. Investors with smaller claims can bring them without counsel, if they cannot find counsel to assist them.

If you are not yet convinced that working with a commission-based advisor can be dangerous to your financial health, perhaps the following quote, provided by Dan Solin, will convince you.

My branch managers only want producers who will pick the gold from their grandmother's teeth. Now that we have the gun to your head and we are into your pockets, do as you are told, sell what we want you to sell when we want you to sell it, or we'll fire you and hire someone else. Then we will sue you for what we lent you and make damn well sure that you never see your book of business again.

The source is an unnamed former Vice President of Sales of a major Broker-Dealer. The source is unnamed because arbitration cases prevent disclosure. Dan Solin has represented an ex-broker who worked for two major firms, and the ex-broker testified to almost precisely this speech being given to him. Dan added that he has reviewed tens of thousands of pages of internal broker-dealer documents and that in his view this statement accurately reflects the prevailing views of management in the brokerage industry.

Once again, the only way to avoid any conflict of interests is to work with an advisor on a fee-only basis. That assures alignment of interests and unbiased advice. No matter how good an advisor's intentions are, it is too easy to be swayed from those good intentions by commission-based compensation.

MISTAKE 42

◆

Do You Spend Too Much Time Managing Your Portfolio?

Inactivity strikes us as intelligent behavior.
—Warren Buffett, 1996 Annual Report
of Berkshire Hathaway

You shouldn't spend time on your investments. That will just tempt you to pull up your plants and see how the roots are doing, and that's very bad for the roots. It's also very bad for your sleep.
—Paul Samuelson, quoted in Jonathan Burton,
Investment Titans

Investors spend an absurd amount of time trying to control the one thing they can do the least about, which is their raw investment performance. They attempt to pick hot stocks, find star fund managers and guess the market's direction. Yet it is extraordinarily difficult, if not impossible, to do any of these things.   —Jonathan Clements, *Wall Street Journal*, July 2, 1999

Indexing is a marvelous technique. I wasn't a true believer. I was just an ignoramus. Now I am a convert. Indexing is an extraordinary sophisticated thing to do. . . . If people want excitement, they should go to the racetrack or play the lottery.
—Douglas Dial, portfolio manager, CREF Stock
Account Fund, in W. Scott Simon, *Index Mutual Funds*

There's something in people, you might even call it a little bit of a gambling instinct . . . I tell people [investing] should be dull. It shouldn't be exciting. Investing should be more like watching paint dry or watching grass grow. If you want excitement, take $800 and go to Las Vegas.
—Paul Samuelson, *Bloomberg* (September 1999)

Shortly after my first book was published, I received a call from a doctor who told me this story. He had been in practice only a few years and had a wife and a young child, with one more on the way. He had seen many of his friends generate large profits from trading stocks and he had gotten caught up in the euphoria of the bull market and the advent of day trading. After putting in his typical long day at the office he would come home not to his wife, but to his computer and the Internet. He spent hours studying charts and investment reports and following the chat boards. He was caught up in the excitement of the greatest bull market ever, the technology revolution that was going to change the world, access to information that the Internet provided, the hype surrounding the success of day traders, and so on. The dramatic expansion of the coverage of financial markets by the press and media helped fuel all this interest in active management and the "take control of your portfolio" mentality. Within just a few months he had turned his small investment stake into about $100,000. Unfortunately, his wife no longer had a husband, and his child no longer had a father, the doctor now being married to his computer. As his wife began to seriously question their marriage, luckily for him, he lost all his profits within a few months.

Fortunately for the doctor, he recognized that his original gains were likely a matter of luck, similar to a hot hand at the craps table. He also recognized that he was not paying attention to the most important part of his life, his family. Someone suggested that he read my book. After doing so, he called to thank me not only for helping him find the winner's game in investing but also the winner's game in life.

Indexing, and passive investing in general, although possibly having the "disadvantage" of being boring, guarantees that you receive market returns in a low-cost and tax-efficient manner; it also frees you from spending any time at all watching CNBC and reading financial publications that are basically not much more than what Jane Bryant Quinn called "investment pornography." And it frees you too, from spending time on the Internet studying charts and reading chat-room posts that have in all likelihood even less value than that found in financial publications. Instead, you can spend your time with your family, doing community service, reading a good book, or pursuing your favorite hobby. Remember, investing was never meant to be exciting, despite what Wall Street and the financial press want you to believe. Investing is supposed to be about achieving your financial goals with the least amount of risk.

In my particular case, I get to spend my time coaching my children's sports team. Over the years I have coached my daughters in soccer, basketball, and softball, and have attended their sporting events and dance recitals. I am also an avid reader. While reading about ten to fifteen investment books a year as part of my research, I also read another forty to fifty books annually, ranging from spy novels to great literature, from history to historical fiction.

I admit it. Indexing, and passive investing, is boring. As Jonathan Clements said, "Index funds are tough to get excited about. But I love them just the same."[1] If anyone needs to get a great deal of excitement in life from investing, perhaps he or she should seriously consider getting another life. Personally, I get my excitement by participating in and attending sporting events and from my passion, whitewater rafting. There is no question in my mind that I can get all the excitement I need from life staring a class V+ rapid in the face. I have been on over forty whitewater adventures, on over twenty different rivers, in ten different states, many of them containing class V and class V+ rapids. I have even experienced the thrill of going overboard on a Class V rapid on the Youghiogheny River in Maryland. That, by the way, is a thrill one can do without. And, very important, I have been able to share many of those experiences with my family, especially my oldest daughter, Jodi. She loves the sport so much she took canoeing classes while attending Emory University and trained to be a guide. As to getting excitement from my investments, I have a special "entertainment" account, typically holding just two to four stocks, representing no more than about one percent of my net worth.

Here is another tale that made me realize how adopting passive investing as the basis for your investment strategy can improve your life as well. About a year after my first book was published, I became friends with a sophisticated investor with an MBA from the Wharton School of University of Pennsylvania. The investor also had about thirty years of experience in financial management, including his last position as assistant treasurer of a Fortune 500 company. After meeting with one of the partners of my firm, and having read my book, he became a client. He was so convinced that this was the winning strategy that he wanted to help others benefit from adopting its principles. Eventually, he became a financial advisor. In short order, he completed the extensive educational requirements for his Certified Financial Planning (CFP) certificate. He then related to me the following story.

My friend used to spend many hours every day reading various financial publications, researching individual stocks, and watching the financial news. And this was after putting in a long and full day at the office. After learning of and adopting the principles of MPT and passive investing, he found that he no longer needed to do those things. He recognized that they were just noise that would, at best, distract him from the winner's game. He and his wife sat down and calculated that he had actually recaptured six weeks per year of his life. It is one thing to decide to spend six weeks a year in productive activities; however, as he discovered, not only are these particular activities highly likely to prove nonproductive, they are likely to prove counterproductive because of the expenses and taxes incurred when implementing an active strategy. And that doesn't even include placing a value on the most precious resource individuals have—their time.

Ted Cadsby, President and CEO of CIBC Securities, put it this way: "Success in investing (as in much of life) is very much dependent upon putting probabilities in your favour—getting them working for you, not against you. And putting market odds in your favour couldn't be easier, because the best investment strategy is basically to do nothing!"[2]

Richard Bernstein, First Vice President and Chief Quantitative Strategist at Merrill Lynch provided the following highly useful insight: "Today's investors find it inconceivable that life might be better without so much information. Investors find it hard to believe that ignoring the vast majority of investment noise might actually improve investment performance. The idea sounds too risky because it is so contrary to their accepted and reinforced actions."[3] What makes this a particularly interesting statement is that his employer (not to single out Merrill Lynch) is responsible for putting out much of the noise! Many entities (not just investment firms, but magazines like *Money*, media firms such as CNBC, newsletters, and the press in general) have a vested interest in your being hooked on the noise, as that is what produces profits for them. Their interests are not aligned with yours. The winning strategy for them is highly likely to be the losing strategy for you, especially in life.

The final comment on the fact that investors spend too much time on their investments: fifty-six percent of people say they think about money more often than they think about sex.[4] The great tragedy in life is not that the vast majority of investors unnecessarily miss out on market returns that are available to anyone simply by adopting a passive investment strategy. The great tragedy in life is that they also miss out on the really important things in life in pursuit of the Holy Grail of outperformance. That is why this book is not just about helping you avoid the mistakes even smart investors make, but about how to win the game of life.

MISTAKE 43

◆

Did You Begin Your Investment Journey Without a Road Map?

If you don't know where you are going, any road will get you there. —Chinese fortune cookie

No traveler would begin a drive to a place he or she had never been without a road map. Yet only a very small percent of all investors have a written investment plan, or investment policy statement. By developing a plan, many mistakes can be avoided. Therefore, investors should not make any investments until they have answered at least these three important questions.

- *How long is my investment horizon?* Along with stability of earned income, this helps define the *ability* to take risk.

- *What is my tolerance for risk?* This helps define the *willingness* to take risk.

- *What are my financial objectives?* This helps define the need to take risk.

Let's begin with the investment horizon. The length of your investment horizon is important because of the nature of the risks of equity investing. Equity investors must be aware that the longer the investment horizon, the more likely it is that the expected will occur (i.e., stocks will significantly outperform both money market funds and bonds). Conversely, the shorter the horizon, the more likely it is that the unexpected will occur (i.e., stocks will generate negative returns). Therefore, investors with long investment horizons have a greater *ability to take risk* and can thus allocate a greater percentage of their portfolios to equities than investors with shorter investment horizons. A reasonable guideline for an investor's maximum equity exposure is provided in the table we first saw in Mistake 33.

Investment Horizon	Maximum Equity Allocation (%)
0–3 years	0
4 years	10
5 years	20
6 years	30
7 years	40
8 years	50
9 years	60
10 years	70
11–14 years	80
15–19 years	90
20 years or longer	100

Turning to the issue of risk tolerance, you should ask yourself how much you could see your portfolio lose in value without losing sleep. You should not take on so much risk that you are likely to lose sleep worrying. In addition, you should ask yourself how much of a loss you think you could absorb without panicking and selling. These questions help define your *willingness to accept risk*, and play an important role in determining the percentage of equity assets allocated to a portfolio. Investment advisor and columnist Nick Murray provides two very good reasons why understanding your "threshold for pain" is important to successful investing:

1. "Fear leads to panic, panic breeds the inability to distinguish between temporary declines and permanent losses. That, in turn, leads to the well-documented propensity to be massive sellers of good investments near market bottoms."

2. "Success is purely a function of two things. First, recognition of the inevitability of major market declines. Second, an emotional/behavioral preparation to regard such declines as nonevents."[1]

Murray puts it this way: "The governing variable in investment success is not the 'performance' of investments, but the behavior of investors." He continues: "The great enemy of long-term investment success isn't ignorance. It's fear."[2] I would add: the antidotes to fear are a well-thought-out written investment plan; preparation for the inevitable bad times; and the knowledge that bear markets are temporary.

The role that emotion plays in the success of an investment strategy cannot be overemphasized. Its importance is summarized by this quotation from financial advisor and author Ragnar Naess: "Successful investment management depends to a large extent on the emotional stability of the individual, particularly during periods of strain and stress, and on his ability to overcome the severe psychological hurdles present during crucial periods."[3]

A reasonable guideline for your maximum equity exposure is provided in the table we first saw in Mistake 28.

Maximum Tolerable Loss (%)	Maximum Equity Exposure (%)
5	20
10	30
15	40
20	50

(continued)

Maximum Tolerable Loss (%)	Maximum Equity Exposure (%)
25	60
30	70
35	80
40	90
50	100

When evaluating your risk tolerance, you should take the following test; but be sure to be honest with yourself, and not make the mistake of treating what you might think of as the highly unlikely prospect of a severe bear market as impossible. Let's assume you have $100,000 to invest, and you decide that you can absorb a loss of thirty percent without panicking and selling or even losing sleep (life is too short to let the stock market keep you from enjoying it). So you check the table and see that a thirty percent loss corresponds to a seventy percent equity allocation. You then invest $70,000 in equities and $30,000 in fixed income. Now, remember that if a severe bear market does occur, the value of your portfolio will not only drop substantially but the equity portion will fall well below seventy percent. This means that in order to rebalance the portfolio and restore the equity allocation to seventy percent, you must have the courage to *buy more*, just when the world looks darkest and all around may be in a state of panic. If you would not be willing to do so, then you should choose a lower equity allocation.

You should compare the results from the investment horizon question with the results from the risk tolerance question. The equity allocation should be the *lower* of the two numbers. For example, if you have a high tolerance for risk but a short investment horizon, the short investment horizon should determine the equity allocation. Conversely, if you have a long investment horizon but a low risk tolerance, the risk tolerance should determine the equity allocation.

Finally, we turn to the question of financial objectives (*the need to take risk*). Considering only the first two issues—the ability and willingness to take risk—while ignoring the need to take risk is a very serious mistake made by investors and advisors alike. The table below serves as a general guideline to help you match your financial goals with your equity allocation. The financial goal is expressed in terms of the annualized rate of return needed to achieve this goal. The return numbers are based on a balanced portfolio, including equal exposures to the small- and large-cap and value and growth asset classes. Please keep in mind that for two investors with the same equity allocation, the one with the greater allocation to the higher-returning asset classes of small and value will have greater expected returns. Also remember that when we speak of returns on equities, we are always speaking of *expected* returns, not *guaranteed* returns.

Financial Goal (%)	Equity Allocation (%)
5.0	0
6.0	20
7.5	40
9.0	60
10.5	80
12.0	100

Bear in mind the following important points. First, the five percent figure for an all-fixed-income portfolio is based on the prevailing rate on short-term treasury bills. Because equity investors receive an expected return *premium* above the risk-free rate, you should adjust these figures to reflect the current level of the risk-free rate. All other return figures should be adjusted accordingly. For example, if the current rate on short-term Treasuries is four percent, all return figures should be lowered by one percent. Note that if investors are willing to lengthen the maturity of their fixed-income allocation to one to five years, then another 1%–1.5% can be added to expected returns for that portion of the portfolio that is fixed income. All return figures would have to be adjusted to reflect the higher return of the fixed-income component.

Keep in mind that since the above figures are the expected returns, there is approximately a fifty percent probability of the actual returns falling below the objective. Believing that investors prefer a much greater probability than the equivalent of a coin toss, the return figures have been lowered in order to provide a greater likelihood of success. Finally, remember that these returns are all pretax.

Returning to the importance of the individual's financial objectives in determining the appropriate equity allocation, the following example is the best illustration I can think of.

In a discussion with a new client, a fifty-five-year-old investor, I learned that

- He currently had $2.5 million of net assets,

- He wanted to retire in ten years, and

- He was a long-term investor with a high tolerance for risk, evidenced by his current portfolio's equity allocation of almost one hundred percent.

When asked how much money he felt he would need in order to retire comfortably, he responded: "Four million dollars." I asked whether his lifestyle would change much if instead of $4 million he ended up with $6 million. He said: "No." I then asked him if his lifestyle would change if he ended up with just $3 million. He said: "Yes, I would have to keep working." Clearly, the reward of his ending up with more dollars than his goal was far less than the pain of ending up with less. In other words, while he had a long investment horizon (the second-to-die life expectancy between his wife and him was about thirty years), and he apparently had a high risk tolerance (as evidenced by his current one hundred percent equity allocation), his *utility of risk* was very low—the marginal benefit of the upside was very low, while the pain of a downside outcome would be severe. I then showed him that in order to achieve his $4 million goal in ten years, including the savings from his salary over that period, he would need to earn less than the rate of return on a money market account. He didn't *need to take the risk* of an all-equity portfolio to achieve his objective. He ultimately decided to substantially reduce his equity allocation. An irony about investing is that the very people who can most afford to take risk (the very wealthy) have the lowest utility of risk, and therefore the least need to take it.

This example illustrates why you need to address all three issues of investment horizon, risk tolerance, and financial goals so carefully. Determining the correct allocation is simple when the results lead to the same conclusion; it becomes more complex when the conclusions are in conflict. In those cases, there are no right answers. You must weigh the risks and potential rewards of each strategy and then decide on the appropriate one. Having made the decision that is most appropriate for you, you should formalize a written plan and then sign it. Having a written and signed IPS will help you avoid many of the fifty-two investment mistakes that even smart people like you make.

The IPS should include not only the desired asset allocation but also a rebalancing table that will help provide the discipline to stay the course. Rebalancing is a very important part of the winning strategy, as it enables you to maintain control over the risks and rewards of your portfolio. Unfortunately, rebalancing goes against human nature as it requires you to sell some of the recent outperforming asset class and buy some of the asset class that has been the poorest performer. Going against the market is very difficult for most investors. Below is a sample asset allocation and rebalancing table. Keep in mind that there is no correct asset allocation, just one that is correct for each individual investor. It is prudent, however, to build a broad, globally diversified portfolio with exposure to each of the asset classes listed.

Asset Class	Minimum Allocation(%)	Target Allocation(%)	Maximum Allocation (%)
U.S. large	7.5	10	12.5
U.S. large value	15	20	25
U.S. small	7.5	10	12.5
U.S. small value	15	20	25
Real Estate	7.5	10	12.5
Total U.S.	**65**	**70**	**75**
International large value	7.5	10	12.5
International small	3.75	5	6.25
International small value	7.5	10	12.5
Emerging markets	3.75	5	6.25
Total International	**25**	**30**	**35**

This table is for an all-equity portfolio. Remember to include any fixed-income allocation when you calculate your target minimum and maximum allocations.

One last point. Creating a financial plan is not a onetime process. Your financial situation will change over time, if for no other reason than as time marches on your investment horizon changes. Financial planning is a dynamic process that can be impacted by market conditions (bull markets can reduce your need to take risk), changes in employment (altering your risk tolerance), inheritances, and all kinds of unforeseen circumstances. A bear market may even test your assumptions about your own ability to absorb the stomach acid it can create. Once a year you should revisit your financial plan to make sure the assumptions upon which you built the plan still hold true.

PART FOUR

Mistakes Made When Developing a Portfolio

MISTAKE 44

Do You Have Too Many Eggs in One Basket?

Every investor knows that putting too many eggs in one basket is a risky investment decision that can easily be avoided by building a diversified portfolio. Yet many executives and long-term corporate employees end up with a very substantial portion of their assets in the stock of the company for which they work. I have seen numerous cases where employees have as much as eighty percent or even ninety percent of their entire net worth in their employer's stock. Typically, the unusually large share is the result of stock options and savings plans that encourage ownership of corporate stock. My experience has been that in the vast majority of cases, no actual decision was made to hold such a risky portfolio. The person just ended up with the portfolio without thinking about the risks incurred. In addition, in many cases people believe that because they work for the company they *know* just how good an investment they have. Let's examine why holding such an undiversified portfolio is really a poor decision, no matter how good the prospects for the company look (remember the highly likely is not certain). In fact, if an investor takes the time to think about the decision in a rational manner, he would in all likelihood never retain the vast majority of his assets in his own company's (or any other company's) stock.

Whenever I meet with a client who has a large percentage of her assets in her own company's stock, I ask her to put herself in the following situation. She is the single greatest blackjack player in the world, never making a mistake counting cards. A casino has offered her a challenge match in which only one deck of cards will be used. On any individual hand she can bet any amount she likes, from one cent to her entire net worth, let's say $2 million. She can also quit the game at any time. She accepts the challenge and proceeds to bet one cent on every hand. Finally, the perfect situation arises: The dealer is down to only four cards left, all of them kings. The dealer can only deal three cards (because the last one is faceup) and then must shuffle and deal himself one more card. The client is then left with the following situation. She will have twenty points and the dealer will have ten, with one more card to be dealt. With only forty-nine cards remaining, the client will have:

- A 12.5% chance to lose (the four aces and other combinations which add to twenty-one).

- A 30% chance to tie.

- A 57.5% chance of winning.

In all likelihood, this will be the best bet (investment) the client will ever have a chance to make. The odds of winning are 4.6 times (57.5/12.5) greater than the odds of losing, and there is only a one in eight chance of losing. Now, with her spouse looking over her shoulder, I ask: How much of your $2 million net worth would you bet? Very rarely does the answer even approach ten percent of the client's net worth. Most people say something like $5,000 or $10,000. I then ask if she believes that the odds that her company's stock will outperform the market are as good as that blackjack bet. Most will admit that it is not.

What do we learn from the blackjack example? We learn that when the cost of losing (being wrong) is high, people become risk-averse. Even with the odds greatly in their favor, they avoid risk. As we saw earlier, other examples of this behavior are the purchase of homeowner's or life insurance. No one expects either to have their home destroyed or to die in the near future, yet virtually everyone buys insurance because the cost of being wrong is so high. Again, when the cost of losing is high, investors become risk-averse. They do so because although it is *highly unlikely* that if they went uninsured they would suffer a loss, it is *not impossible*.

We can apply the blackjack lesson to the example of investors with the vast majority of their assets in their own company's stock. First, investors who are also employees are actually making a double bet: the company may lay off staff to reduce costs, so their jobs may be in danger at the same time their investments may come under pressure.

Second, there is really no logical reason for investors to believe that their own stock will outperform similar stocks. Obviously, by definition, not all investors' stocks can outperform the average. Some will do better and some will do worse. However, since investors are risk-averse when they might lose a large amount, it doesn't make sense to own only one stock, especially when higher returns are not expected. Even if it were logical to believe that an investor would get higher returns, are the odds against being wrong as great as they are in the blackjack example? If investors wouldn't bet a large amount at the blackjack table with odds as stacked in their favor as they are in the hypothetical example, why should they make a large bet when the odds are far less favorable? Unlike the insurance decision, where investors treat the unlikely as possible, when it comes to their company's stock they treat the unlikely—a sharp drop in their company's stock—as impossible. Many employees of such once high flyers as E-Loan and Silicon Graphics have watched the vast majority of their net worth evaporate because they made the mistake of treating the highly unlikely as impossible.

Some good examples of great companies that ended up providing investors with very poor returns follow.

- Black & Decker: The shares of the "do-it-yourself" toolmaker had risen 500-fold in fifteen years: The 1972 peak was not revisited until 1998.

- Campbell Soup: The 1961 price was not regained until 1982, twenty-one years later.

- Digital Equipment: The shares of this minicomputer maker, which had skyrocketed 1,000-fold from 1967 to 1987, lost eighty-five percent of their value over the next five years.

- Polaroid: The stock price in 1998 was only a third of its price thirty years earlier.

- PG&E: This California utility, a safe "widows and orphans" stock, declared bankruptcy in the first quarter of 2001 as a result of the California energy crisis.

- Xerox: The Cisco or Microsoft of its era was in danger of bankruptcy as we entered 2001.

Microsoft is also the "villain" in an all too familiar tale of the tech wreck of 2000–2001. In this story, a mid-level Microsoft employee exercised his stock options. At the peak, his shares were worth about $1.5 million. By the fall of 2000, when the stock began to dive, the brokerage firm which had provided a margin loan (a loan collateralized by the stock) that allowed the employee to exercise the options began selling shares out of his account to pay off the margin loan. By April 2001, most of his stock was gone and he owed $100,000 in income taxes, more than both his annual salary and his entire savings. His only remaining asset was a modest Seattle home that he was concerned he would also lose.[1]

There are of course many more examples of investors placing too many eggs in one basket, and by agreeing to trading techniques such as margin loans when they did not fully understand the risk involved. Most investors do not really appreciate just how risky owning one stock, or even a small group of stocks, can be. Consider the following: Of the 500 firms selected for the original S&P 500 Index in 1957, only seventy-four remained on the list in 1998, and only twelve outperformed the index over the entire period.[2] Not very good odds of success for anyone trying to pick the one successful company. Vladimir Masek, of my firm, took another look at just how risky even the "safe" stocks of the S&P 500 are. Of the 500 companies in the S&P 500 as of October 1, 1990, only 302 (or 60.4%) were even still in existence ten years later. Of the 302 (which certainly includes survivorship bias; many companies that did not survive in all likelihood produced very poor returns), only seventy-nine (26.2%) beat the Vanguard S&P 500 index fund. Perhaps even more surprising is that seventy-five stocks (24.8%) returned less than riskless one-year treasury bills. Forty-five stocks (14.9%) managed to return less than inflation, as measured by the CPI. And, perhaps most important from a risk management perspective, thirty-two stocks, or 10.6%, had negative returns. Stocks are risky, and diversification reduces risk.

It has been my experience that once people take the blackjack test, they become aware, for the first time, just how risky a decision they have made. Ask yourself: If I currently didn't own any of this particular stock, how much would I buy? And remember, if the answer is less than you currently hold, every day you own the stock, you are effectively buying that amount of stock— because, of course, you don't have to own it. The risk of your portfolio can be substantially reduced by using the proceeds to build a globally diversified portfolio that reflects your unique appetite for risk, investment horizon, and financial goals. Finally, if you are ever tempted to put lots of eggs in one basket, remember that while this is the surest way to make a fortune, it is also the surest way to lose one.

MISTAKE 45
◆

Do You Underestimate the Number of Stocks Needed to Build a Diversified Portfolio?

In December 1968, a paper by J. Evans and S. H. Archer entitled "Diversification and the Reduction of Dispersion: An Empirical Analysis" concluded that an investor needed to construct a portfolio containing as little as fifteen randomly selected stocks before the benefits of diversification (as measured by the standard deviation) were basically exhausted.[1] A similar 1970 study by Lawrence Fisher and James Laurie found that ninety percent of the diversification benefit came from just sixteen stocks and ninety-five percent of the benefit could be captured by just thirty stocks.[2] Some individual investors might feel comfortable managing a portfolio of such limited size on their own. Alternatively they might choose to have their portfolio managed by what is known as a separate account manager. If a much larger number of stocks were needed to achieve effective diversification, it could only likely be achieved in a cost-effective way through the use of mutual funds.

A more recent study, co-authored by Burton Malkiel, John Campbell, Yexiao Xu, and Martin Lettau, argues that a dramatic increase in the volatility of individual stocks, and a declining correlation of stocks within the S&P 500 Index, has led to a significant increase in the number of securities needed to achieve the same level of portfolio risk. Their study, entitled "Have Individual Stocks Become More Volatile?", found that for the two decades prior to 1985, in order to reduce excess standard deviation (a measure of diversifiable portfolio risk) to ten percent, a portfolio would have had to consist of at least twenty stocks. From 1986 to 1997, that figure increased to fifty. Whereas the study found that there was a large increase in the volatility of individual stocks, the authors found no increase in overall market volatility, or even industry volatility. The implication of increased volatility of individual stocks and unchanged volatility of the S&P 500 taken together is that correlations between stocks have declined. Reduced correlation between stocks implies that the benefits of, and the need for, portfolio diversification have increased over time. [3]

The authors offer three explanations for the increased volatility of individual stocks, the first of which is the increased influence of institutional investors over the past forty years. Institutional investors have exhibited a herd mentality; thus, when hundreds of funds and pension plans rush to buy or sell at roughly the same time, price changes are now more exaggerated. A second explanation is the advent of retail day traders. The third explanation is the tendency for companies to go public at a much earlier stage, when they are likely to be more volatile.

Keep in mind that even a portfolio of fifty stocks (and it may be much higher today as the market's volatility has increased since the study was completed) will still leave an investor with ten percent excess (greater than the market's) standard deviation. In addition, while a fifty-stock portfolio might track the S&P 500 Index well over a long period of time (i.e. the portfolio's returns and the Index's returns might be similar), it might present the investor with very large short-term tracking error (i.e. the portfolio's returns and the Index's returns might deviate substantially on a short-term basis). This might not be an acceptable risk for investors. The results of this study are supported by the results of a similar study, "The Truth About Diversification by the Numbers."[4] Ronald J. Surz and Mitchell Price measured the "percent of possible reductions in dispersions of returns achieved by portfolios of various sizes on average" compared to a single stock portfolio (i.e. how much extra effective diversification can be achieved by adding additional stocks to the portfolio). Dispersion of returns refers to how far the individual portfolio returns are scattered from each other. The greater the dispersion, the more likely it is that a portfolio's returns will vary greatly from the market's returns. The study covered the period January 1986-June 1999 and included all stocks within the Compustat database. The following table summarizes their findings.

Number of stocks	15	30	60	Total Market
Standard deviation	16.5%	15.4%	15.2%	14.5%
R-squared	.76	.86	.88	1
Tracking error	8.1%	6.2%	5.3%	
Percent reduction in dispersion of returns	82%	86%	88%	

Even with a portfolio of sixty stocks the percent reduction in dispersion of returns was still below ninety percent. Perhaps more importantly the tracking error to the market was still over five percent per annum. With the historical return to the market (as measured by the S&P 500 Index) being just over eleven, I wonder how many investors would be comfortable with a tracking error that is equal to almost fifty percent of the average market return?

A 1996 study by two University of Nevada Las Vegas professors, Gerald Newbould and Percy Poon, came to an even more dramatic conclusion. They found that "investors needed to hold more than one hundred small-cap or large-cap stocks in order to remain within five percent of average risk, which they define as the average volatility of the 40,000 simulated portfolios created for the study."[5]

Consider now an investor who wants to achieve broad global asset class diversification. He would need to hold over one hundred small-cap and one hundred large-cap stocks. And then he would probably have to add a similar number of small and large value stocks, real estate stocks, foreign large-cap stocks, emerging market stocks, and so on. There is simply no way to achieve this type of diversification by building your own portfolio of individual stocks.

The investment results of the year 2000 perfectly illustrate the risks of targeting narrow market sectors rather than diversifying risk. The *Wall Street Journal's* year-end mutual fund survey found that thirty-four domestic and foreign equity funds experienced twelve-month losses in excess of fifty percent. Two of the funds had assets over $1 billion.[6]

Perhaps the following point is the most dramatic example of the need for and logic of broad diversification as the winning strategy. Although the 1990s witnessed one of the greatest bull markets of all time, twenty-two percent of the 2,397 U.S. stocks in existence throughout the decade had negative returns. Not negative real returns, but negative absolute returns.[7] The implication for individual investors is that broad-based index or passively managed asset class mutual funds (or their equivalent ETF) provide the most effective diversification, and do so at a very low cost. The advent of index and passively managed funds that are also tax-managed basically eliminates any advantages an individually tailored private account might offer. Privately managed stock accounts just cannot achieve the same level of diversification that a fund can. And the evidence is clear that there now is a greater need for diversification than ever before.

MISTAKE 46

◆

Do You Believe Diversification Is Determined by the Number of Securities Held?

Most investors understand the need to diversify their portfolios. They understand that diversification reduces the risk of having all your eggs in one basket. The only truly riskless instruments are short-term U.S. government securities, insured bank CDs, and I-Bonds. Long-term government securities, even Treasury Inflation Protected Securities (TIPS), while having no credit risk, do have price risk until maturity. No matter how safe other investments might look, there is always some degree of risk that the expected return will not be realized. Unfortunately, many, if not most, investors still do not understand how to construct a portfolio that *effectively* diversifies risk.

Far too many investors believe that they can achieve effective diversification by purchasing a large number of either stocks or mutual funds. In order to understand why this idea leads to poor investment decisions, we need to understand the factors that determine returns. Professors Eugene Fama and Kenneth French provided us with the answer when they published their famous paper, "The Cross-Section of Expected Returns," in the June

1992 edition of the *Journal of Finance*. Their study demonstrated that the vast majority of equity returns are explained by the exposure to the risk factors of size (determined by market capitalization) and value (determined by book-to-market). The study showed that portfolios of stocks in the same asset class, such as large-cap growth stocks or small-cap value stocks, have returns that are almost entirely explained by the returns of their respective asset class (not the industry).

Fama and French followed up that paper with an unpublished study covering $70 billion of domestic pension assets. They found that their model explained over ninety-seven of the returns of the portfolios of thirty-one different pension plans.[1] Thus, the return on a stock, or group of stocks, is determined primarily by whether the stock is categorized as small or large, and value or growth. Fama and French found that their three-factor model did not explain the returns of a portfolio of real estate stocks. Therefore, real estate is considered a separate asset class. Also of great importance in explaining returns is whether the equity holdings are domestic or international. This study provided significant insight into how to effectively build a portfolio containing assets that would not have high correlation to each other.

Let's look at two portfolios that potential clients presented to my firm, Buckingham Asset Management, for analysis. In each case, individuals were working with a stockbroker and believed that their portfolios were highly diversified, based on owning a large number of different assets. By putting their portfolios under the microscope of the Fama-French model, it was easy to see that in fact they had minimal diversification: almost all of their assets fell into just one asset class. Thus, the portfolios held assets that had high correlation to each other.

In examining the portfolios, we will use the CRSP definitions for size and value. Stocks ranked in deciles one through five by market capitalization are considered large caps. Stocks that are in deciles six through ten are considered small caps. Stocks ranked in deciles one through three by book-to-market are considered growth stocks. Stocks that are in deciles eight through ten are considered value stocks. Stocks in deciles four through seven by BtM are considered core stocks.

The first example involves an investor who held a portfolio of fourteen stocks and eleven mutual funds (Portfolio A), surely a diversified portfolio. But let's take a closer look. Of the fourteen stocks, twelve were ranked in the top decile of stocks by market capitalization. The other two were in the second and third deciles; thus, they were all large-cap stocks. Of the fourteen stocks, nine would be considered growth stocks, and only one would be considered a value stock. Three of the remaining stocks fell in the fourth decile, just barely missing being classified as a growth stock. Let's now look at the mutual funds. Ten of the eleven were in the first decile by size. The remaining fund fell in the fifth decile, still a large-cap holding, even though it had smallcap in its name (fund names can be misleading). The median market cap was above $1 billion, meaning the weighted average market cap was probably much higher. When ranking by BtM, seven of the eleven fell in the first decile, while the other four fell in the second decile. Once again, the portfolio was heavily concentrated in the asset class of large growth stocks. It is worth noting that the portfolio did have some diversification, as fifteen percent of the assets were international. Also noteworthy is that the investor was holding over eight percent cash, even though he believed he held no cash in this portfolio. The actively managed funds had built up cash positions, thereby reducing the investor's equity exposure to well below the desired level. As we have seen, style drift is just one of the risks of using actively managed funds as the building blocks of a portfolio.

The bottom line was that Portfolio A, despite its diversity in terms of number of holdings, was not diversified at all by asset class (it was virtually an all large-cap growth portfolio)—and that is the only type of diversification that really matters. In fact, because the mutual funds were all investing in the same asset class, it was highly likely that the funds held shares in many of the very same stocks the client owned independently.

The second client, having Portfolio B, was even more diversified in terms of number of holdings, with twenty-two stocks and nineteen mutual funds. The BtM data is only presented for seventeen funds, as Morningstar's database, upon which the analysis is based, did not have complete information. Of the twenty-two stocks, twenty were first decile by size, one was second decile, and one third decile. When looking at BtM, fifteen were first decile and a total of twenty would be considered growth stocks. As the remaining stocks were in deciles four and seven, not a single holding could be considered a value stock. Thus, the stock holdings were basically all large-cap growth stocks. Looking at the mutual funds, we find a similar picture. Of the nineteen mutual funds, eighteen were first decile by size, and the last was second decile. Looking at BtM, of the funds for which data was available there were sixteen that were first decile and one second decile. Looking at the weighted averages we found that ninety-five percent of the portfolio was first decile by size (five percent was fifth decile) and seventy-seven percent was first decile and twenty-one percent second decile by BtM. The bottom line was that despite forty-three different holdings, Portfolio B had virtually no diversification (except for diversifying away the single stock and the single industry risk). Like the first portfolio, it was virtually an all large-cap growth portfolio, with no exposure to small caps and value stocks. The only true diversification was from the sixteen percent allocation to international stocks, though here too it was all large growth—which has a fairly high correlation to U.S. large growth, so it is not as effective a diversifier as one might think. To gain more genuinely effective diversification internationally, one must use the asset classes of international small and emerging markets.

The two portfolios probably performed very well in 1998 and 1999 when large-cap growth stocks exhibited strong performance. Our two investors were probably very happy and didn't think about the logic of diversification. When their assets are all in a well-performing asset class, investors seem to forget the principles of, and reasons for, diversification—no one can predict when an asset class will perform relatively well or relatively poorly.

Both of these investors met with my firm in the summer of 2000, when large-cap growth stocks had already entered what would prove to be a severe bear market (especially for NASDAQ-listed stocks), and value stocks experienced one of their greatest periods of outperformance relative to growth stocks. All of a sudden these same investors became concerned about the performance of their portfolios, as all of their assets seemed to be doing poorly at the same time (again, the high correlation was fine when things were going well). These two portfolios are not unique in their lack of diversification. In fact, they are quite typical in that they hold many stocks/funds, but are very heavily concentrated in the asset class of U.S. large growth stocks.

Another very common example that illustrates the same type of error can be seen in portfolios with holdings of many different actively managed funds within the same fund family. Let's use the example of an investor who seeks diversification. We will assume that to accomplish his diversification, he buys twenty different funds, the ten largest in terms of assets under management from each of Fidelity and Janus (two of the most popular fund families for actively managed funds). When we examine such a portfolio under the microscope of the Fama-French model, we find that in the case of Fidelity, seven of the ten funds were first decile by size and three were second decile. All ten were first decile by BtM. None had international exposure. The results are similar with Janus: seven of the ten are first decile by size and three are second decile. Nine are first decile by BtM, with one in the second decile. While the investor would own twenty different funds, and there would be some international diversification with some of the Janus funds, every single one of the funds is a large-cap growth fund. Thus, the investor achieved very little in terms of effective diversification (with the exception, again, of some international exposure).

Professors Fama and French showed us the way to achieve effective diversification. To do so one must diversify across the asset classes of small and large, growth and value, domestic and international. And the best building blocks are index or passive asset class funds, since they are low cost, tax efficient, and do not style drift.

Portfolio A (CRSP size/BtM rankings and data as of July 31, 2000)

Stocks	Mutual Funds
America Online 1/1	Alliance Technology B 1/1
Bank of America 1/7	Capital World Growth & Inc 1/2
Charter Communications 3/8	Euro Pacific Growth 1/2
Coca-Cola 1/1	Fundamental Investors 1/2
Compaq 1/4	Goldman Sachs Internet B 1/1
E-Trade 2/4	Growth Fund of America 1/1

(continued)

Stocks	Mutual Funds
Eastman Kodak 1/2	New Economy 1/1
Intel 1/1	New Perspective 1/1
Lucent 1/1	Phoenix-Engelman Cap Growth 1/1
Pfizer 1/1	Smallcap World 5/1
Schlumberger 1/2	Washington Mutual Investors 1/2
Transocean Sedco Forex 1/4	
Wal-Mart 1/1	
Walt Disney 1/3	

Source: Morningstar database as of February 28, 2001

Portfolio B (CRSP ranking and data as of August 31, 2000)

ADC Telecommunications 1/1	AIM Global Telecom and Tech 1/1
American Home Products 1/1	Alliance Premier Growth 1/1
Art Technology Group 3/1	Alliance Technology 1/1
BP Amoco 1/3	ASAF Marsico Capital Growth 1/1
Bristol Myers Squibb 1/1	Dreyfus Premier Tech Growth 1/1
Cisco Systems 1/1	Dreyfus Premier Worldwide Growth 1/1
EMC 1/1	Janus Overseas 1/1
GE 1/1	Jundt Opportunity 1/1
Guidant 1/1	Kemper Technology 1/1
Intel 1/1	MainStay Blue Chip Growth 1/1
Lucent 1/3	MFS Research Growth and Income 1/1
McLeod USA A 2/4	MFS Strategic Growth 1/1
Medtronic 1/1	New Perspective 1/1
Merck 1/1	Putnam Vista 1/1
Microsoft 1/1	Seligman Communications & Information 2/2
Nokia ADR 1/1	SunAmerica Style Select Focus II 1/1
Nortel 1/2	Van Kampen Emerging Growth 1/1

Pfizer 1/1	SunAmerica Focused TechNet 1/n.a.
Schering Plough 1/1	Dreyfus High Yield Strategies 1/n.a.
Tyco Int'l 1/2	
Wells Fargo 1/3	
WorldCom 1/7	

Source: Morningstar database as of February 28, 2001

Fidelity	Janus
Magellan 1/1	Worldwide 1/1
Growth and Income 1/1	Twenty 1/1
Contrafund 2/1	Mercury 1/1
Growth Company 1/1	Growth and Income 2/1
Blue Chip Growth 1/1	Overseas 1/1
Equity-Income 2/1	Aspen Worldwide Growth Inst. 1/1
Puritan 2/1	Enterprise 2/1
Spartan U.S. Equity Index 1/1	Olympus 1/1
Fidelity 1/1	Global Technology 2/1
Aggressive Growth 1/1	Balanced 1/1

Source: Morningstar database as of February 28, 2001

MISTAKE 47

◆

Do You Confuse Indexing with the Exclusive Use of an S&P 500 Fund?

Investors often confuse indexing with the exclusive use of the most popular indexing vehicles, an S&P 500 fund, or the equivalent ETF known as a SPDR (pronounced as Spider). They may also make the mistake of believing that by purchasing an

S&P 500 Index fund, they will own a highly diversified asset with holdings in five hundred different companies. Investors may therefore content themselves with holding an S&P 500 Index fund as the sole asset in their portfolio. However, investors building such a portfolio are not really getting effective diversification. The lack of diversification arises both from how the stocks are selected by Standard & Poor's for inclusion in the index and also from the market cap weighting mechanism used to calculate the index.

Not only does an S&P 500 Index fund not own an equal amount of 500 different companies, but most investors are surprised at just how skewed the index is toward the largest-cap stocks. As of year-end 1999 the S&P 500 weightings were:

- The largest 50 stocks:60%
- The largest 100 stocks: 75%
- The largest 200 stocks: 88%
- The largest 300 stocks: 95%[1]

Here is another interesting statistic: As we began the second quarter of 2000, the weighted average market cap of the S&P 500 stocks was $143 billion, yet only sixteen stocks were larger than the average! If the 500 stocks in the index were equally weighted (an S&P 500 Index fund that was equally weighted—instead of market cap weighted—would have an equal dollar amount invested in each of the 500 stocks), the average market cap would have been just $24 billion, or one sixth of the actual weighted average of the S&P 500.[2]

The S&P 500's weighted average market cap of $143 billion makes it a first (largest cap) decile fund. As we entered 2001, the BtM of the S&P 500 was 0.21, placing it in the second decile. So an S&P 500 Index fund is very large cap and very growth-oriented. Therefore, even though you own five hundred stocks, you haven't achieved effective diversification. That should not be construed to mean either that it is a poor investment or that you shouldn't own this type of fund. It does mean, however, that if you want to diversify your portfolio beyond the asset class of large-cap growth stocks, you need to broaden the portfolio's holdings.

Total Stock Market (TSM) funds were created to help investors achieve greater diversification than just an S&P 500 Index fund achieves. The appeal of owning the entire market is intuitively attractive from a diversification perspective. However, once again the market cap weighting mechanism that is used to make index funds easy to manage provides a far different outcome from what one would expect. Market cap weighting means that a stock's weighting in an index is based on the total market cap of the individual stock as a percent of the total market cap of all the stocks contained in the index. For example, as I wrote this, the two largest stocks in the S&P 500 Index, GE and Microsoft, made up about ten percent of the entire index. An examination of the 1999 CRSP data reveals that a total market portfolio (CRSP deciles one through ten) had a weighting of ninety-four percent large cap (deciles one through five by market cap) and a weighting of just eight percent of value (deciles eight through ten by BtM). Almost seventy percent of the portfolio is large-cap growth stocks (deciles one through five by size and one through three by BtM). Again, a total market fund is not inherently bad. It is not, however, a well-diversified portfolio in terms of asset class diversification. You should only want to own a total market fund if that is the asset allocation (mostly large-cap growth) you seek.

You should understand that there is no correct asset allocation. You should determine the amount of exposure that you want to each of the five major U.S. asset classes (large, large value, small,

small value, and real estate), and then construct a portfolio based on that allocation. Having said that, as a general rule, broader diversification than is achieved by owning only an S&P 500 or Total Stock Market fund is the more prudent strategy. There are two main reasons.

The first argument in favor of broader diversification is that the S&P 500 is a highly concentrated large growth fund, and even a TSM fund is dominated by the large growth asset class (about seventy percent). There have been very long periods when any one asset class has produced very low returns. For example, for the twenty-five-year period 1966–90 while riskless one-month bank CDs were returning 8.3% per annum, the asset class of large growth returned just 8.2%. For that full twenty-five-year period, risk and reward were not related in that the risk of underperformance did manifest itself in terms of poor returns. The (ex-post) results were much worse than the (ex-ante) expected returns. That twenty-five-year period might have been an individual's entire investment horizon. During that same time period, small and large value stocks returned 15.2% and 12.6%, respectively, and smallcaps, as represented by the asset class of CRSP deciles six through ten (smallest half) returned 11.2%. In my opinion, the risk of that type of performance occurring in any asset class is reason enough to create a more diversified portfolio. Therefore, you should avoid having too many eggs in one basket, or asset class, even if that basket holds five hundred or even five thousand stocks.

The second reason for broad asset class diversification is that financial history provides us with substantial evidence that markets are not always totally rational—bubbles do occur from time to time. This can happen in any asset class. With a portfolio that consists of only an S&P 500 or a TSM fund, you run the risk that a bubble occurs in the asset class in which you have all, or the vast majority, of your eggs. Thus, you should consider building a diversified portfolio that is more diversified by asset class than is a TSM fund. As a starting point, you might consider what has become known as the "coward's portfolio." It is known as the "coward's" portfolio because it owns equal percentages of the five major asset classes—a five by twenty portfolio, five asset classes, twenty percent each—not placing any "bets" on any one asset class. The use of the term "coward" is not to be taken in any way as a pejorative one. More conservative investors might want to tilt the portfolio more toward large-cap growth stocks, and very aggressive investors might want to tilt more toward riskier small and value stocks. One other point: You should only own real estate in a tax-deferred account due to its poor tax efficiency. If you cannot own real estate in a tax-deferred account then you should restrict your diversification to a four by twenty-five portfolio.

The strategy of diversification should also be implemented in the international portion of a portfolio. International assets provide diversification benefits to an all-domestic portfolio. Many investors use an EAFE Index fund to accomplish this objective. However, the EAFE Index fund is similar to an S&P 500 Index fund in that it is essentially a large-cap growth fund. To achieve more effective diversification, you should consider including in your portfolio funds that cover the asset classes of international large value, international small, international small value, and emerging markets.

MISTAKE 48

◆

Do You Consider Your Home as Your Exposure to Real Estate?

Diversification across asset classes is an important component of any investment plan. Put simply, diversification reduces risk by not putting all your eggs in one basket. It is also important to diversify across asset classes that have low correlation. Real estate is an asset class that not only has its own risk and reward characteristics but also has a relatively low correlation with other U.S. equity asset classes. It is therefore a good diversifier of risk and should be considered when constructing an asset allocation plan. A problem arises, however, when investors consider their own home as their real estate allocation.

A home is clearly real estate. However, it is very undiversified real estate. First, it is undiversified by type. There are many types of real estate: office, warehouse, industrial, multifamily residential, hotel, and so on. Owning a home gives an investor exposure to just the residential component of the larger asset class of real estate. Even then, by excluding multifamily residences, it is only exposure to the single-family component.

A second problem is that a home is undiversified geographically. Home prices might be rising in one part of the country and falling in another.

A third problem is that home prices may be more related to exposure to an industry than to real estate in general. For example, in the 1980s home prices in Texas, and in oil-producing regions in general, collapsed when oil prices collapsed. In the late

1990s, home prices in Silicon Valley skyrocketed, riding the technology boom (and, of course, the rise in home prices could reverse now that the boom has turned into a bust). Homes in other areas of the same state experienced a totally different pricing environment. This creates another problem in that often your employment prospects are highly correlated with the value of your home. This problem would be further compounded if your investment portfolio were loaded with assets with exposure to the same industry to which your home is exposed. This is often true of executives who own stock in their company and/or have stock options. It is also true of employees who invest in their employer's stock through retirement plans. The following situation is a good example of the problem.

Seattle used to be considered a one-company (Boeing) town. A senior executive at Boeing owns an expensive home in Seattle. She has the vast percentage of her financial assets invested in Boeing stock. She contributes to Boeing's retirement plan, purchasing more Boeing stock, and also has stock options. She thought she had some diversification of assets because her home was considered real estate exposure—not Seattle, nor Boeing, nor airline, nor even oil price exposure. There were several periods when Boeing was impacted by a recession in the airline industry. The company's stock, reflecting those troubles, fell sharply. Strike one for our investor. Boeing reacted by laying off employees, including our investor. Strike two. With unemployment rising, Seattle home prices collapsed. Strike three for our unlucky investor. The problem was that all of the risks—employment, equity, home—to which our investor was exposed were highly correlated.

The bottom line is that owning a home and considering it exposure to real estate is like being a senior executive with lots of stock and options in Microsoft and thinking you have exposure to large growth stocks. The correlation of any one stock to the overall asset class of equities, or large growth stocks, might turn out to be very low. Stocks might be up overall, but your stock might be down. Similarly, real estate might be up, but the price of your home might be down. Therefore, as a general rule, you should not consider your home as your exposure to real estate. About the only real protection a home provides is against inflation in construction costs. And since in many parts of the country land is by far a more important component of home prices than the cost of construction, it may not be much protection at all (besides providing a roof protecting your head).

Let's now turn to how a home is financed. If a home is financed with a fixed-rate mortgage, that mortgage effectively is a short (negative) bond position and should be considered so when looking at your overall portfolio. The fixed rate on the mortgage does provide inflation protection. A fixed-rate mortgage also has a "put" feature. If interest rates decline, the put (putting the mortgage back to the lender by paying it off) allows the borrower to refinance the mortgage at the then current rate. This provides protection against falling interest rates (for those on fixed incomes) and deflation. If a home were financed with an adjustable rate mortgage, the risk picture would be considerably different, as the rate on the mortgage would move up or down as interest rates changed. Therefore, it is very important that you consider how a home is financed in developing an asset allocation strategy.

The best way to gain exposure to the broad equity real estate asset class is to own an index or passively managed REIT (Real Estate Investment Trust) fund that invests in all equity REITs. For the period 1975–2000 REITs provided a rate of return of 16.5%. This compares to a return of 16.1% for the S&P 500 Index. It is also worth noting that in 1977 when the S&P 500

Index was down 7.2%, REITs were up 18.0%. In 1981, the next year of negative performance by the S&P 500 Index (it fell by 4.9%), REITs were up 6.1%. In 1984 and 1992, when the S&P 500 Index rose just 6.3% and 7.7%, REITs returned 21.8% and 28.3%. Of course, there are also periods when the S&P 500 Index outperformed REITs. For example, from 1998 to 1999 the S&P 500 Index outperformed REITs by 24.7% per annum to −8.9% per annum. And, finally, in 2000 REITs outperformed the S&P 500 by 28.4% to −9.1%.* The combination of the lack of predictability of returns, the low correlation, and their inflation hedge makes a strong case for including REITs as an asset class in an investment portfolio.

MISTAKE 49

◆

Do You Use Long-Term Bonds or Bond Funds for Your Fixed Income Allocation?

Many investors utilize long-term bonds or bond funds rather than short-term fixed-income assets, or inflation protected securities, for the fixed income portion of their portfolio. To understand why this is a mistake we need to examine the role that fixed-income assets play in a portfolio. Are fixed-income assets expected to generate income that is needed to meet living expenses? Or, are fixed-income assets being used to reduce the risks of an equity portfolio? For the vast majority of investors

---

*The return represents the return of the Dimensional Fund Advisors' REIT fund, a passively managed fund that owns all equity REITs.

(with the exception of retired individuals), the overriding motivation for including fixed-income assets is risk reduction. Assuming that current income is not the primary reason for holding fixed-income assets, we can determine the strategy that is most likely to produce the desired results.

We begin with the following facts:

- Academic research has determined that fixed-income markets are just as efficient as, and possibly even more so than, the equity markets. Far fewer fixed-income fund managers have demonstrated the ability to outperform the market (by guessing the direction of interest rates) than would be randomly expected. In fact, a comprehensive study on bond mutual funds found that they underperformed their benchmark index by 0.85% per annum.[1] Furthermore, a Vanguard study found that the performance of bond funds was correlated with only one thing: expenses. The lower the expenses, the higher the returns. Managers were unable to add value by guessing the direction of interest rates.[2] Bond fund managers charge Georgia O'Keeffe prices and deliver paint-by-numbers results. The obvious conclusion: If you are going to use a mutual fund for fixed-income investing, buy the one that matches the risk (credit and maturity) profile you seek and has the lowest expenses for that category.

- Academic research has determined that over long periods of time, although investors are compensated for accepting the risk of owning longer maturity fixed-income assets, this relationship breaks down beyond two to three years. Therefore, if a fixed income investor is seeking the highest expected return over a thirty-year period, he or she should buy a two- to three-year note and continually roll it over (instead of buying a thirty-year bond).[3]

Research on the relationship between risk and return has shown that, for the period 1964–2000:

- Holding one-month short-term U.S. Treasury bills provides what is considered a risk-free rate of return (historically about 6.5%) and has a standard deviation of just over one percent per annum.

- Extending the maturity to one year increases returns above the risk-free rate by about one percent while increasing the standard deviation to about two percent.

- Extending the maturity to five years adds only another 0.3% (total premium above the risk-free rate of about 1.3%) to returns, yet the standard deviation more than *triples*, to 6.4%. Extending the maturity to twenty years causes returns to *fall* almost 0.5% (total premium above the risk-free rate of about 0.8%), yet the standard deviation almost *doubles* again, to 11.2%.[4]

There is another reason not to hold long-term fixed-income instruments. As we saw earlier, the main reason for holding fixed-income assets is to provide a safety net to anchor your portfolio during bear markets. The more stable fixed-income part of your portfolio allows you to stay disciplined. Unfortunately, long-term bonds can have high correlation with the equity portion of your portfolio at just the wrong time. There may be moments when interest rates rise, bond prices fall, and the stock market falls all at the same time. Just when you need low correlation, you may get high correlation. The following table shows the correlations between government instruments of various maturities and the S&P 500 and EAFE indices.[5] Note that the lower the correlation, the more effective the diversification, and the lower the overall risk of the portfolio. Note also the low correlation between short-term maturities and both U.S. and international equities.

Quarterly Correlation Data

Maturity	Correlation with S&P 500 Index 1964–2000	Correlation with EAFE Index 1969–2000
One month	−0.09	−0.16
Six months	0.01	−0.05
One year	−0.07	−0.23
Five years	0.27	0.20
Twenty years	0.33	0.24

As these figures demonstrate, the risk of having high correlation between equities and fixed-income instruments can be avoided by buying short-term fixed-income instruments; they have essentially no correlation with equities.

Armed with the preceding information, we can now determine the winning strategy for the fixed-income portion of our portfolio. For the vast majority of investors using fixed-income assets to reduce the risk of an equity portfolio, the winning strategy seems obvious: Own only very short-term fixed-income assets (or inflation protected securities). Here's why.

Since the main purpose of fixed-income assets is to reduce the volatility of the overall portfolio, investors should include fixed-income assets that have low volatility. Short-term fixed-income assets have both low volatility and low correlation with the equity portion of the portfolio. By limiting the maturity of the fixed-income portion of the portfolio to just one year, we get most of the yield benefit and accept only moderate risk (a standard deviation of only two percent). The combined benefit of lower volatility of the asset class itself, and the reduced volatility of the overall portfolio, seems a well worth the price paid for giving up the extra 0.3% that could be gained by extending the maturity of the fixed-income assets to five years. Remember, in a 60% equity/40% fixed-income portfolio, that extra 0.3% becomes only a 0.12% (0.3% × 40%) added return on the overall portfolio.

We can further improve on this scenario by including international short-term fixed-income assets within the fixed-income allocation, as long as these assets are fully hedged against currency risk. The reason is that their inclusion should further reduce volatility, since not all international fixed-income markets fluctuate in the same direction at the same time and/or by the same amount. The lack of perfect correlation will reduce the overall volatility of the fixed-income portion of the portfolio.

These conclusions are supported by studies that have demonstrated that portfolios that are 60% S&P 500 Index/40% Lehman Bond Index have historically provided lower returns, with the same degree of risk, than 70% S&P 500 Index/30% cash portfolios. Moving the bond portion of the portfolio to cash may have reduced the portfolio's return. However, this was more than offset by the higher returns provided by the ten percent greater equity allocation. In addition, the reduced volatility of the cash position itself (as compared to the volatility of previously held bonds) served to offset the risk incurred by raising the equity allocation ten percent.

We can now explore other reasons why long-term bond funds should not be the investment vehicle of choice for fixed-income investors.

A primary reason to exclude bond funds is they have no effective maturity. If you buy a bond fund that has an average maturity of twenty years, it will probably always have a maturity of about that level. If you happen to buy a bond fund and interest rates go up, you may never recoup the loss of principal, because the bond fund never matures. If, however, you buy an individual bond, in order to recoup your principal, you need only wait for the bond to mature. With very short-term fixed-income funds, the standard deviation is very low, which limits risk. In addition, individual issues within a short-term fund are rolling over so quickly to current rates that risk is further reduced.

Another reason to exclude bond funds is that it is very hard to see how they can add value if they cannot correctly forecast interest rates—and there is no evidence this can be done. You certainly don't need to pay a bond fund a 0.5% fee or more simply to buy government bonds. Individuals can buy these directly from the government or very cost effectively from a discount broker. And since there is no credit risk in owning government bonds, there is no benefit to diversifying credit risk across various issues. Just buy the bond that matches the maturity you seek. If you seek higher yields available from corporate bonds, there is plenty of good public information available on credit quality by rating agencies such as Moody's and S&P. You don't need to pay a fund to get that information. Once you determine the amount of credit and maturity risk you are willing to accept, you can buy the appropriate bonds directly from a discount broker. It is also worth noting that the extra yield you are likely to gain by buying a corporate bond fund, instead of individual government bonds, is likely to be offset by the fund's expenses. Any extra yield probably is not worth the credit risk accepted.

The evidence seems to present a compelling case that today's investors have far too great an allocation of long-term bonds in their portfolios. You would likely benefit from reducing or eliminating your allocations to long-term fixed-income assets and replacing them with short-term fixed-income assets, or the new inflation-protected securities known as TIPS and I-Bonds. They provide stability and low correlation, and they protect you against inflation, which long-term bonds do not.

MISTAKE 50

◆

Do You Purchase Products Meant to Be Sold, Not Bought?

Recent tax law changes, including the lowering of capital gains tax rates, should have wiped out sales of variable annuities (VAs). Unfortunately for investors, however, they are still being aggressively and successfully marketed. The reason: Investors are not fully informed and they are being exploited by aggressive salespeople whose only interest is in collecting the large commissions these products offer.

A VA is a mutual fund-type account wrapped inside an insurance policy. The insurance component allows the investment earnings to be tax-deferred. Unfortunately, the tax deferral is just about the only good thing you can say about these investment products. Virtually everything else about them is not only bad, it is really bad. The negatives include:

- The generally high cost of the insurance wrapper.
- The high operating expenses of the investment account component.
- The lack of passive, low-cost investment choices inside most annuity wrappers.
- The lack of liquidity.
- The loss of the potential for a step-up in basis for the estate of the investor (when a holding's cost basis becomes the current market value rather than the original purchase price,

typically resulting in much lower capital gains taxes when the holding is eventually sold by the beneficiary).

- Perhaps worst of all, the annuity converts low-taxed capital gains into highly taxed ordinary income.

What is perhaps the most amazing fact about annuities is how many are sold to people holding them inside an account that is already tax-deferred. Since the only real benefit of this high-cost product is the tax efficiency, selling this product to an investor to hold inside an account that is already tax-deferred borders on the criminal.

The bottom line is that the tax deferral comes at a very high price. The 1997 Tax Act cut capital gains tax rates while leaving ordinary income tax rates high. Thus, the benefit of wrapping an annuity around your equity portfolio virtually vanished for almost all asset classes. As a Forbes column stated: "That should have stopped annuity sales cold."[1] And if that didn't do the trick, the recent introduction of tax-managed mutual funds by such fund families as DFA and Vanguard should have. Tax-managed funds take the tax efficiency benefit of passive investing to an even higher level. These new funds have basically eliminated any financial argument for purchasing a VA and using it as a vehicle for equity investing. (The one exception to this would be the asset class of real estate. Because of the requirement that REITs have to distribute virtually all of their income, real estate is a very tax inefficient asset class. Of course, most investors don't need an annuity; they can simply hold their real estate assets inside an IRA, SEP, or tax-deferred plan.) Unfortunately for investors, because of the self-interest of salespeople, there does not appear to be any slowdown in annuity sales. In fact, they continue strong. According to Michael Lane, former President of Advisor Resources for AEGON Financial Services, they exceeded $20 billion in 1999, and likely did so again in 2000.

Let's take a quick look at the insurance "benefit" these products tout. The insurance typically guarantees that when you die, the value of your account will be at least as great as the money you originally put in—unless you get a contract that steps up the insurance coverage over time, all you are insured for is the starting value. If the account has indeed grown, you still get only the value of the account. What is the economic value of that life insurance? It is safe to say that with the vast majority of annuities sold today, almost all the money you are assessed for "mortality and expenses" winds up in either the salesperson's or the insurance company's pocket. Even if you get a periodic step-up in protection, the economic value of the insurance is negligible.

Put simply, annuities are costly to own. Expenses—portfolio management fees, plus that "mortality" charge—average in excess of two percent a year, but can range as high as three percent, or more. Surrender charges are common, starting out typically at seven percent and reaching as high as nine percent if you cash out in the first year, and declining to zero in the seventh year or even as long as the tenth year. Also, if you cash out before you reach the age of fifty-nine and a half, you have to pay a tax penalty, except under certain narrow circumstances.

Consider the experience that the no-load fund giant T. Rowe Price had when it sent potential customers software to help them determine whether VAs were right for them.[2] The program factored in the investor's age, income, tax bracket, and investment horizon—and it regularly told potential buyers that they would be better off in a plain old fund, let alone a low-cost, tax-efficient, passively and tax-managed fund. An educated consumer, as it turned out, was not a good prospect for annuities.

There are a handful of exceptions to the high-cost rule, which include AEGON, Schwab, TIAA-CREF, and Vanguard. They are mostly sold to people with existing VAs through "section 1035" *tax-free* exchanges. Existing holders of VAs are looking to escape from their current high costs and poor investment choices. Unfortunately, the surrender charges often keep investors trapped for an extended period. The analysis to find out when and if a 1035 exchange makes sense is fairly straightforward. Your financial advisor/accountant can help you with the calculation.

If the terms of VAs are so bad, why do so many people buy them? The answer is that the tax-deferral sales pitch mesmerizes them. Fortunately, the tax deferral comes much cheaper and more effectively through low-cost, tax efficient mutual funds that are both passively and tax-managed. A tax-managed mutual fund has another advantage over the supposedly tax-favored annuity. With mutual funds, you may escape the capital gains tax altogether by either giving the fund shares to charity or leaving them in your estate (where you receive a step-up in basis upon death as previously described). No such option is available to an annuity holder. Transfer or bequeath an annuity to anyone but your spouse and you trigger recognition of the full appreciation as income. (Note that recently enacted changes in the new tax law regarding inheritance may affect the conclusions drawn here, as might future changes.)

About the only legitimate remaining use of a VA is for creditor protection. Many states, among them, New York, Florida, and Texas, protect assets in VAs from creditors to one degree or another. The laws, however, are complex. Therefore, before you purchase (or get talked into) an annuity for this specific purpose, you should consult your attorney. Doctors worried about malpractice suits, for example, might want to consider VAs. If this is the case, then you shouldn't pay a penny more than you have to in expenses.

Given that there are an estimated $1 trillion of annuities outstanding, there are lots of opportunities to lower expenses and improve investment returns. If you are currently holding a high-cost annuity, you should check out one of the low-cost, no-surrender-charge annuities. If the applicable surrender charge period is over, or even nearly over, the decision to make the tax-free "section 1035" exchange will be easy. Section 1035 of the tax code allows investors to swap one similar annuity for another without triggering a tax, as would be the case if an investor sold one annuity and then bought another. Whatever you do, do not succumb to the sales pitch for the new "bonus" annuities. This is a new and aggressive tactic of the industry, to keep investors imprisoned in high-cost product, and generate new and even larger commissions for the sales force. Annuity holders with a few years left in their surrender charge period are approached with the following "typical" story.

> I understand that you are unhappy with your current VA because of poor performance of the investment choices. I also understand that you have a three percent surrender charge left. We are going to "help" by giving you an up-front "bonus" of three percent to cover the surrender charge. It will not cost you anything to switch.

Unfortunately, the only "bonus" is to the salesperson. The new sale starts the surrender period all over again, and the surrender period of the new product is often even longer and more expensive than on the original annuity. The surrender charge period may now be extended to as many as ten years, and the prepayment penalty increased from 7% to as much as 9%. Given that the annuity holder will now be locked into another high-cost (or even higher cost) product for a much longer time, you might ask: Where's the bonus? It is likely to be in the form of higher commissions to the sales force. It appears that the SEC is coming down hard on this practice. On June 5, 2000 the commission issued an "investor alert" and placed a brochure on its Web site to help investors understand the benefits, costs, and risks of variable annuities, which combine features of mutual funds and insurance.[3] You should also be aware that the insurance industry has already been hit with a round of lawsuits on suitability of annuity sales and turnover. Maybe the real bonus in bonus annuities will be new business for the trial lawyers.

MISTAKE 51

◆

Do You Chase the IPO Dream?

One of the more costly mistakes investors make is to buy initial public offerings (IPOs). Like the variable annuities just discussed, IPOs are products meant to be sold, not bought. Wall Street loves IPOs because they generate great fee income. Desperately searching for the next Microsoft, AOL, or Cisco, investors seem to buy IPOs with the same frenzy with which they buy lottery tickets. Unfortunately, all too often they end up with the next E-Loan, Priceline, or mortgage.com. Let's look at the reality of actual performance.

A study covering the period 1970–90 examined the returns from a strategy of buying every IPO at the end of the first day's closing price and then holding each investment for five years. The average return provided by this strategy was just five percent per annum; it was also seven percent per annum *less* than a benchmark of companies of similar market capitalization.[1]

University of Florida finance professor Jay Ritter looked at 1,006 IPOs that raised at least $20 million from 1988 to 1993. He found that the median IPO underperformed the Russell 3000 by thirty percent in the three years after going public. He also found that forty-six percent of IPOs produced negative returns.[2]

Another study examining the performance of IPOs issued in 1993, and how they performed through the period of mid-October 1998, found that the average IPO had returned just one third as much as the S&P 500 Index. Amazingly, over one half were trading below their offering price, and one third were down over fifty percent![3]

A U.S. Bancorp Piper Jaffray study covering the period May 1988–July 1998 and 4,900 IPOs found that by July 1998, less than one third of new issues were above their IPO price. In addition, almost a third weren't even trading any longer (having gone bankrupt, been acquired, or no longer trading in an active market).[4]

A study covering the period 1988–95 and 1,232 IPOs found very similarly disappointing results, with twenty-five percent of all offerings actually closing the first day of trading below their offering price.[5] This study also found that the IPOs defined as "extra hot," meaning they rose sixty percent or more on the first day of trading, were the very worst performers going forward—over the next year they underperformed the market by two to three percent *per month*.[6]

The year 1999 was a spectacular one for IPOs, with 555 companies raising a record $73.6 billion. The amount raised surpassed the previous record, set in 1996, by almost fifty percent. For all IPOs the median first day performance was thirty percent. However, as a *BusinessWeek* article noted, "investors who bought at the first day's closing price didn't do nearly as well. For all IPOs, the median increase three months after day one was zero, which means that half of all issues lost money."[7] Even more amazing, nearly three quarters of all U.S. Internet-related IPOs since mid-1995 were trading below their offering price at the beginning of 2000.[8] The first quarter of 2000 was not much better. According to Thompson Securities Data Company, the 146 companies that went public experienced an average first-day rise of an incredible ninety-eight percent. By April 6, 2000, almost ninety percent were trading below their opening day's closing price, and almost thirty percent were trading below their IPO price.[9]

The persistent underperformance of IPOs continued throughout 2000. One study examined the performance of IPOs brought to market by four of the largest investment banking firms: Goldman Sachs; Credit Suisse First Boston; Merrill Lynch; and Morgan Stanley Dean Witter.[10] The following table compares the companies' closing price on August 24, 2000, with the closing prices on the first day of trading.

Firm	Number of Deals	Average Post-IPO Performance (%)
Goldman Sachs	54	+0.9
Credit Suisse First Boston	50	−2.3
Merrill Lynch	27	−10.5
Morgan Stanley Dean Witter	34	−14.7

Another study looked at the performance of the dot.com IPOs. The study examined the performance of 170 dot-com IPOs brought to market by eight of Wall Street's largest investment banking firms, beginning in 1996. For institutional investors, these dot.com stocks were trading on average at a sixty-eight percent premium to their IPO price. However, these same IPOs proved to be sucker's bets for retail investors as they were trading at a twenty-three percent discount to the first day's closing price.[11] By March 2001, of all the 1999 and 2000 Internet IPOs only seven percent were trading above their IPO price.[12]

Whereas 2000 was a great year for the Wall Street investment banks as they raised a record $97.9 billion from 443 IPOs, it did not prove as rewarding for investors.[13] In 1999, the average IPO experienced a first-day price rise of 122%. In 2000, the average first-day rise was 13.8%. Far more important, sixty-four percent of all the IPOs issued in 2000 closed the year below their IPO price. In addition, the average IPO ended the year down nineteen percent from its IPO price.[14] By comparison the S&P 500 only fell about nine percent. Another great year for the investment bankers who earned their fees from the offerings, possibly a great year for the institutional investors who receive the vast majority of the IPO (and often quickly flip their shares to the retail public), and another poor year for the general public. As a further example, of the 268 IPOs issued during the "six-month IPO bonanza" from October 1999 to March 2000, by March 2001 almost eighty percent were trading below their IPO price.[15] And, finally during the most hectic six-week period for IPOs in history, from January 31, 2000, through March 10, 2000, the date the NASDAQ market peaked in value, a total of seventy-seven companies went public. Almost half of them doubled or better by the close of the first day of trading, and nearly a quarter tripled in value. On average, one year later, stocks that quadrupled the first day they traded had fallen ninety-one percent; stocks that tripled had lost eighty-seven percent; those that doubled were down eighty-three percent; and those that did not even double were down *just* sixty-six percent. Only three of the companies were selling at more than they sold for on the first day of trading, and only four were valued above their offering prices.[16]

Here is one more bit of anecdotal evidence against the wisdom of investing in IPOs, unless you are lucky enough to get them at the pre-opening price. The academic studies usually measure returns on an investable strategy. They therefore typically use the price at the close of the first day of trading. Unfortunately, many investors may not be so lucky to buy at the close. Let's look at the case of one of the reddest hot of all IPOs. VA Linux Systems set a new record for the single greatest one-day appreciation for an IPO with its offering on December 9, 1999. The headline of the following day's *Wall Street Journal* screamed: "VA Linux Registers Pop." The IPO price was 30 and the stock closed at 239.25, a pop of almost 700%. However, the stock opened at 299 and rose to 320, before falling about 81 points to its final closing price. Trading volume was an enormous 7.6 million shares, especially considering that the total outstanding shares were 4.4 million. It is obvious that there was a great deal of money lost by investors who bought the stock after the initial offering. The one-day loss for a buyer at the opening price was twenty percent, and the loss grew to forty percent after just five days of trading. The *Journal*, however, focused on the gains from the IPO price, not the huge losses experienced by most retail investors.[17]

Another amusing tale about the VA Linux offering: One of my co-workers, Vladimir Masek, received a cold call from a broker at Edward Jones. The broker offered him the "opportunity" to get in at 280, on the first day of trading. Vladimir asked him, "Who is VA Linux?" The broker replied that they were a wonderful new company with an operating system that would put Microsoft out of business, etc. Vladimir then told the broker that he knew very well what Linux is. In fact, he was probably one of the first one hundred or so people in this country ever to install the system on his computer and play with it. Yet he had never heard of VA Linux. The broker had absolutely no idea that Linux is freely distributable, is a wonderful technology, and is good for users, but that there did not appear to be any way for VA Linux to profit from the technology. The broker never called Vladimir again.

You might believe that you can increase the odds of finding the winning IPOs by purchasing only the IPOs of companies that had received early funding from big-name venture capital funds. Obviously, these are highly sophisticated investment firms, which had performed thorough due diligence on their investments before proceeding. Let's look at the results of such a strategy. The following table shows the returns of IPOs launched between January 1, 1999, and June 30, 2000. The returns are market cap weighted returns through November 8, 2000.

Venture Capital Firm	Number of Deals	Average Return Since First Day of Trading (%)
Bay Partners	6	170
Lightspeed	13	128
Crosspoint Ventures	12	37
Kleiner Perkins	23	32
Mayfield	13	−15
Accel Partners	16	−27
CMGI@ Ventures	5	−51
Sequoia Capital	23	−52
Softbank	17	−67
Vulcan Ventures	23	−73
Hummer Winblad	6	−88
Idealab!	7	−91

If we averaged the return figures from the twelve firms, the average would be a negative eight percent. In addition, only four of the twelve firms had IPOs that they had backed show positive returns.[18]

In the face of this poor performance, why do investors continue to chase the latest IPO? There are two explanations for this seemingly irrational behavior. First, unless an investor happens to read scholarly publications such as the *Journal of Finance*, he or she is unlikely to be aware of the facts. Second, even when informed, investors often act in what appear to be irrational ways. In this case, it is another example of *the triumph of hope over experience*. Investors seem to be willing to accept the high probability of low returns in exchange for the small chance of a home run or, possibly even more important, a great story to tell at the next cocktail party.

There is an old saying in sports that sometimes the best trades are the ones you don't make. You can avoid the mistake of investing in IPOs by remembering that while IPOs have provided huge profits for the Wall Street firms that market them, they have generated very poor returns for investors. IPOs are investments best avoided. Yes, it is possible that by investing in an IPO you might be buying the next Microsoft, but it is far more likely that you will end up owning an asset that delivers poor returns.

MISTAKE 52

◆

Is Your Withdrawal Assumption Rate in Retirement Too Aggressive?

Unfortunately, this is not only a very common mistake, but one with the potential for a devastating impact: running out of assets to support your expected lifestyle. Let's see why this is true.

From an investment perspective, the key question when approaching retirement is: What should my portfolio value be in order to provide a high level of confidence that the assets will not be exhausted during my life? A retiree must address the following issues:

- What is my (and my spouse's, if any) life expectancy?
- What will be the level of inflation?

- What will be the portfolio's investment returns?

- What pretax dollars do I want to be able to withdraw to maintain my desired lifestyle?

Time, inflation, and expected returns take on greater significance in retirement. During your working life, a few bad years of high inflation or negative investment returns can be overcome. You can add savings or work longer to make up for any portfolio shortfall. In retirement, however, money is being withdrawn all the time, both in good and bad years.

Let's first address the issue of life expectancy. Most individuals underestimate their life expectancy. For example, the average couple, when both individuals are sixty-five, has a second-to-die life expectancy of well over twenty years. In addition, when determining how long you'll need your assets to last in retirement, you should not simply take average life expectancies as your guide. An average results in approximately a fifty percent chance of living longer. The table below, a safer benchmark, is based on a probability of only a twenty percent chance of outliving the expected time frame. For example, a sixty-year-old male has only a twenty percent chance of living beyond twenty-seven more years.

Investment Horizon to Plan on When Developing a Retirement Plan

At Age	Female	Male
55	36	32
60	31	27
65	27	22
70	22	18

Source: National Center for Health Statistics

269

Note that a married couple's second-to-die life expectancy is greater than the longer of the two individual life expectancies.

Turning to the issue of investment returns and inflation, a common investor mistake is the singular use of averages when projecting returns. A useful analogy is the case of a man drowning in a lake that has an average depth of six inches. The man didn't realize that he jumped into the part of the lake that was ten feet deep. Investors planning retirement need to be sure they don't unexpectedly drown in the deep part of the lake. Let's see how that might happen.

For the period 1926–97, a portfolio consisting of 75% S&P 500 Index and 25% U.S. government bonds returned an average of ten percent. During the same time period, the inflation rate was three percent. Therefore, the real (inflation adjusted) rate of return for this 75/25 portfolio was seven percent. You might conclude that you could withdraw $70,000 per year from a $1 million portfolio and maintain the same real income in the long term, increasing the $70,000 by the future rate of inflation. The problem with this approach is that inflation rates and investment returns vary each year, and using averages may cause unexpected and unpleasant surprises. If you retire before the start of a bull market, it is likely that you could withdraw seven percent per year and maintain a portfolio in excess of $1 million. Retiring at the beginning of a bear market, however, can produce very different results. For example, had you retired in 1972 and withdrawn seven percent of your original principal every year, you would have run out of funds within ten years, by the end of 1982! This is because the S&P 500 Index declined by approximately forty percent in the 1973–74 bear market.

Systematic withdrawals during bear markets exacerbate the effects of the market's decline, causing portfolio values to fall to levels from which they may never recover. For instance, if an investor withdraws seven percent in a year when the portfolio declines by twenty percent, the result is a decline in the portfolio of twenty-seven percent in that year. A thirty-seven percent increase is now required in the next year just to get even, plus another seven percent for the annual withdrawal (a total of forty-four percent) to make up for the prior year's decline.

Given the possibility of a market decline occurring at the very early stages of retirement, investors need to determine how much money they can withdraw annually and still have only a minimal risk that they might outlive their assets. On the basis of historical evidence, investors with a thirty-year or longer investment horizon should not withdraw more than four percent of the starting value of a portfolio. This amount can be increased every year by the previous year's inflation rate, thereby maintaining the same level of real purchasing power. With at least a fifty percent allocation to equities, the historical evidence suggests that you will have less than a five percent chance of outliving your assets with this strategy. Note that even a seventy-five-year-old investor has an investment horizon of about fifteen years. At fifteen years the maximum suggested withdrawal rate is still just six percent.

Using a four percent withdrawal rate, it is easy to calculate the portfolio size needed to feel comfortable about retirement. Investors can estimate the amount of pretax income desired (after subtracting any Social Security and pension income) and then multiply that figure by twenty-five (inverse of four percent). For example, investors needing $50,000 a year in pretax income after taking into account social security (and so on) need to achieve a portfolio of $1,250,000 ($50,000 × 25). Using the six percent withdrawal rate the multiplier would be about seventeen.

You can avoid the mistake of being too aggressive in your assumptions by using the following tables as a guideline. The numbers under the percent withdrawal columns represent the likelihood of not running out of money while you are still alive. The tables are for various investment horizons/life expectancies. As your horizon shortens you can begin to withdraw, with a high degree of safety, slightly larger percentages, but probably far less than most investors would assume.

Odds (%) of Not Running Out of Money (30-Year Time Periods Between 1926 and 1996) Withdrawal % Initial Year*

Asset Allocation	4%	5%	6%	7%
100% stocks	95	85	68	59
75% stocks/25% bonds	98	83	68	49
50% stocks/50% bonds	95	76	51	17
25% stocks/75% bonds	71	27	20	12
100% bonds	20	17	12	0

Odds (%) of Not Running Out of Money (20-Year Time Periods Between 1926 and 1996 Withdrawal % Initial Year*

Asset Allocation	4%	5%	6%	7%
100% stocks	100	88	75	63
75% stocks/25% bonds	100	90	75	61
50% stocks/50% bonds	100	90	75	55
25% stocks/75% bonds	100	82	47	31
100% bonds	90	47	20	14

Odds (%) of Not Running Out of Money (Fifteen-year Time Periods Between 1926 and 1996) Withdrawal % Initial Year*

Asset Allocation	4%	5%	6%	7%
100% stocks	100	100	91	63
75% stocks/25% bonds	100	100	95	82
50% stocks/50% bonds	100	100	93	79
25% stocks/75% bonds	100	100	89	70
100% bonds	100	100	71	39

*Initial dollar amount inflated in subsequent years based on actual inflation to maintain same standard of living.
Source: Study by Phillip L. Cooley, Carl M. Hubbard and Daniel T. Walz, using data from Ibbotson Associates. Stocks are represented by S&P 500 Index and bonds are represented by long-term, high-grade corporates.

These three tables suggest that there is another common error made by investors. As they approach retirement, many investors become too conservative in their equity allocation. There are logical reasons to be more (but not too) conservative. First, your investment horizon has become shorter. Second, your tolerance for risk is lower as your ability to generate earned income is likely to be substantially less or even nonexistent. Third, you may be relying on an old adage which states that your equity allocation should equal no more than one hundred less your age. While this may have been a reasonable guideline fifty years ago, when life expectancies were much shorter, such a formula would now result in an asset allocation with too high a likelihood of failure.

Using the tables above, we can see that in order to have a likelihood of success of ninety percent or greater, an investor with a thirty-year horizon would need to limit withdrawals to just four percent per annum; a twenty-year horizon would require limiting withdrawals to five percent per annum; and a fifteen-year horizon would require limiting withdrawals to six percent per annum. Note that in each case to achieve that ninety percent likelihood of success requires an equity allocation of at least fifty percent or so.

Note also that if you plan on having a higher withdrawal rate, then you really need to have a high allocation to equities to maintain even a reasonable chance of not running out of funds.

Remember that it is wise to plan your retirement with conservative assumptions about the withdrawal percentage while maintaining an equity allocation of at least fifty percent. Very wealthy investors with no need to take risk can use a lower equity allocation.

Conclusion

I have personally tried to invest money, my client's and my own, in every single anomaly and predictive result that academics have dreamed up. And I have yet to make a nickel on any of these supposed market inefficiencies. An inefficiency ought to be an exploitable opportunity. If there's nothing investors can exploit in a systematic way, time in and time out, then it's very hard to say that information is not being properly incorporated into stock prices. Real money investment strategies don't produce the results that academic papers say they should.

—Richard Roll, financial economist and principal of the portfolio management firm, Roll and Ross Asset Management, *Wall Street Journal*, December 28, 2000

As I traipse around the country speaking to investing groups, or just stay in my cage writing my articles, I'm often accused of "disempowering" people because I refuse to give any credence to anyone's hope of beating the market. The knowledge that I don't need to know anything is an incredibly profound form of knowledge. Personally, I think it's the ultimate form of empowerment. You can't tune out the massive industry of investment prediction unless you want to: otherwise, you'll never have the fortitude to stop listening. But if you can plug your ears to every attempt (by anyone) to predict what the markets will do, you will outperform nearly every other investor alive over the long run. Only the mantra of "don't know, and I don't care" will get you there. —Jason Zweig

"This time it's different." Those are the four most dangerous words in the English language for investors. Yes, the world is changing at a very rapid pace, probably faster than ever. Computer technology, the Internet, telecommunications, and biotechnology are all contributing to the incredible pace of change. The investment world is also changing rapidly. Individual investors not only have access to the same timely information as do institutional investors but they now have far more investment options, including such new instruments as ETFs, TIPS, and I-Bonds. The financial world is a far different place than it was just a few years ago. However, none of this in any way changes the basic principles of investing. Passive investors outperform active investors with about the same predictability that one expects from spawning salmon, migrating whales, and the swallows of Capistrano. If you follow the eleven simple steps listed below you will avoid making the mistakes that even smart investors make. As Ted Cadsby stated: "While investors can be irrational, and markets move in exaggerated ways in the short term, a long-term and disciplined approach to investing can overcome both of these problems."[1]

1. Listen carefully to the words of Gary Belsky and Thomas Gilovich:

   - *Any individual who is not professionally occupied in the financial services industry (and even most of those who are) and who in any way attempts to actively manage an investment portfolio is probably suffering from overconfidence. That is, anyone who has confidence enough in his or her abilities and knowledge to invest in a particular stock or bond (or actively managed mutual fund or real estate investment trust or limited partnership) is most likely fooling himself.*

- *Most such people—probably you—have no business at all trying to pick investments, except perhaps as sport. Such people—again, probably you—should probably divide their money among several index funds and turn off CNBC.*[2]

2. Unless it is for entertainment value, turn off CNBC, cancel your subscriptions to financial trade publications, and don't visit Internet chat boards that tout great funds, great stocks, or new and interesting investment strategies. If you need or enjoy the excitement of active investing, set up an entertainment account with five to ten percent of your assets and go ahead and *"play the market."* The odds are you will underperform, but you won't go broke.

3. Determine your unique risk tolerance, need to take risk, investment horizon, and cash flow needs.

4. Build a globally diversified portfolio of passive asset class/index funds and/or ETFs consisting of multiple asset classes. For the equity portion, you should strongly consider including such risky asset classes as small caps, value stocks, real estate, international stocks, and even emerging markets. Too many investors confuse indexing with the exclusive use of an S&P 500 Index fund or a Total Stock Market fund. As Peter Bernstein stated: "If I am going to own an S&P 500 index fund, which I used to think was the answer to all maidens' prayers, I'm buying a very undiversified portfolio in which the greatest weights are the stocks that have gone up the most. Is that really how I want to invest?"[3] Nobel Prize winner William Sharpe agrees with Bernstein. "While its all right to tilt a portfolio in a direction—say, small stocks over large, or growth over value—investors should temper their enthusiasm."[4]

5. Write and sign an IPS. Review it annually to remind your-self why you adopted your strategy and to see if personal circumstances have caused changes to your original assumptions.

6. Using guidelines established in your IPS, regularly rebal-ance your portfolio to its targeted asset allocation. Checking your portfolio on a quarterly basis is more than sufficient. Checking it any more often is only likely to cause you to take actions you would probably be better off not taking.

7. Allocate your most tax efficient asset classes to your tax-able accounts, and your least tax efficient asset classes to your tax-deferred accounts. Whenever possible, use tax-managed funds for taxable accounts.

8. Tax-manage your portfolio throughout the year.

9. Save as much as you can as early as you can.

10. Understand the true cost of major expenditures.

11. Enjoy your life.

By following the advice in this book, you can avoid the invest-ment mistakes that even the smartest people make. Your tuition will have been only the cost of this book. On the other hand, you could choose to play the game of picking stocks, timing the mar-ket, and investing in actively managed funds. If you follow that path, consider the following caution: Every few years the market hands out tuition bills that are much more expensive than the cost of this book. The bursting of the NASDAQ bubble in 2000 was the equivalent of a doctoral degree—and the tuition for doctoral degrees is very expensive.

For those interested in learning more about MPT and the EMT, consider reading my first two books. I hope that the knowledge you gain from them will help you avoid what Richard Thaler cautions us against, and what I will conclude with: "If you are prepared to do something stupid repeatedly, there are many professionals happy to take your money."[5]

Exhibit A: The Risk of Diversification

Investors Confuse Ex Ante Facto Strategy with Ex Post Facto Outcome

Annual Returns (%) 1973–2000

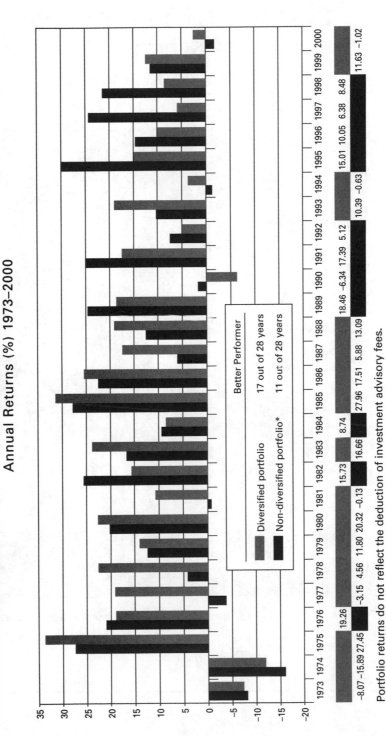

Portfolio returns do not reflect the deduction of investment advisory fees.

Shading indicates the higher returning portfolio *60% S&P 500/4 0% Lehman Govt./Corp. Bond index
Source: Dimensional Fund Advisors, Inc.
Asset class data includes simulated and live returns. For portfolio construction, simulated data is used prior to the inception of the live portfolios. Simulated data does not reflect deductions of fund expenses. Nor do simulated returns represent results of actual trading.

Exhibit B: The Periodic Table of Returns

Can You Pick the Next Winner?

Asset Class Returns 1976–2000

1976	53. 6	51.1	47.7	39.2	23.8	11.5	6.7
1977	74.1	33.2	26.8	21.8	18.0	−2.2	−7.2
1978	65.5	42.2	25.8	21.8	9.4	6.9	6.6
1979	43.2	38.0	33.2	25.9	18.4	4.3	−0.8
1980	41.9	35.5	32.4	29.7	29.1	18.8	18.0
1981	13.5	10.5	9.3	6.1	−2.7	−4.7	−4.9
1982	37.7	28.3	28.0	23.9	21.4	2.5	0.8
1983	44.2	39.7	32.4	31.5	30.9	29.6	22.5
1984	21.8	12.0	10.1	7.6	6.3	5.1	-6.7
1985	67.3	60.1	34.7	32.2	29.9	24.7	11.8
1986	70.2	50.1	24.8	18.5	18.4	16.9	6.9
1987	70.6	31.2	6.7	5.2	−6.1	−6.3	−9.3
1988	33.5	28.8	26.8	26.0	22.9	16.8	14.5
1989	31.5	29.3	25.5	24.7	19.6	10.2	6.7
1990	−3.2	−15.6	−16.0	−16.8	−20.8	−21.6	−22.1
1991	44.6	40.3	39.4	34.4	30.5	12.3	7.1
1992	31.1	28.3	26.3	23.3	7.7	-3.1	−18.4
1993	47.2	33.5	24.7	22.5	21.0	20.3	10.0
1994	12.4	8.8	3.1	3.6	3.4	1.3	−4.5
1995	38.4	37.4	34.5	32.1	12.1	11.5	0.5
1996	33.8	24.5	23.1	20.2	17.6	7.8	2.3
1997	33.4	32.3	28.1	22.8	19.4	−3.1	−25.1
1998	28.6	14.9	12.0	8.0	−5.5	−7.3	−15.4
1999	29.8	21.0	20.2	16.3	14.1	4.8	−2.0
2000	28.4	9.0	−0.2	−3.6	−5.4	−9.3	−14.0

- S&P 500
- US Large Cap Value Stocks Size Deciles 1–5
- US Small Cap Stocks Size Deciles
- US Small Cap Value Stocks Size Deciles 6–10
- US REITS
- International Value Stocks
- International Small Company Stocks

Source: Dimensional Fund Advisors, Inc.

APPENDIX A

♦

Disclaimers It's Likely You'll Never Hear From Mutual Fund Companies

The following suggested disclaimers that follow are ones the SEC should require in the prospectus of any actively managed mutual fund. They might just prevent you from making some of the fifty-two mistakes even smart people make. Although each one might not be appropriate to all actively managed funds, each one is appropriate to some, if not most. Many of the suggestions are based on very specific incidents.

- This fund carries a 12b-1 fee. The fee is compensation to a salesperson. The payment of this fee provides an incentive for a salesperson to recommend this fund over a similar (or even superior) fund that would provide them with less compensation. Although this type of fee structure is not in the investor's best interests, we chose it because we believe it will attract more assets to our fund. There is evidence to suggest that these fees and incentives will increase investor cash inflow to the fund. However, please note that if such an increase did occur, providing the fund with economies of scale, there is no reason for you to expect us to lower our fee, passing on to you those economies of scale. In addition, any such increase in fund assets resulting from the 12b-1 fees is likely to make it more difficult for the fund to outperform its benchmark, not only because of the fee itself but also because our market impact costs will increase.

- This fund is an actively managed fund. Before investing, you should be aware that the historical evidence on the performance of actively managed funds is that they have performed very poorly. While it is true that by investing in this fund you will have a small hope of outperformance, it is far more likely that the fund will underperform its benchmark. Note also that there is a very good reason that the SEC requires that we advise investors that past performance is not an indicator of future performance: there is no evidence of any persistence of fund manager outperformance. You should also note that even for the small number of funds that have managed to outperform their benchmark, the size of the average outperformance has been less than the size of the average underperformance, especially after taxes. Thus, the decision to invest in this fund is similar to the decision to purchase a lottery ticket. You trade off the great likelihood of underperformance for the small hope of large outperformance.

- This fund charges a significantly higher fee than a similar index fund. In addition to this high fee, because the fund is actively managed, it will incur significantly greater trading costs that are not explicitly accounted for. These costs include bid-offer spreads, commissions, and market impact costs. Though you will not receive a bill for these expenses, they do reduce your returns in the same manner as operating expenses. The combination of these expenses creates a very high hurdle for the fund to overcome. In fact, the historical evidence suggests that the odds are very low that the fund will be successful in its efforts. We don't offer index funds because while they are profitable for investors, they are not profitable for us.

- This international fund is actively managed. Our strategy is based on exploiting inefficiencies (mispricings) in foreign markets. However, there is no evidence that foreign markets are any less efficient than U.S. markets. In addition, even if there are inefficiencies in overseas markets, the greater operating expenses make it just as difficult, if not more so, for an actively managed fund to outperform a passive strategy than it does in the U.S. markets. Not only are the costs of the bid-offer spreads greater, but commissions and custodial fees are also greater. In addition, we incur the cost of stamp duties that are not incurred in the United States. Thus, as with domestic actively managed funds, our efforts to outperform the market are not just likely to prove nonproductive. They are likely to prove counterproductive because of the expenses and taxes incurred.

- The high expenses of the fund are not a reflection of our confidence in the fund manager's ability to beat the market. Instead, they are simply a reflection of our view that we can get away with charging such a high expense.

- This fund is managed with total disregard to tax considerations. It is to be expected that the fund will realize and distribute a high portion of its total return in the form of capital gains. These gains are taxable. In addition, a large percentage of the capital gain distributions are likely to be in the form of short-term gains. These gains are taxed at the higher ordinary income tax rates. Once the burden of capital gain taxes is considered, the historical evidence suggests that the fund has an almost insurmountable hurdle in its effort to outperform its benchmark.

- The assets under management of this fund have increased dramatically. You should note that as the assets under management increase, it is less likely that the fund will be able to beat its benchmark. One reason is that as its assets increase, it must become more diversified. As the fund's diversification increases, the fund will look more and more like its benchmark index. The investor is therefore paying large fees for little differentiation from the benchmark. Thus, the fund's costs for the differentiated portion of the portfolio are being spread out over a smaller and smaller percentage of our assets. As the fund grows larger, it will tend to become what is referred to as a "closet" index fund (an actively managed fund whose holdings so closely resemble the holdings of an index fund that investors are unknowingly paying very large fees for minimal differentiation). In addition, the increased assets will lead to increased market impact costs whenever we decide to buy or sell a particular stock. This will also negatively affect our ability to outperform.

- The assets under management of this fund have increased dramatically. The rapid increase has masked our tax inefficiency, as fund distributions have been spread out over a larger shareholder base. Should inflows slow down, or redemptions occur, the fund's tax efficiency is likely to decline sharply. Thus, the past tax efficiency of the fund should not be considered a predictor of future tax efficiency.

- This fund has underperformed its benchmark. While we are disappointed that we have not delivered on our objective, in order to attract better talent we are raising our fees. This will increase the already substantial burden we have in trying to meet our objective of outperformance. There is, of course, no guarantee, or even any evidence to suggest that by raising fees we will be able to increase the likelihood of outperformance.

- The historical performance of our family of funds is misleading for several reasons. First, there is survivorship bias in the data. Several of our funds that experienced poor returns were merged into other funds in order to make their poor performance disappear. The poor performance of those funds is not reflected in the returns of the merged fund. However, investors did actually experience those poor returns; we just don't report them any longer. The result is that the returns to investors in our family of funds are over-stated. Second, we employ the strategy of incubating funds. We seed several new funds with very small amounts of our own capital. We know that some will do poorly. However, the SEC allows us to send them to the mutual fund grave-yard. No tombstone will ever appear showing the evidence of their poor performance. While the poor returns will mag-ically disappear, we will bring to life the one good per-former and market its great investment performance. Thus, the historical performance of the funds that we promote in our advertisements is not a reflection of the actual returns that were and/or could have been earned by investors.

- This fund has a large amount of unrealized capital gains. The management has become concerned that those unreal-ized gains are scaring away potential new investors. In order to solve this problem and attract new investors, we are con-sidering realizing those gains. The fund will sell the stocks in which it has large unrealized gains and immediately buy them back. We recognize that existing shareholders will then have to pay taxes on the required distribution. We also recognize that the fund will incur unnecessary transactions costs as it realizes the gains and repurchases the same secu-rities. Despite the obvious conflict of interest, we retain the right to take such action.

In case you think that this last item is such a blatant case of abuse of shareholders that it could not happen, think again. It is exactly what happened to shareholders in the Stagecoach Strategic Growth Fund. In late 1997, the fund made a capital gain distribution of twenty-seven percent of assets. This large distribution was made despite the fund returning just 7.7% for the year, dramatically underperforming both the market and the average mutual fund. The fund's management cited as the main reason for the unusually large distribution the concern that a large unrealized gain was scaring away potential new investors.[1]

One more suggested disclaimer:

- This fund is an enhanced index fund. Enhanced indexing is an oxymoron—the investing equivalent of putting both a humidifier and a dehumidifier in the same room and letting them fight it out. If we really believed we could identify the few stocks that will outperform, we would only own those and none of the others. Enhanced indexing, through stock selection and marketing timing efforts, is simply a scheme to extract larger fees from the pockets of investors.

APPENDIX B

◆

Disclaimers It's Likely You'll Never Hear From Financial Publications, the Financial Media, or an Investment Bank

The investment world would be a far better and safer place if investment banks and the financial media covering the world of Wall Street were required to make the following disclosures. Again, these disclaimers just might prevent you from making some of the fifty-two mistakes even smart investors make.

- Regarding the advice you are about to hear or read: We are in business to provide profits to our shareholders. In order to maximize our profits, we use attention-getting headlines such as *sell stocks now*! Our goal is to turn the boring world of investing into an exciting industry. Much of what you will hear is simply investment pornography, a speculative orgy pretending to know what cannot be known. We sell noise, not disciplined investment strategies designed to provide investors with the greatest likelihood of achieving their financial objectives. If we told you to simply buy and hold index funds, there would be little reason for you to tune us in or subscribe to our publication. Our objective of selling magazines and generating advertising revenue presents us with a conflict of interest that we choose to ignore. Our interests are simply not aligned with those of our viewers and readers. We are not about creating wealth. We are about creating sensationalism, the noise to stir you into action you would be better served not taking. We recognize that not only is passive management is boring, but if we told you to buy and hold a globally diversified portfolio of passive asset class or index funds, what would be left to say? We can't keep repeating the same story every week.

- The following list of best buy funds has no predictive value. If it did, the buy list we publish or announce every year (week, or month, as the case may be) would contain the same names each time. Note that we make no representation as to our ability to spot next year's top funds or stocks. As you can see from the following list of our previous best buys and their performance against their appropriate benchmark, there is a lack of persistence of performance. If we really could identify the winners ahead of time, we would make far more money selling that information than publishing it. Following the recommendations of this buy list is likely to prove dangerous to your financial health.

- While the strategy and the stocks we recommend appear to have outperformed the market, there is a long way between the success of a strategy and the successful implementation of a strategy. Strategies have no costs. If we had considered operating expenses and trading costs (and taxes), it is very likely that the apparent success of our strategy would not only have disappeared, it would have produced below benchmark results.

- Regarding the following forecast: We recommend that the advice you are about to read or hear be considered only for its entertainment value.

- The fund manager you are about to hear from may have his own agenda. He may have already purchased the stocks he recommends and therefore wants you to buy them. This would drive the price up. This would then allow him to sell the shares at a higher price than he can currently.

- The guru you are about to hear from (read about) has made many forecasts. Some have been correct and many have been incorrect. Her track record has been the equivalent of a coin toss. However, her latest forecast has turned out to be correct. We will only tell you about her latest forecast and will not provide you with any record regarding the outcome of previous forecasts. And, unless her new forecast turns out to be accurate, we will not remind you of the forecast you are about to hear. You should be aware that, as Winston Churchill said, "the greatest lesson in life is to know that even fools are right sometimes." Unfortunately, if we did provide you with strict accountability, it would likely result in lower ratings (subscription sales) as the game would be ruined, because you would ignore the forecasts.

- Our brokerage firm makes money the old-fashioned way: We charge outrageously high fees and create lots of turn-over in our clients' accounts.

- Our brokerage firm makes money only when you take action. Our brokers have a strong incentive to get customers to trade even when it might be in the clients' best interests to do nothing.

- Our brokerage firm only offers actively managed funds. We recognize that index funds are likely to provide our clients with greater returns. However, we would make less money. Our primary concern is providing our shareholders with the greatest returns, and our brokers with the highest commissions, not providing our customers with the best investment vehicles.

- Over the years we have managed to gradually transfer the assets of our clients to our own name and those of our brokers.

Two further disclaimers were requirements suggested by John Merrill in his book *Beyond Stocks*:

- *The views expressed are the views of our guest and not of this network. They may be unfounded, biased, self-serving and completely at odds with your long-term investment success. No due diligence on all past recommendations has been attempted.*

- *Warning! The following market analysis will likely be hazardous to your long-term investment strategy if acted upon. It is designed to motivate you to be a short-term trader (most of whom eventually fail) instead of a long-term investor (most of whom succeed).*[1]

Disclaimers should also be required of investment bankers and security analysts. I offer the following:

- The following guest works at an investment banking firm. As such, his views are extremely biased. His main objective is to win investment banking business from the companies he is assigned to cover. He is under tremendous pressure to see everything in a positive light. If he did not do so, not only might he lose investment banking business, but the target firm might also cut off all access as punishment. You should also be aware that analysts issue earnings estimates that are six percent higher and put out twenty-five percent more buy recommendations when their firm has an investment banking relationship with the company involved. They should be considered promoters of the interests of their employer, the investment banking firm.[2]

In case you think the issue of analysts feeling pressure to see everything in a positive light is not real, one more example will enlighten you. In the summer of 1998, Ashok Kumar, an analyst at Piper Jaffray, downgraded the stock of Gateway from a *strong buy* to a simple *buy*. Now keep in mind, Kumar did not issue a sell or even a hold recommendation. He simply warned investors that "The long-term growth rate implicit in the current price of the stock may be unrealistic." During the next Gateway conference call, Kumar found that he couldn't ask any questions. After the call, a couple of portfolio managers that did business with Piper Jaffray called Kumar's boss and told him that "If this guy doesn't stop pissing on the stock, we'll yank our business." When Kumar gave similar warnings on Dell's stock, he was kicked off the company's conference call with analysts.[3] The danger of candid, unbiased commentary is very clear to analysts.

Another tale is even more revealing. Credit Suisse First Boston (CSFB) banking analyst Mike Mayo had become a guru for his December 1994 forecast that bank stocks were bottoming out and would stage a rally. He made a gutsy call and turned out to be right. Over the next few years the Standard & Poor's bank index rose 254%. Thinking (mistakenly) that he could change the ratings game on Wall Street—he actually thought he could be honest and tell people to *sell*—in the spring of 1999, Mayo stated: "In no uncertain terms sell bank stocks." He turned out to be right. Banks began to issue earnings warnings, and from their peak on July 7th to the end of 1999, the benchmark index fell twenty-one percent. This was the worst performance relative to the S&P 500 Index in fifty-four years. It continued to tumble through February 2000.

How did Mayo fare? After many irate calls from their investment banking clients (including at least one that threatened to cease all underwriting and trading business with CSFB), Mike Mayo was fired. Why? Was it for making a great forecast? In fact, his forecast had just earned him the *Wall Street Journal*'s number two ranking in its annual stock-picking poll. He also came out second in *Institutional Investors*' 2000 ranking. The answer is obvious. Wall Street's interests are simply not aligned with those of investors. Their interests are to increase investment banking profits. In order to do that, they must keep their investment banking clients happy. This is why you see virtually no negative recommendations from them. As *Fortune* magazine put it: "If, in fact, stocks are headed for a disastrous slide, you won't hear it from the researchers paid to predict it." *Fortune*'s article pointed out that more than seventy percent of the 27,000 First Call Thomson Financial analyst recommendations are either buys or strong buys. How likely is it that seventy percent of the stocks will outperform the market? Amazingly, only one percent are sell recommendations. How likely is that only one percent of stocks will underperform the market?[4]

Two more examples of the extreme conflict of interest faced by analysts:

- Marvin Roffman was an analyst at Janney Montgomery Scott in 1990. He was at the firm for sixteen years and had been in the business for thirty. He followed the gaming industry and put out a report that called an investment in Trump's Taj Mahal in Atlantic City too risky. Donald Trump demanded he be fired, and he was, within days. Trump's company filed for bankruptcy shortly thereafter.[5]

- Richard Lilly was an analyst at J. W. Charles Securities in 1992. Convinced he had uncovered fraud in a company he had previously been recommending, he was about to issue a sell recommendation. The company learned what he was planning and threatened both Lilly and the firm. He refused to comply and sent letters to the media and investors outlining his concerns. He was fired. Shortly thereafter, the company collapsed.[6]

The results of a study done by Roni Michaely of Cornell and Kent Womack of Dartmouth are quite revealing on the issue of analyst bias. "Conflict of Interest and the Credibility of Underwriter Analyst Recommendations," compared recommendations made by underwriters and non-underwriters of 391 companies that conducted IPOs in 1990 and 1991. They tracked stock performance for up to two years after the IPO date. They found significant evidence of bias and possible conflict of interest between an analyst's responsibility to his investing clients and his incentive to market stocks underwritten by his firm. The study also concluded that contrary to conventional wisdom the market doesn't come close to recognizing the full extent of this bias. They found that the stocks of companies that were recommended only by analysts from the underwriting firms were terrible performers. After two years, the average IPO recommended only by non-underwriters outperformed the group recommended by their own underwriter by more than fifty-five percent. They considered that a logical explanation for this underperformance is that the analysts know that they are misleading the public, but do so anyway because they have been directed to or because it is good for their compensation.[7]

Another study, "The Relation Between Analysts' Forecasts of Long-Term Earnings Growth and Stock Price Performance Following Equity Offerings," turned up similar results. The study found that, in general, sell-side analysts' long-term growth forecasts are systematically overly optimistic around equity offerings and that analysts employed by the lead managers of the offerings make the most optimistic growth forecasts. The study concluded that there was a positive relationship between the fees paid to the affiliated analysts' employers and the level of the affiliated analysts' growth forecasts.[8]

One of my favorite examples of the potential for bias in analysts' forecasts and the lack of value of such forecasts goes as follows. On May 31, 2000, Goldman Sachs analyst Anthony Noto ranked thirty-two e-commerce companies he covered into three groups in terms of likely survival: winners; a middle tier; and losers.[9] Of the eight winners, eighty-eight percent (all except Amazon.com) were Goldman Sachs investment banking clients. Only one of the nine middle tier companies, and none of the fifteen losers, were Goldman clients. Let's roll the videotape.

An investor who had purchased on June 1, 2000, the stocks of the companies Noto had forecast to be the winners by December 26 of that same year would have experienced an average loss of seventy-three percent. One would have been slightly better off actually purchasing the stocks of the companies he forecast as the losers; then the loss would have been only seventy-two percent. It is also worth noting that during the same time frame the S&P 500 Index fell from 1449 to 1315. Including dividends, the loss to an investor would have been slightly less than nine percent.

The bottom line is that it is time for the SEC to take action. Whenever an analyst recommends a company, full disclosure of any conflict of interest should be required. The recommendation should disclose conflicts such as that the analyst's firm may have or be seeking a business relationship with the company; the investment bank may have an equity interest in the company; and the analyst's compensation may be tied to his or her ability to generate investment banking business.

Glossary

Active management The attempt to uncover securities the market has either under- or overvalued; also the attempt to time investment decisions in order to be more heavily invested when the market is rising and less so when the market is falling.

Alpha A measure of performance against a benchmark. *Positive alpha* represents outperformance; *negative alpha* represents underperformance.

Arbitrage The process by which investors exploit the price difference between two exactly alike securities by simultaneously buying one at a lower price and selling the other at a higher price (thereby avoiding risk). This action locks in a risk-free profit for the arbitrageur (person engaging in the arbitrage) and eventually brings the prices back into equilibrium.

Asset allocation The process of determining what percentage of assets should be dedicated to which specific asset classes

Asset class A group of assets with similar risk and reward characteristics. Cash, debt instruments, real estate, and equities are examples of asset classes. Within a general asset class, such as equities, there are more specific classes such as large and small companies and domestic and international companies.

Barra Indices The Barra Indices divide the three major S&P indices (400 for mid-cap, 500 for large cap, and 600 for small cap) into growth and value categories. The top fifty percent of stocks as ranked by book-to-market value are considered value stocks and the bottom fifty percent are considered growth stocks. This creates both value and growth indices for all three S&P indices.

Basis point One one-hundredth of one percent, or 0.0001

Benchmark An appropriate standard against which actively managed funds can be judged. Actively managed large-cap growth funds should be judged against a large-cap growth index such as the S&P 500, while small-cap managers should be judged against a small-cap index such as the Russell 2000.

Bid-offer spread The bid is the price at which you can sell a security, and the offer is the price you must pay to buy a security. The spread is the difference between the two prices and represents the cost of a round-trip trade (purchase and sale) excluding commissions.

Book-to-market value (BtM) The ratio of the book value per share to the market price per share, or book value divided by market capitalization

Book value An accounting term for the equity of a company. Equity is equal to assets less liabilities; it is often expressed in per share terms. Book value per share is equal to equity divided by the number of shares.

Call An option contract that gives the holder the right, but not the obligation, to buy a security at a predetermined price on a specific date (*European call*) or during a specific period (*American call*)

Churning Excessive trading in a client's account by a broker seeking to maximize commissions, regardless of the client's best interests. Churning is a violation of NASD rules and is illegal.

Closet index fund An actively managed fund whose holdings so closely resemble the holdings of an index fund that investors are unknowingly paying very large fees for minimal differentiation

Coefficient of correlation A statistical term describing how closely related the price movement of different securities or asset classes is; the higher the coefficient, the more prices move in the same direction

Concave investing Specifically the opposite of convex investing. Investors follow a strategy of purchasing yesterday's underperformers (buying low) and selling yesterday's outperformers (selling high)

Convex investing The tendency for individual investors to buy yesterday's top performing stocks and mutual funds (buying high) and sell yesterday's underperformers (selling low)

CPI Consumer Price Index

Correlation In mathematics, correlation is the measure of the linear relationship between two variables. Values can range from +1.00 (perfect correlation) to −1.00 (perfect negative correlation). An example of a strong positive correlation would be stocks of two oil companies. A strong negative correlation might exist between an oil company (that benefits from rising oil prices) and an airline company (that would benefit from a fall in oil prices).

CRSP Center for Research in Security Prices

Data mining A technique for building predictive models of the real world by discerning patterns in masses of data

Diamond An exchange traded fund that replicates the Dow Jones Industrial Index

Distressed stocks Stocks with high book-to-market values and/or low price-to-earnings ratios. Distressed stocks are generally considered to be value stocks.

DJIA Dow Jones Industrial Average

EAFE Index The Europe, Australasia, and Far East Index, similar to the S&P 500 Index in that it consists of the stocks of the large companies from the EAFE countries. The stocks within the index are weighted by market capitalization.

Efficient market A state in which trading systems fail to produce returns in excess of the market's overall rate of return because everything currently knowable about a company is already incorporated into the stock price. The next piece of available information will be random as to whether it will be better or worse than the market expects. An efficient market is also one in which the trading costs are low.

Emerging markets The capital markets of less developed countries that are beginning to develop characteristics of developed countries, such as higher per capita income. Countries typically included in this category would be Brazil, Mexico, Thailand, and Korea.

Efficient market theory (EMT) A hypothesis explaining how markets work. See efficient market.

Exchange traded fund (ETF) For practical purposes these act like open-ended, no-load mutual funds. Like mutual funds, they can be created to represent virtually any index or asset class. However, they are not actually mutual funds. Instead, these new vehicles represent a cross between an exchange-listed stock and an open-ended, no-load mutual fund. Like stocks (but unlike mutual funds), they trade throughout the day.

Ex ante facto Before the fact

Expense ratio The operating expenses of a fund expressed as a percentage of total assets. These expenses are subtracted from the investment performance of a fund in order to determine the net return to shareholders.

Ex post facto After the fact

5%/25% rule Numerical formula used to determine the need to rebalance a portfolio

Fundamental security analysis The attempt to uncover mis-priced securities by focusing on predicting future earnings

Futures contract An agreement to purchase or sell a specific collection of securities or a physical commodity, at a specified price and time in the future. For example, an S&P 500 futures contract represents ownership interest in the S&P 500 Index, at a specified price for delivery on a specific date on a particular exchange.

Growth stock A stock trading, relative to the overall market, at a high price-to-earnings ratio (or at a relatively low book-to-market ratio) because the market anticipates rapid earnings growth, relative to the overall market

Hedge fund A fund that generally has the ability to invest in a wide variety of asset classes. These funds often use leverage in an attempt to increase returns.

I-Bond A bond that provides both a fixed rate of return and an inflation protection component. The principal value of the bond increases by the total of the fixed rate and the inflation component. The income is deferred for tax purposes until funds are withdrawn from the account holding the bond.

Index fund A passively managed fund that seeks to replicate the performance of a particular index (such as the Wilshire 5000, the S&P 500, or the Russell 2000) by buying all the securities in that index, in direct proportion to their weight, by market capitalization, within that index, and holding them

Initial public offering (IPO) The first offering of a company's stock to the public

Institutional fund A mutual fund that is not available to individual investors. Typical clients are pension and profit-sharing plans and endowment funds.

Institutional-style fund A mutual fund that is available to individual investors, under certain conditions, such as through registered investment advisors. These advisors require their clients to commit to the same type of disciplined, long-term, buy-and-hold strategy that is typical of institutional investors.

Investment pandering Advice on market or securities values that is designed to titillate, stimulate, and excite you into action but has no basis in reality

Investment pornography Extreme examples of investment pandering

Leverage The use of debt to increase the amount of assets that can be acquired, for example, to buy stock. Leverage increases the riskiness of a portfolio.

Loser's game A game in which, while it is not impossible to win, the odds of winning are so low that it does not pay to play

Market capitalization The market price per share times the number of shares

Market cap weighting The ownership of individual stocks determined by their percentage of market capitalization relative to all market capitalization of all stocks within an index, or other benchmark. An index fund's holdings are market cap weighted, not equally weighted.

Micro cap The smallest stocks by market capitalization: The ninth and tenth CRSP deciles. Other definitions used are the smallest five percent of stocks and stocks with a market capitalization of less than about $200 million.

Modern portfolio theory (MPT) A body of academic work founded on the following concepts. First, markets are too efficient to allow returns in excess of the market's overall rate of return to be achieved through trading systems. Active management is therefore counterproductive. Second, asset classes can be expected to achieve, over sustained periods, returns that are commensurate with their level of risk. Riskier asset classes, such as small companies and value companies, will produce higher returns as compensation for their higher risk. Third, diversification across asset classes can increase returns and reduce risk. For any given level of risk, a portfolio can be constructed that will produce the highest expected return. Finally, there is no right portfolio for every investor. Each investor must choose an asset allocation that results in a portfolio with an acceptable level of risk.

Mortgage-backed security (MBS) A financial instrument representing an interest in assets that are mortgage related (either commercial or residential)

MPT Modern portfolio theory

NAIC National Association of Investment Clubs

NASD The National Association of Securities Dealers

NASDQ or NASDAQ The National Association of Securities (Automated) Quotations. A computerized marketplace in which securities are traded, frequently called the "over-the-counter market"

NASDAQ 100 Index The one hundred largest capitalization stocks on that exchange.

NAV Net asset value

No-load A mutual fund that does not impose any charge for purchases or sales

Nominal returns Returns that have not been adjusted for the negative impact of inflation

NYSE New York Stock Exchange

Out of sample Data from a study covering different time periods or different geographic regions from the original study

P/E ratio The ratio of stock price to earnings. Stocks with high price-to-earnings ratios are considered growth stocks; stocks with low P/E ratios are considered value stocks.

Passive asset class funds Funds that buy and hold all securities within a particular asset class. The weighting of each security within the fund is typically equal to its weighting, by market capitalization, within the asset class. Each security is then typically held until it no longer fits the definition of the asset class to which the fund is seeking exposure. For example, a small company might grow into a large company and then no longer fit within the small company asset class. Fund managers may also use common sense and research to implement screens to eliminate certain securities from consideration (in an attempt to improve risk-adjusted returns). To be considered a passive fund, however, those screens cannot be based on any technical or fundamental security analysis. Examples of passive screens would be: minimum market capitalization; minimum number of years of operating history; and minimum number of market makers in the company stock.

Passive management A buy-and-hold investment strategy, specifically contrary to active management. Characteristics of the passive management approach include: lower portfolio turnover; lower operating expenses and transactions costs; greater tax efficiency; fully invested at all times; and a long-term perspective.

Prudent Investor Rule A doctrine imbedded within the American legal code stating that a person responsible for the management of someone else's assets must manage those assets in a manner appropriate to the financial circumstance and tolerance for risk of the investor

Put An option contract that gives the holder the right, but not the obligation, to sell a security at a predetermined price on a specific date (*European put*) or during a specific period (*American put*)

Qubes (QQQ) An exchange traded fund that tracks the NASDAQ 100 Index

Real returns Returns that reflect purchasing power as they are adjusted for the negative impact of inflation

Rebalancing The process of restoring a portfolio to its original asset allocation. Rebalancing can be accomplished either through adding newly investable funds or by selling portions of the best performing asset classes and using the proceeds to purchase additional amounts of the underperforming asset classes.

Registered investment advisor A designation representing that a financial consultant's firm is registered with the appropriate state regulators and that the RIA representatives for that firm have passed the required exams

REIT Real Estate Investment Trust, a trust available to investors through the purchase of shares in it

Risk premium The higher *expected*, not guaranteed, return for accepting the possibility of a negative outcome

Russell 2000 The smallest 2,000 of the largest 3,000 stocks within the Russell Index. Generally used as a benchmark for small-cap stocks

Retail funds Mutual funds that are sold to the general public, as opposed to institutional investors

ROA Return on assets

S&P 400 Index A market cap weighted index of 400 mid-cap stocks

S&P 500 Index A market cap weighted index of 500 of the largest U.S. stocks designed to cover a broad and representative sampling of industries

S&P 600 Index A market cap weighted index of 600 small-cap stocks

SEC Securities and Exchange Commission

Sharpe ratio A measure of the return earned above the rate of return earned on riskless short-term U.S. treasury bills relative to the risk taken, with risk being defined as standard deviation of returns. Example: The return earned on an asset was ten percent. The rate of one-month Treasury bills was four percent. The standard deviation was twenty percent. The Sharpe ratio would be equal to ten percent minus four percent (six percent) divided by twenty percent, or 0.3.

Short selling Borrowing a security for the purpose of immediately selling it; with the expectation that the investor will be able to buy the security back at a later date, at a lower price

Spiders (SPDR) Exchange traded funds that replicate the various Standard & Poors Indices

Standard deviation A measure of volatility, or risk. For example, given a portfolio with a twelve percent annualized return and a eleven percent standard deviation, an investor can expect that in thirteen out of twenty annual periods (about two thirds of the time) the return on that portfolio will fall within one standard deviation, or between one percent (12% − 11%) and twenty-three percent (12% + 11%). The remaining one third of the time an investor should expect that the annual return will fall outside the 1% − 23% range. Two standard deviations (11% × 2) would account for ninety-five percent (19 out of 20) of the periods. The range of expected returns would be between −10% (12% − 22%) and 34% (12% + 22%). The greater the standard deviation, the greater the volatility of a portfolio. Standard deviation can be measured for varying time periods—that is, you can have a monthly standard deviation or an annualized standard deviation measuring the volatility for a given time frame.

Style drift The moving away from the original asset allocation of a portfolio, either by the purchase of securities outside the particular asset class a fund represents or by not rebalancing to adjust for significant differences in performance of the various asset classes within a portfolio

Tactical Asset Allocation (TAA) The attempt to outperform a benchmark by actively shifting the portfolio's exposure to various asset classes (the portfolio's asset allocation)

TIPS Treasury Inflation Protected Security. A bond that receives a fixed stated rate of return, but also increases its principal by the changes in the Consumer Price Index. Its fixed-interest payment is calculated on the inflated principal, which is eventually repaid at maturity.

Tracking error The amount by which the performance of a fund differs from the appropriate index or benchmark. More generally, when referring to a whole portfolio, the amount by which the performance of the portfolio differs from a widely accepted benchmark, such as the S&P 500 Index or the Wilshire 5000 Index

Turnover The trading activity of a fund as it sells securities from a portfolio and replaces them with new ones. Assume that a fund began the year with a portfolio of $100 million in various securities. If the fund sold $50 million of the original securities and replaced them with $50 million of new securities, it would have a turnover rate of fifty percent.

Value stocks Companies that have relatively low price-to-earnings ratios or relatively high book-to-market ratios. These are considered the opposite of growth stocks.

Variable Annuity An investment product with an insurance component. Taxes are deferred until funds are withdrawn.

WEBS World Equity Benchmark Securities are exchange traded funds that track various foreign country indices such as the United Kingdom, German, and French equivalents of the S&P 500 Index.

Winner's Game A game in which the odds of winning are reasonably high, and the prize of winning is commensurate with the risk of playing

Suggested Reading

The following books are highly recommended for those wishing to expand their knowledge of the subjects covered in this book:

- Gary Belsky and Thomas Gilovich, *Why Smart People Make Big Money Mistakes.*
- Bill Bernstein, *The Intelligent Asset Allocator.*
- Peter Bernstein, *Capital Ideas.*
- Peter Bernstein, *Against the Gods.*
- John Bogle, *Common Sense on Mutual Funds.*
- Charles Ellis, *Winning the Loser's Game.*
- Richard Ferri, *All About Index Funds.*
- Martin Fridson, *Investment Illusions.*
- Howard Kurtz, *The Fortune Tellers.*
- Burton G. Malkiel, *A Random Walk Down Wall Street.*
- Bill Schultheis, *The Coffeehouse Investor.*
- Jeremy Siegel, *Stocks for the Long Run.*
- William Sharpe, *Portfolio Theory and Capital Markets.*
- Hersh Shefrin, *Beyond Greed and Fear.*
- William Sherden, *The Fortune Sellers.*
- W. Scott Simon, *Index Mutual Funds.*

- Nassim Nicholas Taleb, *Fooled by Randomness*.
- Bruce J. Temkin, Don Phillips, and Deborah Thomas, *The Terrible Truth About Investing*.
- Ben Warwick, *Searching for Alpha*.

For those interested in learning more about the history of financial follies there are three excellent books. The first is Charles MacKay's *Extraordinary Popular Delusions and the Madness of Crowds* (1841). MacKay noted: "Every age has its peculiar folly: some scheme, project, or fantasy into which it plunges, spurred on by the love of gain, the necessity of excitement or the force of imitation." His book is as relevant today as it was when it was first published almost 150 years ago. The others are *Devil Take the Hindmost*, by Edward Chancellor, and *Irrational Exuberance*, by Robert J. Shiller.

Acknowledgments

No book is ever the work of one individual. This book is no exception. I thank my partners at Buckingham Asset Management and BAM Advisor Services, Paul Forman, Steve Funk, Ed Goldberg, Joe Hempen, Mont Levy, Irv Rothenberg, Bert Schweizer III, and Stuart Zimmerman, for their support and encouragement. I would also like to thank Bob Gellman, Rick Hill, Vladimir Masek, and especially Wendy Cook for their contributions. Vladimir, thank you very much for your valuable insights and editorial suggestions. Any errors are certainly mine.

A special note of thanks to my good friend Larry Goldfarb, who not only provided editorial assistance but has also contributed greatly to the organization and structure of my first two books. My appreciation is expressed to Truman "Mac" Talley, who has been my editor for over five years for all three of my books. His many contributions to each of these efforts have been incalculable. I would be remiss if I did not note the contributions of my agent, Sam Fleishman. I cannot imagine a better relationship between author and agent.

I also thank the people at DFA, especially Weston Wellington. I have learned much from DFA and Wes. He seems to always be able to explain difficult concepts in an easy and often humorous way.

I would also be remiss if I did not thank the many friends I have made on the Web sites *www.indexfunds.com.* and Vanguard

ACKNOWLEDGMENTS

Diehards. I have learned much from them through our long discussions.

I also thank Dan Solin, an attorney specializing in securities cases. He provided me with valuable insights and information.

Finally, I thank my family: Jodi, Jennifer, and Jacquelyn, thanks for allowing me to monopolize our computer for over one year, for the third time now. I especially thank the love of my life, my wife, Mona. She showed tremendous patience in reading and rereading numerous drafts. I also thank her for her tremendous support and understanding for the lost weekends and the many nights that I sat at the computer well into the early morning hours. She has always provided whatever support was needed, and then some.

Notes

Introduction
1. *Wall Street Journal*, December 24, 1998.

Mistake 1
1. *Wall Street Journal*, April 6, 1998.
2. *New York Times*, March 30, 1997.
3. Quoted in Jonathan Burton, *Investment Titans*, p 218.
4. Brad Barber and Terrance Odean, "Trading Is Hazardous to Your Wealth: The Common Stock Investment Performance of Individual Investors," *Journal of Finance*, April 2000.
5. Brad Barber and Terrance Odean, "Boys Will Be Boys: Gender, Overconfidence and Common Stock Investment," *Quarterly Journal of Economics*, February 2001.
6. Brad Barber and Terrance Odean, "Do Investors Trade Too Much?" *American Economic Review*, December 1999.
7. Brad Barber and Terrance Odean, "The Internet and the Investor," *The Journal of Economic Perspectives*, (Winter 2001).
8. Salomon Smith Barney, *Market Perspective*, March 27, 2001.
9. John Liscio, "The U.S.: Love It, Don't Leave It." *Dow Jones Asset Management*, November–December 1999.
10. Jonathan Clements, *25 Myths You've Got to Avoid*, p. 55.
11. James H. Smalhout, "Too Close to Your Money?" *Bloomberg Personal*, November 1997.

12. David Dreman, *Contrarian Investment Strategies*, p. 81.
13. Quoted in *Wall Street Journal*, August 6, 1998.

Mistake 2

1. *Wall Street Journal*, November 27, 2000.
2. SmartMoney.com, On the Street, Matthew Goldstein, "Where's the Little Guy?" December 11, 2000.
3. Ibid.
4. Ibid.
5. *Morningstar FundInvestor*, January 2001.
6. *New York Times*, March 9, 1997.
7. TheStreet.com, January 17, 2001.

Mistake 3

1. Quoted in *Fortune*, September 25, 1989.
2. *Fortune*, February 5, 2001.
3. Quoted in Victoria Collins, *Invest Beyond.com*, p 35.
4. *Money*, November 2000.

Mistake 4

1. Gary Belsky and Thomas Gilovich, *Why Smart People Make Big Money Mistakes*.

Mistake 5

1. Jonathan Clements, 25 *Myths You've Got To Avoid*, p. 33.
2. Quoted in Ben Warwick, *Searching for Alpha*, p. 17.
3. Jonathan Clements, 25 *Myths You've Got To Avoid*, p. 54.
4. John Bogle, "Investing with Simplicity," keynote speech, Philadelphia, Pa., October 3, 1998.
5. Dean LeBaron and Romesh Vaitilingam, *The Ultimate Investor*, p. 201.

Mistake 6

1. Henry Fielding, *The True Patriot*.
2. Quoted in Edward Chancellor, *Devil Take the Hindmost*, p. 69.
3. Robert Shiller, *Irrational Exuberance*.
4. Ibid.
5. *Wall Street Journal*, April 4, 2000.

Mistake 7

1. *Rekenthaler Report*, post 354.
2. *New York Times*, January 14, 2001.
3. Ibid.

Mistake 8

1. *Financial Planning*, February 1997.
2. Cited in the *Wall Street Journal*, May 16, 1997.
3. Cited in the *St. Louis Post-Dispatch*, September 24, 1999.

Mistake 11

1. Thomas Gilovich, R. P. Vallone, and Amos Tversky, "The Hot Hand in Basketball: On the Misperception of Random Sequences." *Cognitive Psychology*, 17:295–314.
2. Micropal: CRSP 1–10 universe.
3. *New York Times*, April 4, 1999.
4. Jonathan Clements, *25 Myths You've Got to Avoid*, p. 86.
5. *Kiplinger's* (January 2000).

Mistake 12

1. Gur Huberman, *Familiarity Breeds Investment* (September 1999).
2. Kenneth R. French and James M. Poterba, "Investor Diversification and International Equity Markets," *American Economic Review*, vol. 81, no. 2, 222–26.

3. Ibid.
4. D. Glassman and L. Riddick, "What Is Home Asset Bias and How Should It Be Measured?" University of Washington working paper.
5. Hersh Shefrin and Meir Statman, "Behavioral Portfolio Theory," 1997 paper.
6. F. Heath and A. Tversky, "Preference and Belief: Ambiguity and Competence in Choice Under Uncertainty," *Journal of Risk and Uncertainty* 4, 4–28.
7. David Laster, *Journal of Investing*, Fall 1998.
8. David Blitzer, *Outpacing the Pros*, p. 114.

Mistake 13

1. Gary Belsky and Thomas Gilovich, *Why Smart People Make Big Money Mistakes*

Mistake 14

1. *Financial Advisor* (March 2001).

Mistake 15

1. Christopher R. Blake and Matthew R. Morey, "Morningstar Ratings and Mutual Fund Performance," *Journal of Financial and Quantitative Analysis* (September 2000).
2. Diane Del Guerico and Paula A. Tkac, "Star Power: The Effect of Morningstar Ratings on Mutual Fund Flows," Federal Reserve Bank of Atlanta, Working Paper 2001–15.
3. Prem C. Jain and Joanna Shuang Wu, "Truth in Mutual Fund Advertising: Evidence on Future Performance and Fund Flows," *Journal of Finance* 55, 937–958.
4. John Bogle, "The Stock Market Universe—Stars, Comets, and the Sun," speech before the Financial Analysts of Philadelphia, February 15, 2001.

5. *InvestmentNews*, March 29, 1999.

6. *New York Times*, April 4, 1999.

7. Blake and Morey, "Morningstar Ratings and Mutual Fund Performance."

8. *Investment Advisor* (September 1994).

9. *Journal of Financial Planning* (September 2000).

10. *St. Louis Post-Dispatch*, November 10, 2000.

11. *Wall Street Journal*, December 22, 1998.

12. *In the Vanguard* (Autumn 2000).

13. Amy C. Arnott, Beyond the Stars: The New Category Rating," *Morningstar Mutual Funds*, summary section, vol. 29, issue 2, Dec. 6, 1996.

Mistake 16

1. Mark Carhart, "On Persistence in Mutual Fund Performance," *Journal of Finance* (March 1997).

2. *Wall Street Journal*, April 4, 1997.

3. *Dow Jones Asset Management* (January-February 1998).

4. Burton G. Malkiel, *A Random Walk Down Wall Street*.

5. John Bogle, *Bogle on Mutual Funds*.

6. *Wall Street Journal*, May 10, 1999.

7. *Barron's*, May 7, 2001.

8. *Wall Street Journal*, October 9, 2000.

9. Ibid.

10. Ibid.

11. http://news.morningstar.com/doc/article/0,1,4689,00.html.

Mistake 17

1. Russ Wermers in *Journal of Finance* (August 2000).

2. *St. Louis Post-Dispatch*, August 12, 1997.

3. Dimensional Fund Advisors.

4. *New York Times*, July 11, 1999.

5. John Bogle, *Common Sense on Mutual Funds*, p. 286.
6. Scott West and Mitch Anthony, *Storyselling for Financial Advisors.*

Mistake 18

1. See *http://www.indexfunds.com/articles/20000729_marcial_com _act_LP.htm*, July 29, 2000. by Larry Putnam, contributing writer.
2. James Choi, "The Value Line Enigma," *Journal of Financial and Quantitative Analysis* (September 2000).
3. *New York Times*, June 27, 1999.
4. *Journal of Financial and Quantitative Analysis* (September 2000).
5. Choi, "The Value Line Enigma."
6. D. Keim and A. Madhavan, "The Cost of Institutional Equity Trades," *Financial Analysts Journal*, July-August 1998, p. 50–69
7. B. Barber, R Lehavy, M. McNichols, and B. Trueman, "Can Investors Profit from the Prophets? Security Analyst Recommendations and Stock Returns," *Journal of Finance* (April 2001).
8. D. Keim and A. Madhavan, "The Cost of Institutional Equity Trades," *Financial Analysts Journal*, 54, p. 50–69.
9. Russ Wermers, "Mutual Fund Performance: An Empirical Decomposition into Stock-Picking Talent, Style, Transactions Costs, and Expenses," *The Journal of Finance*, Vol. 55, No. 4, (August 2000).
10. *Seattle Times*, May 5, 2001.

Mistake 20

1. *Smart Money* (June 2001).
2. *Fortune*, August 16, 1999.

3. Ibid.
4. Ibid.

Mistake 21

1. *www.gsm.ucdavis.edu/~bmbarber*.
2. John Nofsinger, *Investment Madness*, p. 72.

Mistake 22

1. John Bogle, *Bogle on Investing*, p. 89.
2. Richard E. Evans and Burton G. Malkiel, *The Index Fund Solution*.
3. Lipper Analytical Service.
4. *BusinessWeek*, February 22, 1999.
5. William Sherden, *Fortune Sellers*, p. 121.

Mistake 23

1. John Bogle, *Common Sense on Mutual Funds*, p. 119.
2. Lipper Analytical Service.
3. Mark M. Carhart, *"On Persistence in Mutual Fund Performance,"* doctoral dissertation, University of Chicago, December 1994.
4. *The Index Insider* (January 2001).

Mistake 24

1. "Ranking Mutual funds on an After-Tax Basis," Stanford University Center for Economic Policy Research Discussion Paper, 344.
2. Richard Evans, *The Index Fund Solution*, p. 59.
3. James Garland, "The Tax Attraction of Tax-Managed Index Funds," *Journal of Investing* (Spring 1997).
4. Robert D. Arnott and Robert H. Jeffrey, "Is Your Alpha Big Enough to Cover Your Taxes?" *Journal of Portfolio Management* (Spring 1993).
5. *Wall Street Journal*, June 10, 1997.

6. Schwab Center for Investment Research, "How Tax Efficient Are Tax-Managed Funds?" vol. I, issue II (October 1998).
7. Robert D. Arnott, Andrew L. Berkin and Jia Ye, "How Well have Taxable Investors Been Served in the 1980s and 1990s,"*Journal of Portfolio Management* (Summer 2000).
8. KPMG, *Tax-Managed Mutual Funds and the Taxable Investor*.

Mistake 25

1. *Financial Analysts Journal* (July-August 1986).
2. Dimensional Fund Advisors.
3. Roger G. Ibbotson and Paul D. Kaplan, "Does Asset Allocation Policy Explain 40%, 90%, or 100% of Performance?", *Financial Analysts Journal* (January–February 2000).
4. Moon Kim, Ravi Shukla, and Michael Tomas. "Mutual Fund Objective Misclassification," *Journal of Economics and Business*, July/August 2000.
5. Dan diBartolomeo and Erik Witkowski, "Mutual Fund Misclassification: Evidence Based on Style Analysis," *Financial Analysts Journal* (September-October 1997).
6. George Arrington, "Chasing Performance Through Style Drift," *Journal of Investing* (Summer 2000).
7. Stephen J. Brown and William N. Goetzmann, Brown is at the NYU Leonard Stern School of Business and Goetzman at the Yale School of Management, "Mutual Fund Styles," June 6, 1996, *http://viking.somyale.edu/will/styles/styles.htm*.

Mistake 26

1. *New York Times*, January 24, 1999.
2. Datastream.
3. "Untangling Emerging Markets," *New York Times*, January 24, 1999.
4. Quoted in *The New York Times*, January 24, 1999.

Mistake 27

1. *InvestmentNews*, December 1, 1997.
2. *Forbes*, January 11, 1999.
3. *Journal of Finance*, "The Performance of Hedge Funds: Risk, Return and Incentives," June 1999.
4. *Wall Street Journal*, February 22, 2001.
5. *BusinessWeek*, September 17, 2001.
6. *BusinessWeek*, February 21, 2000.
7. *BusinessWeek*, September 17, 2001.

Mistake 28

1. *Journal of Portfolio Management* (Fall 1999).

Mistake 29

1. Nissam Nicholas Taleb, *Fooled by Randomness*, p. 26.
2. John Bogle, *Common Sense on Mutual Funds*, p. 245.
3. Ibid. p. 255.
4. *Wall Street Journal*, April 23, 1999.

Mistake 30

1. Piscataqua Research, Inc. Portsmouth, N.H. and Dimensional Fund Advisors.
2. T. Daniel Coggin and Charles A. Trzcinka, "A Panel Study of Equity Pension Fund Manager Style Performance," *Journal of Investing* (Summer 2000).
3. *Pension & Investments*, June 26, 2000.
4. Forbes.com, June 1, 2001.
5. *Dow Jones Asset Management* (November–December) 1998.

Mistake 34

1. John Bogle, *Bogle on Investing*, p. 55.
2. *Wall Street Journal*, March 14, 2000.

Mistake 35

1. Tweedy, Browne Fund Inc., Tweedy Browne Global Value Fund and Tweedy, Browne American Value Fund Semi-Annual Investment Manager's Report, September 30, 1998.

Mistake 37

1. *New York Times*, January 10, 2001.

Mistake 38

1. John Bogle, *Common Sense on Mutual Funds*, p. 20.
2. John D. Stowe, "A Market Timing Myth," *Journal of Investing* (Winter 2000).
3. *Worth* (September 1995).
4. *BusinessWeek*, March 9, 1998.
5. Ibid.
6. National Bureau of Economic Research, Working Paper 4890, October 1994.
7. W. Scott Simon, *Index Mutual Funds*.
8. Andrew Metrick, "Performance Evaluation with Transactions Data: The Stock Selection of Investment Newsletters," *Journal of Finance* (October 1999).
9. *American Association of Individual Investors Journal* (September 1996).
10. David Dreman, *Contrarian Investment Strategies*, p. 57.
11. Ted Cadsby, *The 10 Biggest Investment Mistakes Canadians Make*, p. 87.
12. Quoted in John Merrill, *Beyond Stocks*, p. 230.
13. Quoted in Jonathan Burton, *Investment Titan*, p. 38.

Mistake 39

1. William Sherden, *The Fortune Sellers*.
2. *Forbes*, December 26, 1988, p. 94.

3. *Industry Week*, April 20, 1992, p. 76.
4. Burton Malkiel, *A Random Walk Down Wall Street*, p. 179.
5. *Wall Street Journal*, January 2, 2001.
6. Benjamin Mark Cole, *The Pied Pipers of Wall Street*, p. 93.
7. *St. Louis Post-Dispatch*, January 6, 2001.
8. *USA Today*, July 9, 2001.
9. *Financial World*, November 1980.
10. David Dreman, *Contrarian Investment Strategies*, p. 91.
11. *Fortune*, June 11, 2001.
12. *St. Louis Post Dispatch*, October 4, 1997.
13. Peter Lynch, *One Up on Wall Street*, p. 60.
14. *BusinessWeek*, June 25, 2001.
15. Sherden, *The Fortune Sellers*.

Mistake 42

1. Jonathan Clements, *25 Myths You've Got to Avoid*, p. 95.
2. Ted Cadsby, *The 10 Biggest Investment Mistakes Canadians Make*, p. 36.
3. Richard Bernstein, *Navigating The Noise*, p. xii.
4. *Ladies Home Journal* (October 1998).

Mistake 43

1. Nick Murray, *Investment Advisor* (April 1996).
2. Nick Murray, *The Craft of Advice*.
3. Ragnar D. Naess, *Readings in Financial Analysis and Investment Management*.

Mistake 44

1. *New York Times*, April 18, 2001.
2. *New York Times*, April 22, 2001.

Mistake 45

1. J. Evans and S. H. Archer, "Diversification and the Reduction of Dispersion: An Empirical Analysis," *Journal of Finance* (December 1968).
2. Lawrence Fisher and James Lorie, "Some Studies of Variability of Returns on Investments in Common Stocks," *Journal of Business*, vol. 43, no. 2 (April 1970).
3. *Bloomberg Wealth Manager*, (July-/August 2000).
4. Ronald J. Surz and Mitchell Price, "The Truth About Diversification by the Numbers," *Journal of Investing* (Winter 2000).
5. *Wall Street Journal*, January 29, 2001.
6. *Wall Street Journal*, January 8, 2001.
7. *In The Vanguard* (Winter 2001).

Mistake 46

1. Dimensional Fund Advisors.

Mistake 47

1. *Bloomberg Personal Finance* (April 2000).
2. Ibid.

Mistake 49

1. C. R. Blake, E. J. Elton, and M. J. Gruber, "The Performance of Bond Mutual Funds," *Journal of Business*, 66 (July):1993, p. 371–403.
2. John Bogle, *Bogle on Mutual Funds*.
3. Dale L. Domian, Terry S. Maness and W. Reichentstein, *Journal of Portfolio Management* (Spring 1998).
4. David Plecha, Dimensional Fund Advisors, "Fixed Income Investing," working paper, June 2001.
5. Ibid.

Mistake 50

1. *Forbes*, February 9, 1998.
2. Ibid.
3. *www.cbsmarketwatch.com*, June 6, 2000.

Mistake 51

1. *Journal of Finance* (March 1995).
2. *Wall Street Journal*, February 24, 1999.
3. *Fortune*, November 23, 1998.
4. *Wall Street Journal*, March 30, 1999.
5. *Journal of Finance*, June 1999.
6. *Wall Street Journal*, February 24, 1999.
7. *BusinessWeek*, February 7, 2000.
8. *The Economist*, February 26, 2000.
9. *St. Louis Post-Dispatch*, April 6, 2000.
10. *BusinessWeek*, September 18, 2000.
11. *www.msnbc.com/news/429141.asp*.
12. *Wall Street Journal*, March 7, 2001.
13. "The Year the Bubble Burst," *SmartMoney.com*, January 3, 2001.
14. *Wall Street Journal*, January 2, 2001.
15. *Wall Street Journal*, March 7, 2001.
16. *New York Times*, March 8, 2001.
17. Dimensional Fund Advisors, From the Research Desk, December 1999.
18. *BusinessWeek*, December 11, 2000.

Conclusion

1. Ted Cadsby, *The 10 Biggest Investment Mistakes Canadians Make*, p. 10.
2. Gary Belsky and Thomas Gilovich, *Why Smart People Make Big Money Mistakes*, p. 162.

3. Quoted in Jonathan Burton, *Investment Titans*, p. 218.
4. Quoted in Ibid., p. 237.
5. Richard Thaler, *The Winner's Curse*, p. 5.

Appendix A
1. *Wall Street Journal*, April 23, 1998.

Appendix B
1. John Merrill, *Beyond Stocks*.
2. Howard Kurtz, *The Fortune Tellers*, p. 209.
3. Ibid., p. 69.
4. *Fortune*, February 5, 2001.
5. Benjamin Cole, *The Pied Pipers of Wall Street*, p. 81.
6. Ibid., p. 83.
7. Roni Michaely and Kent Womack, "Conflict of Interest and the Credibility of Underwriter Analyst Recommendations," *The Review of Financial Studies 1999*.
8. Patricia M. Dechow, Richard Sloan and Amy Hutton, "The Relation Between Analysts' Long-Term Earnings Forecasts and Stock Price Performance Following Equity Offerings," *Contemporary Accounting Research*, vol. 17, no. 1 (Spring 2000).
9. *Forbes*, January 22, 2001.

Index

INDEX

INDEX